THE ULTIMAT
MEDITERRANEA
COOKBOOK FOR BEGINNERS

1500 Days of No-fuss & Delicious Mediterranean Recipes to Build Healthy

Eating Habits and Lifestyle | 60 Days Meal Plan to Kickstart!

KELLY V. HENNINGS

Table of Contents

Introduction

There is a quotation by George Herbert that says, "Living well is the best revenge." The Mediterranean diet could be summed up in this quotation. For Mediterranean people, eating a diet that mostly consists of grains, vegetables, and legumes, with modest amounts of dairy, eggs, chicken, and even fewer amounts of red meat, is the norm. But eating out with friends and engaging in regular exercise are also important. This diet will transport you in spirit to a sunny vacation in Greece, Italy, or the south of France.

There is a common thread among the people who live in the region, even though there isn't a singular "Mediterranean diet" that all people in such countries as France, Spain, Italy, Greece, Turkey, and Israel, adhere to. Technically, they consume a diet that is low in saturated fat and high in monounsaturated fatty acids, fiber, and antioxidants.

The World Health Organization, the Harvard School of Public Health, and Oldways introduced the concept of a Mediterranean diet in 1993. The diet is based on research that dates back to Dr. Ancel Keys, who in 1958 began a fifteen-year study spanning seven nations. The outcomes of numerous investigations that came after were impressive. People in Mediterranean nations were usually healthier and experienced fewer heart attacks. According to the studies, La Cucina Povera was indeed healthier than modern diets popular in more developed and industrialized regions of the world.

The Mediterranean diet is derived from the traditional foods consumed by people in the Mediterranean region, particularly in Crete. You'll be on the right track if you remember to "eat like your ancestors." Your forefathers did not consume soft drinks, processed foods, or fast food, and you should not either.

Although the goal of this diet is overall health rather than weight loss, it is nevertheless feasible to lose weight on it, especially if your regular eating habits are more in line with the standard American diet of processed foods and unhealthy fats. According to the Mayo Clinic, the Mediterranean diet is particularly beneficial for heart health, lowering the risk of cancer and cancer mortality, as well as lowering the occurrence of Parkinson's and Alzheimer's diseases. The Mediterranean diet receives good marks from U.S. News & World Report in the areas of Best Diets for Healthy Eating, Best Diets Overall, and Easiest Diet to Follow. So, let's learn about the Mediterranean diet.

Chapter 1
Basics of Mediterranean diet

What is the Mediterranean Diet?

The Mediterranean diet isn't really a diet, at least not in the typical you-can't-eat-that sense, unlike many other diets. It serves more as a guide for leading a long, healthy, and fulfilling life. You might need to change your outlook on life and your way of thinking, but you won't need to give up anything other than poor health and unsightly body fat. In return, you'll need to eat a lot of deliciously flavored meals, discover some physically demanding hobbies you enjoy doing, and enjoy more time with your friends and family. All right? In that case, this might be the "diet" you've been looking for!

WHAT MAKES THE MEDITERRANEAN DIET DIFFERENT FROM OTHER DIETS?

Wonderful question. The general consensus among health professionals for the past few decades has been that eating a diet low in fat and carbs is essential to maintaining a healthy weight and preventing disease. Unfortunately, science doesn't support this theory. To produce energy, combat disease, and maintain normal brain function, your body requires healthy fats and adequate carbohydrates.

MEDITERRANEAN DIET PYRAMID

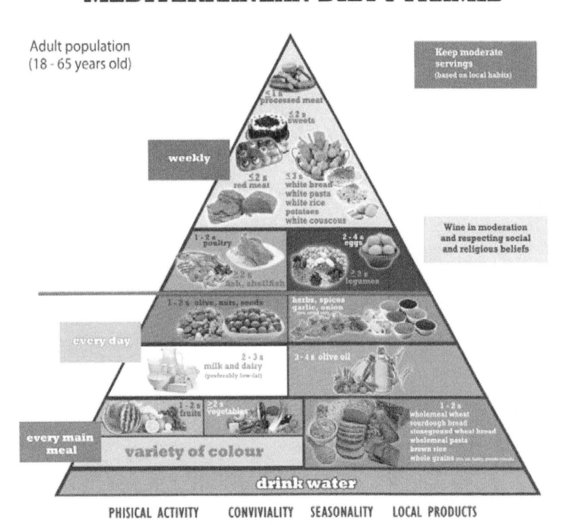

THE FOOD PYRAMID FOR THE MEDITERRANEAN DIET

The food pyramid of the Mediterranean diet allows for any type of food but arranges it in a hierarchy. Here, the top of the food pyramid represents fatty meats and sweets, which should only be consumed in moderation. At the base of the food pyramid, which should make up the majority of every meal, are foods rich in nutrients, beneficial carbohydrates, and necessary fats. Fresh fruits and vegetables, lentils, whole grains, herbs, olive oil, and spices are some of these wholesome foods.

Fish and seafood, which should be consumed at least twice per week, make up the second-largest layer of the food pyramid. Beneath meats and sweets is the third layer, which consists of dairy products like cheese, yogurt, eggs, and poultry, all of which should be consumed in moderation daily or weekly. You should consume a sufficient amount of water and a moderate amount of wine in addition to adhering to the food pyramid.

MEDITERRANEAN DIET

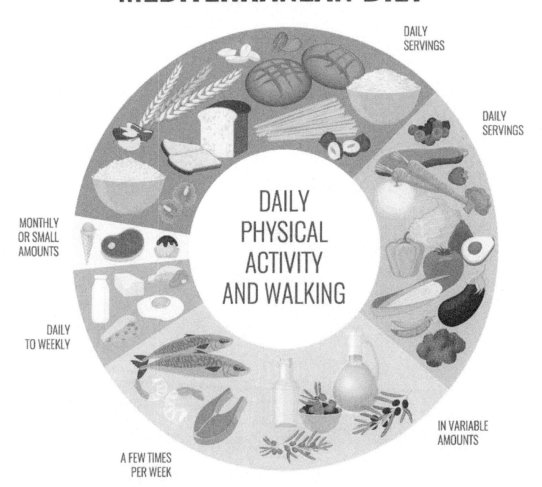

DAILY
SERVINGS

DAILY
SERVINGS

MONTHLY
OR SMALL
AMOUNTS

DAILY
PHYSICAL
ACTIVITY
AND WALKING

DAILY
TO WEEKLY

IN VARIABLE
AMOUNTS

A FEW TIMES
PER WEEK

The Mediterranean Lifestyle

Living in a country with plenty of sunshine near the Mediterranean Sea makes staying healthy simple. Part of the Mediterranean diet entails adopting a little bit of a vacation-mode mentality, at least for a few moments throughout the day. With the ocean air, sunshine, and decent wine, how could you be stressed out and lacking in energy?

Slow down at mealtimes: Calculate how long one of your typical family dinners lasts. Then, try extending it by only ten minutes, so you have time to talk to the others at your table. Please eat at a table with all TVs, phones, and devices off. You'll be headed toward the leisurely meal that is typical of Mediterranean areas.

Savor a glass of wine: Wine helps to slow down your dinners. Serve wine (not necessarily an expensive bottle) on nights when you have time to enjoy it, or with a leisurely lunch on weekends. It is customary to drink wine only with food.

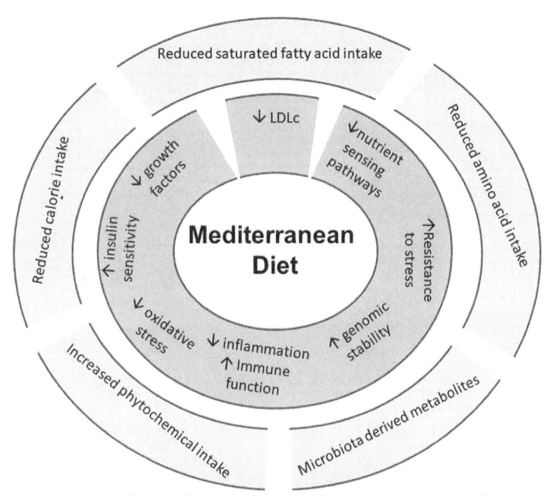

Move that body more often: Even if you eat the healthiest diet, your body won't be completely fit unless you exercise. Maintaining a strong body makes almost everything simpler and helps prevent back and shoulder injuries. Consider engaging in everyday exercise as a form of pain prevention. It is a wonderful stress-relieving method as well. Better health results from short bursts of exercise, even if they only last ten minutes.

Get a sound sleep: Every night, try to get seven to eight hours of sleep. We must emphasize this. We all know folks who have transformed their entire lives simply by obtaining enough sleep on a daily basis. Your body won't function as well even with the best diet and fitness regimen in the world if you don't get enough sleep. Make it a high priority.

Benefits of the Mediterranean Diet

Fad diets come and go because they are difficult to maintain and have short-term effects. The Mediterranean diet, on the other hand, is here to stay. It's not only delicious and filling, but it's also simple to follow for the rest of your life. Furthermore, it is supported by extensive research on heart disease and a variety of other benefits.

LOWERS THE RISK OF HEART DISEASE

According to numerous studies conducted over many years, the Mediterranean diet lowers the overall risk of death from cardiovascular disease, including heart attack and stroke. By lowering plaque buildup in the arteries, lowering cholesterol levels, and promoting stronger, less rigid, and healthier blood vessels, the eating pattern improves overall health.

WEIGHT MANAGEMENT BENEFITS

The Mediterranean way of eating can nevertheless help you lose weight, especially belly fat, and make it simpler to maintain a healthy weight, even though there is no emphasis on calories, even those from fat.

MAY REVERSE METABOLIC SYNDROME

High triglycerides, low HDL ("good") cholesterol, high blood pressure, high blood sugar or insulin resistance, and extra belly fat are all hallmarks of metabolic syndrome. They raise your risk of diabetes and heart disease when combined. The chance of getting metabolic syndrome is lower in people who follow a Mediterranean-style diet, and research has shown that doing so can even help reverse the condition.

ASSISTS IN MANAGING DIABETES

This healthy eating pattern provides several advantages if diabetes runs in your family, if you already have diabetes, or if you have prediabetes. A significant factor in this is the emphasis on good fats. Because it contains little processed carbs and added sugar, the diet has been demonstrated to enhance blood glucose levels. Furthermore, it appears that olive oil in particular can lower the chance of developing diabetes.

IMPROVES BRAIN HEALTH AND COGNITIVE FUNCTION

The impact of nutrition on cognitive performance and brain health at all stages of life—not only with aging—is another topic under investigation by experts. For instance:

- Pregnancy, and the fetus, can be healthier when the Mediterranean diet is followed.
- According to an Australian study, the Mediterranean diet may help people with early-stage Alzheimer's disease or those who are at risk for the condition to halt its course.
- In your twenties and thirties, sticking to the diet seems to make depression less common as you become older.

MAY REDUCE THE RISK OF CANCER

The abundant antioxidants in the Mediterranean diet can shield your DNA and cells from oxidative damage, which promotes the development of cancer cells. Particularly, eating a Mediterranean-style diet may lower your chance of developing breast, endometrial, bladder, prostate, and colorectal cancers.

Chapter 2
Start your Mediterranean Diet Journey

Foods to Focus on

- **Fruits and vegetables:** Plant foods make up the majority of the diet and are represented at the top of the food pyramid. Phytonutrients are unique substances found in plants that protect them from pests and diseases. These phytonutrients in plants can also protect us from sickness when we eat the plants. Fruits and vegetables high in fiber can lower our chance of developing chronic diseases and add bulk to our meals, making us feel full and content.
- **Nuts and seeds:** Although nuts and seeds have some protein, their main lipids are monounsaturated and polyunsaturated fats, which are good fats that lower the risk of disease. Additionally containing fiber, protein, and phytonutrients are whole nuts and seeds.
- **Beans, legumes, and whole grains:** Common ingredients in Mediterranean cuisine, these include lentils, black beans, pinto beans, cannellini beans, and chickpeas (also known as garbanzo beans). They are abundant in fiber, protein, and energy-boosting B vitamins. Consuming more whole grains, beans, and other legumes is linked to a lower risk of disease.
- **Olives and olive oil:** A daily intake of olives and/or olive oil is required for those adhering to the Mediterranean Diet. Monounsaturated fatty acids and antioxidants are abundant in olives, which are good for the heart. Furthermore, the olive fruit (yes, it qualifies as a fruit) has high levels of iron and fiber.
- **Herbs and spices:** In addition to offering potent phytonutrients, numerous herbs and spices help to create the distinct flavor profiles that are prevalent in Mediterranean cuisine. Your meals' nutrition, color, and fresh flavors will all be increased by using a range of herbs and spices.
- **Oily fish and seafood:** According to 2006 research published in the Journal of the American Medical Association, eating seafood two to three times per week lowers the risk of death from any cause, which is why it has a prominent place on the Mediterranean diet pyramid. According to a 2007 study published in The Lancet, it is crucial throughout pregnancy and aids in the growth of a child's brain and eyes. An investigation published in Neurology in 2012 found a connection between it and better memory in older people. Few meals have the necessary omega-3 fats that are present in fish.
- **Poultry, eggs, cheese, and yogurt:** These are examples of foods that are consumed frequently but in lower quantities as we approach the pyramid's tip. Red meat is consumed less frequently and in smaller amounts than poultry. A cheap source of complete protein, eggs are also one of the few naturally occurring sources of the brain- and immune-strengthening nutrients choline and vitamin D. Yogurt and cheese are other common sources of protein. These foods contain calcium and potassium, which are essential for bone health, as well as probiotics, which support a healthy immune system.

Foods to Enjoy in Moderation

If you notice the food pyramid you will see the words "less often" with meats and sweets, which indicates they are only occasionally consumed.

- **Red meat:** While red meat contains essential nutrients like iron, vitamin B12, and protein, a 2012 study published in the Archives of Internal Medicine found that consuming other protein sources like fish, beans, or nuts frequently or in place of red meat can reduce your risk for several diseases and early death. Consume red meat in moderation as a side dish.
- **Sweets:** In the Mediterranean diet, cakes, ice cream, cookies, pastries, and candies are only consumed on special occasions. We advise reducing your sugar intake gradually. Reduce the number of baked products you consume while substituting fruit for dessert twice a week.
- **Wine:** Sipped slowly, wine is a key component of the Mediterranean diet and enhances the flavor and enjoyment of food. Dietary Guidelines for Americans, currently revised, describe moderate consumption as two 5-ounce glasses of wine for men and one for women per day. These dosages seem to offer the best balance of health benefits and dangers.

Foods to Cut Back on

Processed meats: Processed meats like deli meats, sausage, salami, and bacon often include a lot of salt and fillers. Prosciutto and other cured meats are preferred but are only consumed sometimes.

Added sugars: We're not referring to sugars found naturally in fruits, vegetables, or dairy products; rather, we're referring to sugars that have been added to a product. These days, they may be found in just about anything, including bread, yogurt, sauces, and drinks, and you may not even be aware of how much you are ingesting. On food labels, look for "added sugars." Additionally, you can typically cut the sugar in any recipe by a few tablespoons. When eating the Mediterranean diet, honey is a common sweetener, but keep in mind that it's still regarded as added sugar.

Refined grains: During the milling process, refined grains lose their bran and germ, which also removes much of the B vitamins, iron, and phytonutrients that are present. They can frequently be found in bread, desserts, granola bars, some cereals, and savory or sweet snacks. They are identified on food labels as wheat flour, rice flour, and any flour or grain without the word "whole" in front of them (except oats as they are always whole grain).

Sodium: The majority of the sodium in our diet comes from processed items like fast food, frozen pizzas, frozen dinners, processed meats, and sauces rather than from the saltshaker. When purchasing items like beans, tomatoes, and broth that are canned, look for no-salt-added or lower-sodium labels. We suggest kosher or sea salt instead of regular table salt in our recipes since the larger granules mean you need less per serving. However, a small amount of salt is necessary when cooking to bring out the taste of the other ingredients.

Empty-calorie beverages: The only things that sports drinks, energy drinks, sweetened iced teas, and sodas add to your diet are calories and sugar. The bottom line is to drink water. (And the occasional bottle of wine; we'll also give you your coffee!)

Follow the 8 DIETARY COMMANDMENTS

ADOPT GREENS
no day without greens and
other vegetables

SAY YES
to fish and legumes

TAKE TO FRUITS
no day without figs or
other fruit

LOVE PLANT FOODS
no day without
walnuts and flaxseeds

DAILY GRAINS
no day without
whole grains and cereals

SAY NO
to meat (beef, lamb, pork)

ENJOY
moderate alcohol consumption,
mainly in the form of
red wine, recommended
at dinner.

AVOID FATS
no more butter and cream - to be
replaced by extra virgin olive oil

BONUS FOOD FOR THE HARD WORK - Plus a deep, dark, sinfully rich chocolate!

8 Principles of the Mediterranean Diet

The Mediterranean diet emphasizes the same basic food groups that you are already familiar with, albeit they are almost certainly cooked and served differently. Equally significant to the food consumed is how it is consumed—more slowly, deliberately, and with family and friends. The following are the eight straightforward principles of the Mediterranean diet:

1. **Focus on vegetables:** Fresh, vibrant, and in-season veggies are the highlight of every dinner. Eating seasonally ensures that freshness and diversity are always present.
2. **Modify your thoughts about meat:** Small amounts of chicken and beef are recommended in the Mediterranean diet, which prioritizes seafood and high-fiber legumes for protein. That doesn't mean that meat is forbidden, but it is always accompanied by vegetables and consumed in moderation, usually only on special occasions.
3. **Allow spices and herbs to shine:** All herbs and spices, whether dried or fresh, provide your foods' taste, color, and a host of health advantages.
4. **Accept healthy fats:** Mediterranean diet is not always low in fat. Instead, it offers wholesome, superior

sources of fat. Every kitchen must have olive oil in addition to nuts, olives, and seeds.

5. **Eat quality dairy products:** Cheese and plain, unsweetened yogurt are staples of the Mediterranean diet. Similar to meat, they are consumed in smaller portions and frequently with fruits, vegetables, and other staple foods.

6. **Change to ancient grains:** The Mediterranean diet includes whole and cracked ancient grains such as barley, oats, farro, and bulgur in place of white or processed grains that have been depleted of their nutrients. The staple food is bread, but it's often made from fermented sourdough and whole grains.

7. **Make fruit the centerpiece of your dessert:** Fruits are rich in natural sugars, and whether combined with almonds, a small amount of cheese, or a baked treat, they contribute fiber and nutrients while satisfying your sweet taste.

8. **Make eating a celebration:** Gourmet dining is not the focus of Mediterranean cuisine. They emphasize appreciating food's simplicity and taking the time to share its vibrant flavors with loved ones. If at all possible, eat with a loved one at the table and take the time to enjoy the food you are eating and where it came from.

In addition to being a method to eat, the Mediterranean diet is also a way to enjoy food. Commit to not only adhering to the diet but also to emulating a society in which simple preparation of meals and liberal sharing of food are valued, as well as the practice of indulging in leisurely meals accompanied by wine and discussion.

In addition to enhancing your health and assisting with weight loss, a Mediterranean diet can also motivate you to take breaks from your busy schedule at least two or three times every day.

Have fun learning about the Mediterranean diet, spend your weekends at the farmers' market, and turn eating new foods into an adventure. By serving your family and friends these inexpensive but delectable dishes, you can add additional social time to your week.

Living healthfully is important. The Mediterranean diet not only ensures healthy living but also ensures joyful living! So, hopefully, this Mediterranean diet cookbook will help you enjoy healthy and joyful living.

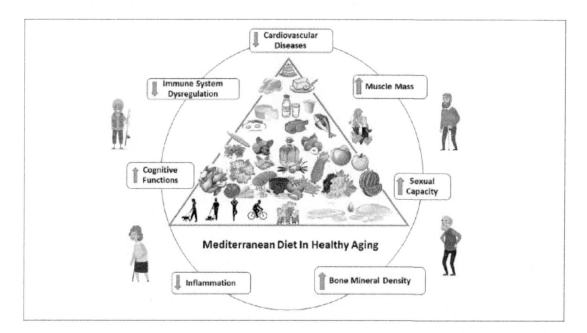

Morning Buzz Iced Coffee

Prep Time: 10 minutes | Serves 1

- 1 cup freshly brewed strong black coffee, cooled slightly
- 1 tablespoon extra-virgin olive oil
- 1 tablespoon half-and-half or heavy cream (optional)
- 1 teaspoon MCT oil (optional)
- ⅛ teaspoon almond extract
- ⅛ teaspoon ground cinnamon

1. Pour the slightly cooled coffee into a blender or large glass (if using an immersion blender).
2. Add the olive oil, half-and-half (if using), MCT oil (if using), almond extract, and cinnamon.
3. Blend well until smooth and creamy. Drink warm and enjoy.

PER SERVING

Calories: 128, Total Fat: 14g, Total Carbs: 0g, Net Carbs: 0g, Fiber: 0g, Protein: 0g; Sodium: 5mg

Mediterranean Frittata

Prep time: 5 minutes | Cook time: 15 minutes | Serves 2

- 4 large eggs
- 2 tablespoons fresh chopped herbs, such as rosemary, thyme, oregano, basil or 1 teaspoon dried herbs
- ¼ teaspoon salt
- Freshly ground black pepper
- 4 tablespoons extra-virgin olive oil, divided
- 1 cup fresh spinach, arugula, kale, or other leafy greens
- 4 ounces quartered artichoke hearts, rinsed, drained, and thoroughly dried
- 8 cherry tomatoes, halved
- ½ cup crumbled soft goat cheese

1. Preheat the oven to broil on low.
2. In small bowl, combine the eggs, herbs, salt, and pepper and whisk well with a fork. Set aside.
3. In a 4- to 5-inch oven-safe skillet or omelet pan, heat 2 tablespoons olive oil over medium heat. Add the spinach, artichoke hearts, and cherry tomatoes and sauté until just wilted, 1 to 2 minutes.
4. Pour in the egg mixture and let it cook undisturbed over medium heat for 3 to 4 minutes, until the eggs begin to set on the bottom.
5. Sprinkle the goat cheese across the top of the egg mixture and transfer the skillet to the oven.
6. Broil for 4 to 5 minutes, or until the frittata is firm in the center and golden brown on top.
7. Remove from the oven and run a rubber spatula around the edge to loosen the sides. Invert onto a large plate or cutting board and slice in half. Serve warm and drizzled with the remaining 2 tablespoons olive oil.

PER SERVING

Calories: 527, Total Fat: 47g, Total Carbs: 10g, Net Carbs: 7g, Fiber: 3g, Protein: 21g; Sodium: 760mg

Green Goddess Smoothie

Prep time: 5 minutes | Cook time: 5 minutes | Serves 1

- 1 small very ripe avocado, peeled and pitted
- 1 cup almond milk or water, plus more as needed
- 1 cup tender baby spinach leaves, stems removed
- ½ medium cucumber, peeled and seeded
- 1 tablespoon extra-virgin olive oil or avocado oil
- 8 to 10 fresh mint leaves, stems removed
- Juice of 1 lime (about 1 to 2 tablespoons)

1. In a blender or a large wide-mouth jar, if using an immersion blender, combine the avocado, almond milk, spinach, cucumber, olive oil, mint, and lime juice and blend until smooth and creamy, adding more almond milk or water to achieve your desired consistency.

PER SERVING

Calories: 330, Total Fat: 30g, Total Carbs: 19g, Net Carbs: 10g, Fiber: 9g, Protein: 4g; Sodium: 36mg

Blueberry Power Smoothie

Prep time: 5 minutes | Cook time: 5 minutes | Serves 1

- 1 cup unsweetened almond milk, plus more as needed
- ¼ cup frozen blueberries
- 2 tablespoons unsweetened almond butter
- 1 tablespoon ground flaxseed or chia seeds
- 1 tablespoon extra-virgin olive oil or avocado oil
- 1 to 2 teaspoons stevia or monk fruit extract (optional)
- ½ teaspoon vanilla extract
- ¼ teaspoon ground cinnamon

1. In a blender or a large wide-mouth jar, if using an immersion blender, combine the almond milk, blueberries, almond butter, flaxseed, olive oil, stevia (if using), vanilla, and cinnamon and blend until smooth and creamy, adding more almond milk to achieve your desired consistency.

PER SERVING

Calories: 460, Total Fat: 40g, Total Carbs: 20g, Net Carbs: 10g, Fiber: 10g, Protein: 9g; Sodium: 147mg

Spiced Orange-Pistachio Smoothie

Prep time: 5 minutes | Cook time: 5 minutes| Serves 1

- ½ cup plain whole-milk Greek yogurt
- ½ cup unsweetened almond milk, plus more as needed
- Zest and juice of 1 clementine or ½ orange
- 1 tablespoon extra-virgin olive oil or MCT oil
- 1 tablespoon shelled pistachios, coarsely chopped
- 1 to 2 teaspoons monk fruit extract or stevia (optional)
- ¼ to ½ teaspoon ground allspice or unsweetened pumpkin pie spice
- ¼ teaspoon ground cinnamon
- ¼ teaspoon vanilla extract

1. In a blender or a large wide-mouth jar, if using an immersion blender, combine the yogurt, ½ cup almond milk, clementine zest and juice, olive oil, pistachios, monk fruit extract (if using), allspice, cinnamon, and vanilla and blend until smooth and creamy, adding more almond milk to achieve your desired consistency.

PER SERVING

Calories: 264, Total Fat: 22g, Total Carbs: 12g, Net Carbs: 10g, Fiber: 2g, Protein: 6g; Sodium: 127mg

Florentine Breakfast Sandwich

Prep time: 5 minutes | Cook time: 5 minutes| Serves 1

- 1 teaspoon extra-virgin olive oil
- 1 large egg
- ¼ teaspoon salt
- ¼ teaspoon freshly ground black pepper
- 1 versatile sandwich round
- 1 tablespoon jarred pesto
- ¼ ripe avocado, mashed
- 1 (¼-inch) thick tomato slice
- 1 (1-ounce) slice fresh mozzarella

1. In a small skillet, heat the olive oil over high heat. When the oil is very hot, crack the egg into the skillet and reduce the heat to medium. Sprinkle the top of the egg with salt and pepper and let it cook for 2 minutes, or until set on bottom.
2. Using a spatula, flip the egg to cook on the other side to desired level of doneness (1 to 2 minutes for a runnier yolk, 2 to 3 minutes for a more set yolk). Remove the egg from the pan and keep warm.
3. Cut the sandwich round in half horizontally and toast, if desired.
4. To assemble the sandwich, spread the pesto on a toasted bread half. Top with mashed avocado, the tomato slice, mozzarella, and the cooked egg. Top with the other bread half and eat warm.

PER SERVING

Calories: 548, Total Fat: 48g, Total Carbs: 8g, Net Carbs: 5g, Fiber: 3g, Protein: 21g; Sodium: 1450mg

Avocado Toast

Prep time: 5 minutes | Cook time: 5 minutes| Serves 2

- 2 tablespoons ground flaxseed
- ½ teaspoon baking powder
- 2 large eggs
- 1 teaspoon salt, plus more for serving
- ½ teaspoon freshly ground black pepper, plus more for serving
- ½ teaspoon garlic powder, sesame seed, caraway seed or other dried herbs (optional)
- 3 tablespoons extra-virgin olive oil, divided
- 1 medium ripe avocado, peeled, pitted, and sliced
- 2 tablespoons chopped ripe tomato or salsa

1. In a small bowl, combine the flaxseed and baking powder, breaking up any lumps in the baking powder. Add the eggs, salt, pepper, and garlic powder (if using) and whisk well. Let sit for 2 minutes.
2. In a small nonstick skillet, heat 1 tablespoon olive oil over medium heat. Pour the egg mixture into the skillet and let cook undisturbed until the egg begins to set on bottom, 2 to 3 minutes.
3. Using a rubber spatula, scrape down the sides to allow uncooked egg to reach the bottom. Cook another 2 to 3 minutes.
4. Once almost set, flip like a pancake and allow the top to fully cook, another 1 to 2 minutes.
5. Remove from the pan and allow to cool slightly. Slice into 2 pieces.
6. Top each "toast" with avocado slices, additional salt and pepper, chopped tomato, and drizzle with the remaining 2 tablespoons olive oil.

PER SERVING (1 TOAST)

Calories: 287, Total Fat: 25g, Total Carbs: 10g, Net Carbs: 3g, Fiber: 7g, Protein: 9g; Sodium: 1130mg

Baklava Hot Porridge

Prep time: 5 minutes | Cook time: 5 minutes| Serves 2

- 2 cups riced cauliflower
- ¾ cup unsweetened almond milk
- 4 tablespoons extra-virgin olive oil, divided
- 2 teaspoons grated fresh orange peel (from ½ orange)
- ½ teaspoon ground cinnamon
- ½ teaspoon almond extract or vanilla extract
- ⅛ teaspoon salt
- 4 tablespoons chopped walnuts, divided
- 1 to 2 teaspoons liquid stevia, monk fruit, or other sweetener of choice (optional)

1. In medium saucepan, combine the riced cauliflower, almond milk, 2 tablespoons olive oil, grated orange peel, cinnamon, almond extract, and salt. Stir to combine and bring just to a boil over medium-high heat, stirring constantly.
2. Remove from heat and stir in 2 tablespoons chopped walnuts and sweetener (if using). Stir to combine.
3. Divide into bowls, topping each with 1 tablespoon of chopped walnuts and 1 tablespoon of the remaining olive oil.

PER SERVING

Calories: 382, Total Fat: 38g, Total Carbs: 11g, Net Carbs: 7g, Fiber: 4g, Protein: 5g; Sodium: 229mg

Greek Yogurt Parfait

Prep time: 5 minutes | Cook time: 5 minutes| Serves 1

- ½ cup plain whole-milk Greek yogurt
- 2 tablespoons heavy whipping cream
- ¼ cup frozen berries, thawed with juices
- ½ teaspoon vanilla or almond extract (optional)
- ¼ teaspoon ground cinnamon (optional)
- 1 tablespoon ground flaxseed
- 2 tablespoons chopped nuts (walnuts or pecans)

1. In a small bowl or glass, combine the yogurt, heavy whipping cream, thawed berries in their juice, vanilla or almond extract (if using), cinnamon (if using), and flaxseed and stir well until smooth. Top with chopped nuts and enjoy.

PER SERVING

Calories: 267, Total Fat: 19g, Total Carbs: 12g, Net Carbs: 8g, Fiber: 4g, Protein: 12g; Sodium: 63mg

Lemon Olive Oil Breakfast Cakes with Berry Syrup

Prep time: 5 minutes | Cook time: 15 minutes| Serves 4

FOR THE PANCAKES

- 1 cup almond flour
- 1 teaspoon baking powder
- ¼ teaspoon salt
- 6 tablespoon extra-virgin olive oil, divided
- 2 large eggs
- Zest and juice of 1 lemon
- ½ teaspoon almond or vanilla extract
- For the Berry Sauce
- 1 cup frozen mixed berries
- 1 tablespoon water or lemon juice, plus more if needed
- ½ teaspoon vanilla extract

TO MAKE THE PANCAKES

1. In a large bowl, combine the almond flour, baking powder, and salt and whisk to break up any clumps.
2. Add the 4 tablespoons olive oil, eggs, lemon zest and juice, and almond extract and whisk to combine well.
3. In a large skillet, heat 1 tablespoon of olive oil and spoon about 2 tablespoons of batter for each of 4 pancakes. Cook until bubbles begin to form, 4 to 5 minutes, and flip. Cook another 2 to 3 minutes on second side. Repeat with remaining 1 tablespoon olive oil and batter.

TO MAKE THE BERRY SAUCE

1. In a small saucepan, heat the frozen berries, water, and vanilla extract over medium-high for 3 to 4 minutes, until bubbly, adding more water if mixture is too thick. Using the back of a spoon or fork, mash the berries and whisk until smooth.

PER SERVING (2 PANCAKES WITH ¼ CUP BERRY SYRUP)

Calories: 275, Total Fat: 26g, Total Carbs: 8g, Net Carbs: 6g, Fiber: 2g, Protein: 4g; Sodium: 271mg

Greek Egg and Tomato Scramble

Prep time: 5 minutes | Cook time: 25 minutes| Serves 4

- ¼ cup extra-virgin olive oil, divided
- 1½ cups chopped fresh tomatoes
- ¼ cup finely minced red onion
- 2 garlic cloves, minced
- ½ teaspoon dried oregano or 1 to 2 teaspoons chopped fresh oregano
- 8 large eggs
- ½ teaspoon salt
- ¼ teaspoon freshly ground black pepper
- ¾ cup crumbled feta cheese
- ¼ cup chopped fresh mint leaves

1. In large skillet, heat the olive oil over medium heat. Add the chopped tomatoes and red onion and sauté until tomatoes are cooked through and soft, 10 to 12 minutes.
2. Add the garlic, oregano, and thyme and sauté another 2 to 4 minutes, until fragrant and liquid has reduced.
3. In a medium bowl, whisk together the eggs, salt, and pepper until well combined.
4. Add the eggs to the skillet, reduce the heat to low, and scramble until set and creamy, using a spatula to move them constantly, 3 to 4 minutes. Remove the skillet from the heat, stir in the feta and mint, and serve warm.

PER SERVING

Calories: 338, Total Fat: 28g, Total Carbs: 6g, Net Carbs: 5g, Fiber: 1g, Protein: 16g; Sodium: 570mg

Egg Baked in Avocado

Prep time: 5 minutes | Cook time: 15 minutes| Serves 2

- 1 ripe large avocado
- 2 large eggs
- Salt
- Freshly ground black pepper
- 4 tablespoons jarred pesto, for serving
- 2 tablespoons chopped tomato, for serving
- 2 tablespoons crumbled feta, for serving (optional)

1. Preheat the oven to 425°F.
2. Slice the avocado in half and remove the pit. Scoop out about 1 to 2 tablespoons from each half to create a hole large enough to fit an egg. Place the avocado halves on a baking sheet, cut-side up.
3. Crack 1 egg in each avocado half and season with salt and pepper.
4. Bake until the eggs are set and cooked to desired level of doneness, 10 to 15 minutes.
5. Remove from oven and top each avocado with 2 tablespoons pesto, 1 tablespoon chopped tomato, and 1 tablespoon crumbled feta (if using).

PER SERVING

Calories: 302, Total Fat: 26g, Total Carbs: 10g, Net Carbs: 5g, Fiber: 5g, Protein: 8g; Sodium: 436mg

Sweet 'n' Savory Toast with Burrata and Berries

Prep time: 5 minutes | Cook time: 5 minutes| Serves 2

- ½ cup mixed frozen berries
- Juice of 1 clementine or ½ orange (about ¼ cup)
- ½ teaspoon vanilla extract
- 1 versatile sandwich round
- 2 ounces burrata cheese

1. To make the berry sauce, in a small saucepan, heat the frozen berries, clementine juice, and vanilla over medium-high heat until simmering. Reduce the heat to low and simmer, stirring occasionally, until the liquid reduces and the mixture becomes syrupy.
2. Cut the sandwich round in half horizontally and toast each half in a toaster or under a broiler.
3. On a rimmed dish, slice the burrata into two slices, reserving the cream.
4. Top each toasted sandwich round half with 1 ounce sliced burrata cheese, the reserved cream, and ¼ cup berry sauce.

PER SERVING (1 TOAST)

Calories: 221, Total Fat: 17g, Total Carbs: 6g, Net Carbs: 5g, Fiber: 1g, Protein: 11g; Sodium: 225mg

Crustless Greek Cheese Pie

Prep time: 15 minutes | Cook time: 45 minutes| Serves 6

- 4 tablespoons extra-virgin olive oil, divided
- 1¼ cups crumbled traditional Greek feta
- 2 tablespoons chopped fresh mint
- 1 tablespoon chopped fresh dill
- ½ teaspoon lemon zest
- ¼ teaspoon freshly ground black pepper
- 2 large eggs
- ½ teaspoon baking powder

1. Preheat the oven to 350°F.
2. Pour 2 tablespoons olive oil into an 8-inch square baking dish and swirl to coat the bottom and about 1 inch up the sides of the dish.
3. In a medium bowl, combine the feta and ricotta and blend well with a fork, crumbling the feta into very small pieces.
4. Stir in the mint, dill, lemon zest, and pepper and mix well.
5. In a small bowl, beat together the eggs and baking powder. Add to the cheese mixture and blend well.
6. Pour into the prepared baking dish and drizzle the remaining 2 tablespoons olive oil over top.
7. Bake until lightly browned and set, 35 to 40 minutes.

PER SERVING

Calories: 182, Total Fat: 17g, Total Carbs: 2g, Net Carbs: 2g, Fiber: 0g, Protein: 7g; Sodium: 322mg

Lemon-Olive Oil Breakfast Pancakes with Berry Syrup

Prep time: 5 minutes | Cook time: 20 minutes| Serves 4

FOR THE PANCAKES

- 1 cup almond flour
- 1 teaspoon baking powder
- ¼ teaspoon salt
- 6 tablespoons extra-virgin olive oil, divided
- 2 large eggs
- Grated zest and juice of 1 lemon
- ½ teaspoon almond or vanilla extract

FOR THE BERRY SYRUP

- 1 cup frozen mixed berries
- 1 tablespoon water or lemon juice, plus more if needed
- ½ teaspoon vanilla extract

TO MAKE THE PANCAKES

1. In a large bowl, combine the almond flour, baking powder, and salt and whisk to break up any clumps.
2. Add 4 tablespoons of olive oil, the eggs, grated lemon zest and juice, and almond extract and whisk to combine well.
3. In a large skillet, heat 1 tablespoon of olive oil over medium heat and spoon about 2 tablespoons of batter for each of the 4 pancakes into the skillet. Cook until bubbles begin to form, 4 to 5 minutes, and flip. Cook 2 to 3 minutes more on the second side. Repeat with the remaining 1 tablespoon of olive oil and the remaining batter.
4. Leftover pancakes can be frozen in an airtight container for up to 2 months.

TO MAKE THE BERRY SYRUP

5. In a small saucepan, heat the frozen berries, water, and vanilla over medium-high heat for 3 to 4 minutes, until bubbly, adding more water if the mixture is too thick. Using the back of a spoon or fork, mash the berries, and whisk until smooth.
6. Refrigerate in an airtight container for 2 to 3 days.

PER SERVING (2 PANCAKES WITH ¼ CUP BERRY SYRUP)

Calories: 379; Total Fat: 35g; Saturated Fat: 5g; Cholesterol: 93mg; Sodium: 273mg; Potassium: 248mg; Magnesium: 71mg; Carbohydrates: 12g; Sugars: 5g; Fiber: 4g; Protein: 8g; Added Sugars: 0g; Vitamin K: 19mcg

Caprese Egg Muffin Cups

Prep time: 10 minutes | Cook time: 25 minutes| Serves 4

- 6 large eggs
- 4 egg whites
- ½ cup 1% milk
- ⅛ teaspoon salt
- Freshly ground black pepper
- 2 teaspoons Italian seasoning
- 1 cup diced tomatoes

- ⅓ cup shredded mozzarella cheese
- ½ cup roughly chopped fresh basil, lightly packed
- Nonstick cooking spray

1. Preheat the oven to 350°F.
2. Whisk together the eggs, egg whites, and milk in a bowl. Season with salt, pepper, and Italian seasoning. Add the tomatoes, mozzarella cheese, and basil to the bowl. Stir until everything is well combined.
3. Coat a 12-cup muffin tin with cooking spray. Fill the muffin cups halfway with the egg mixture.
4. Bake for 20 to 25 minutes, until the centers are set and no longer runny. Allow to cool slightly before serving.
5. Refrigerate in an airtight container for up to 5 days and reheat in the microwave before serving.

PER SERVING (3 MUFFINS)

Calories: 174; Total Fat: 10g; Saturated Fat: 4g; Cholesterol: 288mg; Sodium: 313mg; Potassium: 326mg; Magnesium: 25mg; Carbohydrates: 4g; Sugars: 3g; Fiber: 1g; Protein: 16g; Added Sugars: 0g; Vitamin K: 17mcg

Crostini with Smoked Trout

Prep time: 10 minutes | Cook time: 5 minutes| Serves 4

- ½ French baguette, cut into 1-inch-thick slices
- 1 tablespoon extra-virgin olive oil
- ¼ teaspoon onion powder
- 1 (4-ounce) can smoked trout
- ¼ cup crème fraîche
- ¼ teaspoon chopped fresh dill, for garnish

1. Drizzle the bread on both sides with the olive oil and sprinkle with the onion powder.
2. Place the bread in a single layer in a large skillet and toast over medium heat until lightly browned on both sides, 3 to 4 minutes total.
3. Transfer the toasted bread to a serving platter and place one or two pieces of the trout on each slice. Top with the crème fraîche, garnish with the dill, and serve immediately.
4. Store leftovers at room temperature in an airtight container for 5 to 7 days. If you are making these in advance, it is best to add the crème fraîche and fresh dill just before serving.

PER SERVING

Calories: 265; Total Fat: 8g; Saturated Fat: 2g; Cholesterol: 32mg; Sodium: 467mg; Potassium: 283mg; Magnesium: 33mg; Carbohydrates: 30g; Sugars: 3g; Fiber: 1g; Protein: 17g; Added Sugars: 0g; Vitamin K: 3mcg

Loaded Avocado Sweet Potato "Toast"

Prep time: 5 minutes | Cook time: 15 minutes| Serves 4

- 1 avocado, pitted and peeled
- Salt
- Freshly ground black pepper
- 1 large sweet potato, scrubbed with skin on and cut lengthwise into 4 slices
- 4 eggs
- 1 teaspoon fresh thyme, for garnish

1. Preheat oven to 375°F.
2. In a small bowl, mash the avocado and season with salt and black pepper. Set aside.
3. Place the sweet potato slices on a baking sheet lined with aluminum foil or parchment paper. Bake for 15 to 20 minutes, turning once halfway through. Bake until the sweet potato gets soft, slightly caramelized, and crispy along the edge.
4. Prepare the eggs whichever way you desire: hard-boiled, scrambled, poached, over easy, or sunny-side up.
5. Transfer each sweet potato slice to a plate. Top each slice with a quarter of the mashed avocado and an egg. Sprinkle with salt, black pepper, thyme, and red pepper flakes.
6. Refrigerate the leftovers in an airtight container for 3 to 5 days.

PER SERVING

Calories: 180; Total Fat: 12g; Saturated Fat: 3g; Cholesterol: 186mg; Sodium: 131mg; Potassium: 423mg; Magnesium: 29mg; Carbohydrates: 11g; Sugars: 2g; Fiber: 4g; Protein: 8g; Added Sugars: 0g; Vitamin K: 11mcg

Apple Cinnamon Overnight Oats

Prep time: 15 minutes, plus at least 4 hours refrigeration| Serves 2

1 cup old-fashioned rolled oats
2 tablespoons chia seeds or ground flaxseed
1¼ cups 1% milk
½ tablespoon ground cinnamon
2 teaspoons honey or pure maple syrup
½ teaspoon vanilla extract
Dash salt
1 apple, diced

1. Divide the oats, chia seeds, milk, cinnamon, honey, vanilla, and salt into two mason jars. Place the lids tightly on top and shake until thoroughly combined.
2. Remove the lids and add half of the diced apple to each jar. Sprinkle with additional cinnamon, if desired. Place the lids tightly on the jars and refrigerate for at least 4 hours or overnight.
3. Refrigerate in single-serve airtight containers for up to 3 days.

PER SERVING

Calories: 392; Total Fat: 9g; Saturated Fat: 2g; Cholesterol: 8mg; Sodium: 149mg; Potassium: 598mg; Magnesium: 153mg; Carbohydrates: 65g; Sugars: 17g; Fiber: 13g; Protein: 16g; Added Sugars: 6g; Vitamin K: 3mcg

Tomato and Herb Baked Ricotta Toast

Prep time: 5 minutes | Cook time: 15 minutes| Serves 6

- 2 tablespoons extra-virgin olive oil, divided
- 1 tablespoon red wine vinegar
- 1 garlic clove, minced
- 1 pint cherry tomatoes, halved
- Salt
- Freshly ground black pepper
- 1 (8-ounce) container part-skim ricotta cheese
- ¼ cup coarsely chopped fresh basil
- ¼ cup coarsely chopped fresh parsley
- 2 tablespoons finely chopped fresh oregano
- 1 tablespoon finely chopped fresh rosemary
- 6 (¾-inch-thick) slices sourdough bread

1. Preheat the oven to 400°F.
2. In a medium bowl, whisk together 1 tablespoon of oil and the red wine vinegar. Add the garlic and cherry tomatoes, and season with salt and pepper. Mix until combined and set aside.
3. In another medium bowl, combine the ricotta, basil, parsley, oregano, and rosemary.
4. Line up the sourdough slices on a baking sheet. Brush each side of the bread with the remaining 1 tablespoon of olive oil. Scoop some of the herbed ricotta on top of each slice of bread. Top with the tomato mixture, pressing down so the tomatoes sink into the ricotta. Bake for 10 to 15 minutes, or until the tomatoes begin to blister and the cheese is golden.
5. You can prepare this in advance and refrigerate the tomato mixture and cheese blend in separate airtight containers for up to 7 days.

PER SERVING

Calories: 186; Total Fat: 8g; Saturated Fat: 3g; Cholesterol: 12mg; Sodium: 259mg; Potassium: 165mg; Magnesium: 21mg; Carbohydrates: 20g; Sugars: 2g; Fiber: 1g; Protein: 8g; Added Sugars: 0g; Vitamin K: 50mcg

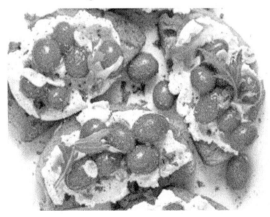

California Egg White Scramble

Prep time: 20 minutes | Cook time: 5 minutes| Serves 4

- 10 large egg whites
- 1 tablespoon chopped fresh parsley
- 1 teaspoon chopped fresh basil
- ½ teaspoon chopped fresh thyme
- Salt
- Freshly ground black pepper
- 1 tablespoon extra-virgin olive oil
- 1 ripe avocado, pitted, peeled, and chopped
- 1 cup halved cherry tomatoes, at room temperature
- 2 tablespoons chopped fresh cilantro
- 1 tablespoon minced jalapeño

1. In a medium bowl, whisk together the egg whites, parsley, basil, and thyme and season with salt and pepper.
2. In a large skillet, heat the olive oil over medium heat. Pour the egg mixture into the skillet and swirl the pan lightly. Scramble the eggs until cooked through but still moist, about 5 minutes.
3. Spoon the eggs onto a platter and top with the avocado, tomatoes, scallion, cilantro, and jalapeño. Serve.
4. Refrigerate the leftovers in an airtight container for 3 to 4 days.

PER SERVING

Calories: 162; Total Fat: 11g; Saturated Fat: 2g; Cholesterol: 0mg; Sodium: 183mg; Potassium: 490mg; Magnesium: 31mg; Carbohydrates: 7g; Sugars: 2g; Fiber: 4g; Protein: 10g; Added Sugars: 0g; Vitamin K: 43mcg

Avocado-Blueberry Smoothie

Prep time: 5 minutes| Serves 2

- ½ cup unsweetened almond milk
- ½ cup low-fat plain Greek yogurt
- 1 ripe avocado, peeled, pitted, and coarsely chopped
- 1 cup blueberries
- ¼ cup gluten-free rolled oats
- ½ teaspoon vanilla extract
- 4 ice cubes

1. In a blender, combine the almond milk, yogurt, avocado, blueberries, oats, and vanilla and pulse until well blended.
2. Add the ice cubes and blend until thick and smooth. Serve.
3. While smoothies are best served fresh, you can refrigerate the mixture in an airtight container for up to 1 day. Be sure to choose a container that the smoothie will fill to the brim to prevent oxidation.

PER SERVING

Calories: 328; Total Fat: 18g; Saturated Fat: 3g; Cholesterol: 4mg; Sodium: 89mg; Potassium: 786 mg; Magnesium: 76mg; Carbohydrates: 38g; Sugars: 16g; Fiber: 10g; Protein: 9g; Added Sugars: 0g; Vitamin K: 36mcg

Shakshuka

Prep time: 10 minutes | Cook time: 30 minutes| Serves 6

- ¼ cup extra-virgin olive oil
- 1 onion, chopped
- 1 green bell pepper, seeded and chopped
- 1 garlic clove, minced
- 1 teaspoon smoked paprika
- ½ teaspoon ground cumin
- ¼ teaspoon red pepper flakes
- Pinch salt
- Freshly ground black pepper
- 1 (28-ounce) can whole peeled tomatoes
- 6 large eggs
- ¼ cup chopped fresh flat-leaf parsley

1. In a large skillet, heat the olive oil over medium heat. Cook the onion, bell pepper, garlic, paprika, cumin, red pepper flakes, salt, and black pepper for about 10 minutes, stirring often, until the vegetables soften.
2. Add the tomatoes with their juices and break apart with a potato masher or spoon. Cook the mixture for 10 minutes.
3. Using a spoon, make six wells in the mixture. Crack an egg into each well.
4. Cover the pan, reduce the heat to low, and simmer for 8 to 10 minutes, until the egg whites set and the yolks are still runny.
5. Garnish with chopped parsley.
6. Refrigerate the leftovers in an airtight container for 5 to 7 days. (The spices will meld and you'll get an even more intense flavor.) It's best to reheat on the stove (not in the microwave) to keep the eggs from getting rubbery.

PER SERVING

Calories: 187; Total Fat: 14g; Saturated Fat: 3g; Cholesterol: 186mg; Sodium: 253mg; Potassium: 411mg; Magnesium: 26mg; Carbohydrates: 8g; Sugars: 5g; Fiber: 3g; Protein: 8g; Added Sugars: 0g; Vitamin K: 52mcg

Greek Yogurt Parfait

Prep time: 10 minutes| Serves 4

- 2 cups low-fat plain Greek yogurt, divided
- 1 cup chopped raspberries, divided
- 1 cup granola
- ¼ cup chopped almonds
- ¼ cup honey

1. Spoon ¼ cup of yogurt into each of four wine glasses or mason jars. Arrange a layer of berries on top; then add ¼ cup more of yogurt. Top with the remaining berries, the granola, and almonds. Drizzle with the honey.

PER SERVING

Calories: 273; Total Fat: 7g; Saturated Fat: 2g; Cholesterol: 7mg; Sodium: 88mg; Potassium: 467mg; Magnesium: 74mg; Carbohydrates: 44g; Sugars: 11g; Fiber: 5g; Protein: 11g; Added Sugars: 17g; Vitamin K: 3mcg

Fresh Fruit Crumble Muesli

Prep time: 20 minutes| Serves 4

- 1 cup gluten-free rolled oats
- ¼ cup chopped pecans
- ¼ cup almonds
- 4 pitted Medjool dates
- 1 teaspoon vanilla extract
- ¼ teaspoon ground cinnamon
- 1 cup sliced fresh strawberries
- 1 nectarine, pitted and chopped
- 2 kiwis, peeled and chopped
- ½ cup blueberries
- 1 cup low-fat plain Greek yogurt

1. In a food processor, combine the oats, pecans, almonds, dates, vanilla, and cinnamon and pulse until the mixture resembles coarse crumbs.
2. In a medium bowl, stir together the strawberries, nectarine, kiwi, and blueberries until well mixed. Divide the fruit and yogurt among four bowls and top each bowl with the oat mixture. Serve.
3. Refrigerate in single-serve airtight containers for up to 2 days.

PER SERVING

Calories: 331; Total Fat: 11g; Saturated Fat: 2g; Cholesterol: 4mg; Sodium: 45mg; Potassium: 668mg; Magnesium: 103mg; Carbohydrates: 51g; Sugars: 28g; Fiber: 8g; Protein: 11g; Added Sugars: 0g; Vitamin K: 6mcg3

Spinach Cheese Pie

Prep time: 5 minutes | Cook time: 25 minutes| Serves 8

- 2 tablespoons extra-virgin olive oil
- 1 onion, chopped
- 1 pound frozen spinach, thawed
- ¼ teaspoon ground nutmeg
- ¼ teaspoon garlic salt
- ¼ teaspoon freshly ground black pepper
- 4 large eggs, divided
- 1 cup grated Parmesan cheese, divided
- 2 puff pastry doughs, at room temperature
- 4 hard-boiled eggs, halved
- Nonstick cooking spray

1. Preheat the oven to 350°F. Spritz a baking sheet with nonstick cooking spray and set aside.
2. Heat a large skillet over medium-high heat. Add the olive oil and onion and sauté for about 5 minutes, stirring occasionally, or until translucent.
3. Squeeze the excess water from the spinach, then add to the skillet and cook, uncovered, so that any excess water from the spinach can evaporate.
4. Season with the nutmeg, garlic salt, and black pepper. Remove from heat and set aside to cool.
5. Beat 3 eggs in a small bowl. Add the beaten eggs and ½ cup of Parmesan cheese to the spinach mixture, stirring well.
6. Roll out the pastry dough on the prepared baking sheet. Layer the spinach mixture on top of the dough, leaving 2 inches around each edge.
7. Once the spinach is spread onto the pastry dough, evenly place the hard-boiled egg halves throughout the pie, then cover with the second pastry dough. Pinch the edges closed.
8. Beat the remaining 1 egg in the bowl. Brush the egg wash over the pastry dough.
9. Bake in the preheated oven for 15 to 20 minutes until golden brown.
10. Sprinkle with the remaining ½ cup of Parmesan cheese. Cool for 5 minutes before cutting and serving.

PER SERVING

Calories: 417;Fat: 28.0g;Protein: 17.0g;Carbs: 25.0g

Sweet Banana Pancakes with Strawberries

Prep time: 5 minutes | Cook time: 15 minutes | Serves 4

- 2 tbsp olive oil
- 1 cup flour
- 1 cup + 2 tbsp milk
- 2 eggs, beaten
- ⅓ cup honey
- 1 tsp baking soda
- ¼ tsp salt
- 1 sliced banana
- 1 cup sliced strawberries
- 1 tbsp maple syrup

1. Mix together the flour, milk, eggs, honey, baking soda, and salt in a bowl.
2. Warm the olive oil in a skillet over medium heat and pour in ⅓ cup of the pancake batter. Cook for 2-3 minutes.
3. Add half of the fresh fruit and flip to cook for 2-3 minutes on the other side until cooked through. Top with the remaining fruit, drizzle with maple syrup and serve.

PER SERVING

Calories: 415;Fat: 24g;Protein: 12g;Carbs: 46g.

Pecan & Peach Parfait

Prep time: 5 minutes | Cook time: 15 minutes | Serves 2

- 1½ cups Greek yogurt
- ½ cup pecans
- ½ cup whole-grain rolled oats
- 1 tsp honey
- 1 peeled and chopped peach
- mint leaves for garnish

1. Preheat oven to 310 °F. Pour the oats and pecans into a baking sheet and spread evenly. Toast for 11-13 minutes; set aside. Microwave honey for 30 seconds. Stir in the peach.
2. Divide some peach mixture between 2 glasses, spread some yogurt on top, and sprinkle with the oat mixture. Repeat the layering process to exhaust the ingredients, finishing with the peach mixture. Serve with mint leaves.

PER SERVING

Calories: 403;Fat: 19g;Protein: 22g;Carbs: 40g.

Avocado & Tuna Sandwiches

Prep time: 5 minutes | Cook time: 15 minutes | Serves 4

- 2 cans tuna, packed in olive oil
- 4 bun breads, sliced in half
- 2 tbsp garlic aioli
- 1 avocado, mashed
- 1 tbsp chopped capers
- 1 tsp chopped fresh cilantro

1. Cut each round of bun in half and set aside. Add the tuna and oil into a bowl, and mix in the aioli, avocado, capers, and cilantro.
2. Mix well with a fork. Toast the bread, remove and spread the tuna salad onto each quarter. Serve warm.

PER SERVING

Calories: 436;Fat: 36g;Protein: 22.9g;Carbs: 5g.

Carrot & Pecan Cupcakes

Prep time: 5 minutes | Cook time: 35 minutes | Serves 6

- 2 tbsp olive oil
- 1½ cups grated carrots
- ¼ cup pecans, chopped
- 1 cup oat bran
- 1 cup whole wheat flour
- ½ cup all-purpose flour
- ½ cup old-fashioned oats
- 3 tbsp light brown sugar
- 1 tsp vanilla extract
- ½ lemon, zested
- 1 tsp baking powder
- 2 tsp ground cinnamon
- 2 tsp ground ginger
- ½ tsp ground nutmeg
- ¼ tsp salt
- 1¼ cups soy milk
- 2 tbsp honey
- 1 egg

1. Preheat oven to 350 °F. Mix whole-wheat flour, all-purpose flour, oat bran, oats, sugar, baking powder, cinnamon, nutmeg, ginger, and salt in a bowl; set aside.
2. Beat egg with soy milk, honey, vanilla, lemon zest, and olive oil in another bowl. Pour this mixture into the flour mixture and combine to blend, leaving some lumps.
3. Stir in carrots and pecans. Spoon batter into greased muffin cups. Bake for about 20 minutes. Prick with a toothpick and if it comes out easily, the cakes are cooked done. Let cool and serve.

PER SERVING

Calories: 346;Fat: 10g;Protein: 13g;Carbs: 59g.

Tomato Scrambled Eggs with Feta Cheese

Prep time: 5 minutes | Cook time: 25 minutes| Serves 4

- ¼ cup olive oil
- 2 Roma tomatoes, chopped
- ¼ cup minced red onion
- 2 garlic cloves, minced
- ½ tsp dried oregano
- ½ tsp dried thyme
- 8 large eggs
- Salt and black pepper to taste
- ¾ cup feta cheese, crumbled
- ¼ cup fresh cilantro, chopped

1. Warm the olive oil in a large skillet over medium heat. Add the chopped tomatoes and red onion and sauté for 10 minutes or until the tomatoes are soft. Add the garlic, oregano, and thyme and sauté for another 1-2 minutes until the liquid reduces.
2. In a medium bowl, whisk together the eggs, salt, and pepper until well combined.
3. Add the eggs to the skillet, reduce the heat to low, and scramble until set and creamy, using a spatula to move them constantly, 3-4 minutes. Remove the skillet from the heat, stir in the feta and cilantro, and serve.

PER SERVING

Calories: 338;Fat: 28g;Protein: 16g;Carbs: 6g

Easy Buckwheat Porridge

Prep time: 5 minutes | Cook time: 45 minutes| Serves 4

- 3 cups water
- 2 cups raw buckwheat groats
- Pinch sea salt
- 1 cup unsweetened almond milk

1. In a medium saucepan, add the water, buckwheat groats, and sea salt and bring to a boil over medium-high heat.
2. Once it starts to boil, reduce the heat to low. Cook for about 20 minutes, stirring occasionally, or until most of the water is absorbed.
3. Fold in the almond milk and whisk well. Continue cooking for about 15 minutes, or until the buckwheat groats are very softened.
4. Ladle the porridge into bowls and serve warm.

PER SERVING

Calories: 121;Fat: 1.0g;Protein: 6.3g;Carbs: 21.5g.

Morning Baklava French Toast

Prep time: 5 minutes | Cook time: 25 minutes| Serves 2

- 2 tbsp orange juice
- 3 fresh eggs, beaten
- 1 tsp lemon zest
- 1⁄8 tsp vanilla extract
- ¼ cup honey
- 2 tbsp whole milk
- ¾ tsp ground cinnamon
- ¼ cup walnuts, crumbled
- ¼ cup pistachios, crumbled
- 1 tbsp sugar
- 2 tbsp white bread crumbs
- 4 slices bread
- 2 tbsp unsalted butter
- 1 tsp confectioners' sugar

1. Combine the eggs, orange juice, lemon zest, vanilla, honey, milk, and cinnamon in a bowl; set aside. Pulse walnuts and pistachios in a food processor until they are finely crumbled. In a small bowl, mix the walnuts, pistachios, sugar, and bread crumbs. Spread the nut mixture on 2 bread slices.
2. Cover with the remaining 2 slices. Melt the butter in a skillet over medium heat. Dip the sandwiches into the egg mixture and fry them for 4 minutes on both sides or until golden. Remove to a plate and cut them diagonally. Dust with confectioners' sugar. Serve immediately.

PER SERVING

Calories: 651;Fat: 30g;Protein: 21g;Carbs: 80g

Brown Rice and Black Bean Burgers

Prep time: 5 minutes | Cook time: 45 minutes| Serves 8

- 1 cup cooked brown rice
- 1 can black beans, drained and rinsed
- 1 tablespoon olive oil
- 2 tablespoons taco or seasoning
- ½ yellow onion, finely diced
- 1 beet, peeled and grated
- 1 carrot, peeled and grated
- 2 tablespoons no-salt-added tomato paste
- 2 tablespoons apple cider vinegar
- 3 garlic cloves, minced
- ¼ teaspoon sea salt
- Ground black pepper, to taste
- 8 whole-wheat hamburger buns

TOPPINGS:

- 16 lettuce leaves, rinsed well
- 8 tomato slices, rinsed well
- whole-grain mustard, to taste

1. Line a baking sheet with parchment paper.
2. Put the brown rice and black beans in a food processor and pulse until mix well. Pour the mixture in a large bowl and set aside.
3. Heat the olive oil in a nonstick skillet over medium heat until shimmering.
4. Add the taco seasoning and stir for 1 minute or until fragrant.
5. Add the onion, beet, and carrot and sauté for 5 minutes or until the onion is translucent and beet and carrot are tender.
6. Pour in the tomato paste and vinegar, then add the garlic and cook for 3 minutes or until the sauce is thickened. Sprinkle with salt and ground black pepper.
7. Transfer the vegetable mixture to the bowl of rice mixture, then stir to mix well until smooth.
8. Divide and shape the mixture into 8 patties, then arrange the patties on the baking sheet and refrigerate for at least 1 hour.
9. Preheat the oven to 400°F.
10. Remove the baking sheet from the refrigerator and allow to sit under room temperature for 10 minutes.
11. Bake in the preheated oven for 40 minutes or until golden brown on both sides. Flip the patties halfway through the cooking time.
12. Remove the patties from the oven and allow to cool for 10 minutes.
13. Assemble the buns with patties, lettuce, and tomato slices. Top the filling with mustard and serve immediately.

PER SERVING

Calories: 544;Fat: 20.0g;Protein: 15.8g;Carbs: 76.0g.

Kale Egg Cupcakes

Prep time: 5 minutes | Cook time: 45 minutes| Serves 2

- 1 whole-grain bread slice
- 4 large eggs, beaten
- 3 tbsp milk
- Salt and black pepper to taste
- ½ tsp onion powder
- ¼ tsp garlic powder
- ¾ cup chopped kale

1. Heat the oven to 350 °F. Break the bread into pieces and divide between 2 greased ramekins. Mix the eggs, milk, salt, onion powder, garlic powder, pepper, and kale in a medium bowl.
2. Pour half of the egg mixture into each ramekin and bake for 25 minutes or until the eggs are set. Serve and enjoy!

PER SERVING

Calories: 213;Fat: 12g;Protein: 17g;Carbs: 13g

Chapter 4
Poultry

Grilled Oregano Chicken Kebabs with Zucchini and Olives

Prep time: 10 minutes |Cook time: 20 minutes| Serves 4

- Nonstick cooking spray
- ¼ cup extra-virgin olive oil
- 2 tablespoons balsamic vinegar
- 1 teaspoon dried oregano, crushed between your fingers
- 1 pound boneless, skinless chicken breasts, cut into 1½-inch pieces
- 2 medium zucchini, cut into 1-inch pieces (about 2½ cups)
- ½ cup Kalamata olives, pitted and halved
- 2 tablespoons olive brine
- ¼ cup torn fresh basil leaves

1. Coat the cold grill with nonstick cooking spray. Heat the grill to medium-high.
2. In a small bowl, whisk together the oil, vinegar, and oregano. Divide the marinade between two large plastic zip-top bags.
3. Add the chicken to one bag and the zucchini to another. Seal and massage the marinade into both the chicken and zucchini.
4. Remove the chicken and zucchini from the skewers and put in a large serving bowl. Toss with the olives, olive brine, and basil and serve.

PER SERVING

Calories:283g,TotalFat:15g,SaturatedFat:3g,TotalCarbs:26g, Fiber:3g, Protein:11g, Sugar:7g, Sodium:575mg,Phosphorus: 111mg,Potassium: 208mg,Cholesterol: 31mg,

Honey Almond-Crusted Chicken Tenders

Prep time: 10 minutes |Cook time: 20 minutes| Serves 4

- Nonstick cooking spray
- 1 tablespoon honey
- 1 tablespoon whole-grain or Dijon mustard
- ¼ teaspoon kosher or sea salt
- ¼ teaspoon freshly ground black pepper
- 1 pound boneless, skinless chicken breast tenders or tenderloins
- 1 cup almonds (about 3 ounces)

1. Preheat the oven to 425°F. Line a large, rimmed baking sheet with parchment paper. Place a wire cooling rack on the parchment-lined baking sheet, and coat the rack well with nonstick cooking spray.
2. In a large bowl, combine the honey, mustard, salt, and pepper. Add the chicken and stir gently to coat. Set aside.
3. Use a knife or a mini food processor to roughly chop the almonds; they should be about the size of sunflower seeds. Dump the nuts onto a large sheet of parchment paper and spread them out. Press the coated chicken tenders into the nuts until evenly coated on all sides. Place the chicken on the prepared wire rack.

4. Bake for 15 to 20 minutes, or until the internal temperature of the chicken measures 165°F on a meat thermometer and any juices run clear. Serve immediately.

PER SERVING

Calories:222g, Total Fat:7g, Saturated Fat: 2g,Total Carbs:29 g, Fiber:2g, Protein:11g, Sugar:11g, Sodium:448mg,Phosphorus: 109mg,Potassium: 176mg,Cholesterol: 26mg,

One-Pan Parsley Chicken and Potatoes

Prep time: 5 minutes |Cook time: 25 minutes| Serves 6

- 1½ pounds boneless, skinless chicken thighs, cut into 1-inch cubes
- 1 tablespoon extra-virgin olive oil
- 1½ pounds Yukon Gold potatoes, unpeeled, cut into ½-inch cubes (about 6 small potatoes)
- 2 garlic cloves, minced (about 1 teaspoon)
- ¼ cup dry white wine or apple cider vinegar
- 1 cup low-sodium or no-salt-added chicken broth
- 1 tablespoon Dijon mustard
- ¼ teaspoon kosher or sea salt
- ¼ teaspoon freshly ground black pepper
- 1 cup chopped fresh flat-leaf (Italian) parsley, including stems
- 1 tablespoon freshly squeezed lemon juice (½ small lemon)

1. Pat the chicken dry with a few paper towels. In a large skillet over medium-high heat, heat the oil. Add the chicken and cook for 5 minutes, stirring only after the chicken has browned on one side. Remove the chicken from the pan with a slotted spoon, and put it on a plate; it will not yet be fully cooked. Leave the skillet on the stove.
2. Add the potatoes to the skillet and cook for 5 minutes, stirring only after the potatoes have become golden and crispy on one side. Push the potatoes to the side of the skillet, add the garlic, and cook, stirring constantly, for 1 minute. Add the wine and cook for 1 minute, until nearly evaporated. Add the chicken broth, mustard, salt, pepper, and reserved chicken pieces. Turn the heat up to high, and bring to a boil.
3. Once boiling, cover the skillet, reduce the heat to medium-low, and cook for 10 to 12 minutes, until the potatoes are tender and the internal temperature of the chicken measures 165°F on a meat thermometer and any juices run clear.
4. During the last minute of cooking, stir in the parsley. Remove from the heat, stir in the lemon juice, and serve.

PER SERVING

Calories:324g, Total Fat:9g, Saturated Fat: 3g,- Total Carbs:45 g, Fiber:5g, Protein:16g, Sugar:7g, Sodium:560mg,Phosphorus: 214mg,Potassium: 782mg,Cholesterol: 30mg,

Romesco Poached Chicken

Prep time: 5 minutes |Cook time: 20 minutes| Serves 6

- 1½ pounds boneless, skinless chicken breasts, cut into 6 pieces
- 1 carrot, halved
- 1 celery stalk, halved
- ½ onion, halved
- 2 garlic cloves, smashed
- 3 sprigs fresh thyme or rosemary
- 1 cup Romesco Dip
- 2 tablespoons chopped fresh flat-leaf (Italian) parsley
- ¼ teaspoon freshly ground black pepper

1. Put the chicken in a medium saucepan. Fill with water until there's about one inch of liquid above the chicken. Add the carrot, celery, onion, garlic, and thyme.
2. Cover and bring it to a boil. Reduce the heat to low (keeping it covered), and cook for 12 to 15 minutes, or until the internal temperature of the chicken measures 165°F on a meat thermometer and any juices run clear.
3. Remove the chicken from the water and let sit for 5 minutes.
4. When you're ready to serve, spread ¾ cup of romesco dip on the bottom of a serving platter. Arrange the chicken breasts on top, and drizzle with the remaining romesco dip. Sprinkle the tops with parsley and pepper.

PER SERVING

Calories:270g, Total Fat:11g, Saturated Fat:3 g,Total Carbs:31 g, Fiber:3g, Protein:13g, Sugar:8g, Sodium:647mg,Phosphorus: 197mg,Potassium: 292mg,Cholesterol: 30mg,

Roasted Red Pepper Chicken with Lemony Garlic Hummus

Prep time: 10 minutes |Cook time: 10 minutes| Serves 6

- 1¼ pounds boneless, skinless chicken thighs, cut into 1-inch pieces
- ½ sweet or red onion, cut into 1-inch chunks (about 1 cup)
- 2 tablespoons extra-virgin olive oil
- ½ teaspoon dried thyme
- ¼ teaspoon freshly ground black pepper
- ¼ teaspoon kosher or sea salt
- 1 (12-ounce) jar roasted red peppers, drained and chopped
- lemony garlic hummus, or a 10-ounce container prepared hummus
- ½ medium lemon
- 3 (6-inch) whole-wheat pita breads, cut into eighths

1. Line a large, rimmed baking sheet with aluminum foil. Set aside. Set one oven rack about 4 inches below the broiler element. Preheat the broiler to high.
2. In a large bowl, mix together the chicken, onion, oil, thyme, pepper, and salt. Spread the mixture onto the prepared baking sheet.
3. Place the chicken under the broiler and broil for 5 minutes. Remove the pan, stir in the red peppers, and return to the broiler. Broil for another 5 minutes, or until the chicken and onion just start to char on the tips. Remove from the oven.
4. Spread the hummus onto a large serving platter, and spoon the chicken mixture on top. Squeeze the juice from half a lemon over the top, and serve with the pita pieces.

PER SERVING

Calories:320g, Total Fat:12g, Saturated Fat: 3g,Total Carbs:40 g, Fiber:5g, Protein:13g, Sugar:8g, Sodium:680mg,Phosphorus: 174mg,Potassium: 349mg,Cholesterol: 23mg,

Tahini Chicken Rice Bowls

Prep time: 10 minutes |Cook time: 15 minutes| Serves 4

- 1 cup uncooked instant brown rice
- ¼ cup tahini or peanut butter (tahini for nut-free)
- ¼ cup 2% plain Greek yogurt
- 2 tablespoons chopped scallions, green and white parts (2 scallions)
- 1 tablespoon freshly squeezed lemon juice (from ½ medium lemon)
- 1 tablespoon water
- 1 teaspoon ground cumin
- ¾ teaspoon ground cinnamon
- ¼ teaspoon kosher or sea salt
- 2 cups chopped cooked chicken breast (about 1 pound)
- ½ cup chopped dried apricots
- 2 cups peeled and chopped seedless cucumber (1 large cucumber)
- 4 teaspoons sesame seeds
- Fresh mint leaves, for serving (optional)

1. Cook the brown rice according to the package instructions.
2. While the rice is cooking, in a medium bowl, mix together the tahini, yogurt, scallions, lemon juice, water, cumin, cinnamon, and salt. Transfer half the tahini mixture to another medium bowl. Mix the chicken into the first bowl.
3. When the rice is done, mix it into the second bowl of tahini (the one without the chicken).
4. To assemble, divide the chicken among four bowls. Spoon the rice mixture next to the chicken in each bowl. Next to the chicken, place the dried apricots, and in the remaining empty section, add the cucumbers. Sprinkle with sesame seeds, and top with mint, if desired, and serve.

PER SERVING

Calories:335g, Total Fat:11g, Saturated Fat: 2g,Total Carbs:30 g, Fiber:4g, Protein:31g, Sugar:12g, Sodium:345mg,Phosphorus: 338mg,Potassium: 672mg,Cholesterol: 60mg,

Sheet Pan Lemon Chicken and Roasted Artichokes

Prep time: 10 minutes |Cook time: 20 minutes| Serves 4

- 2 large lemons
- 3 tablespoons extra-virgin olive oil, divided
- ½ teaspoon kosher or sea salt
- 2 large artichokes
- 4 (6-ounce) bone-in, skin-on chicken thighs

1. Put a large, rimmed baking sheet in the oven. Preheat the oven to 450°F with the pan inside. Tear off four sheets of aluminum foil about 8-by-10 inches each; set aside.
2. Using a Microplane or citrus zester, zest 1 lemon into a large bowl. Halve both lemons and squeeze all the juice into the bowl with the zest. Whisk in 2 tablespoons of oil and the salt. Set aside.
3. Rinse the artichokes with cool water, and dry with a clean towel. Using a sharp knife, cut about 1½ inches off the tip of each artichoke. Cut about ¼ inch off each stem. Halve each artichoke lengthwise so each piece has equal amounts of stem. Immediately plunge the artichoke halves into the lemon juice and oil mixture (to prevent browning) and turn to coat on all sides. Lay one artichoke half flat-side down in the center of a sheet of aluminum foil, and close up loosely to make a foil packet. Repeat the process with the remaining three artichoke halves. Set the packets aside.
4. Put the chicken in the remaining lemon juice mixture and turn to coat.
5. Using oven mitts, carefully remove the hot baking sheet from the oven and pour on the remaining tablespoon of oil; tilt the pan to coat. Carefully arrange the chicken, skin-side down, on the hot baking sheet. Place the artichoke packets, flat-side down, on the baking sheet as well. (Arrange the artichoke packets and chicken with space between them so air can circulate around them.)
6. Roast for 20 minutes, or until the internal temperature of the chicken measures 165°F on a meat thermometer and any juices run clear. Before serving, check the artichokes for doneness by pulling on a leaf. If it comes out easily, the artichoke is ready.

PER SERVING

Calories:832g, Total Fat:80g, Saturated Fat: 21g,Total Carbs:11 g, Fiber:5g, Protein:19g, Sugar:2g, Sodium:544mg,Phosphorus: 238mg,Potassium: 530mg,Cholesterol: 182mg,

Peach-Glazed Chicken Drummies

Prep time: 10 minutes |Cook time: 20 minutes| Serves 4

- 8 chicken drumsticks (about 2 pounds), skin removed
- Nonstick cooking spray
- 1 (15-ounce) can sliced peaches in 100% juice, drained
- ¼ cup honey
- ¼ cup cider vinegar
- 3 garlic cloves
- ½ teaspoon smoked paprika
- ¼ teaspoon kosher or sea salt
- ¼ teaspoon freshly ground black pepper

1. Remove the chicken from the refrigerator.
2. Set one oven rack about 4 inches below the broiler element. Preheat the oven to 500°F. Line a large, rimmed baking sheet with aluminum foil. Place a wire cooling rack on the aluminum foil, and spray the rack with nonstick cooking spray. Set aside.
3. In a blender, combine the peaches, honey, vinegar, garlic, smoked paprika, salt, and pepper. Purée the ingredients until smooth.
4. Add the purée to a medium saucepan and bring to a boil over medium-high heat. Cook for 2 minutes, stirring constantly. Divide the sauce among two small bowls. The first bowl will be brushed on the chicken; set aside the second bowl for serving at the table.
5. Brush all sides of the chicken with about half the sauce (keeping half the sauce for a second coating), and place the drumsticks on the prepared rack. Roast for 10 minutes.
6. Remove the chicken from the oven and turn to the high broiler setting. Brush the chicken with the remaining sauce from the first bowl. Return the chicken to the oven and broil for 5 minutes. Turn the chicken; broil for 3 to 5 more minutes, until the internal temperature measures 165°F on a meat thermometer, or until the juices run clear. Serve with the reserved sauce.

PER SERVING

Calories:1492g, Total Fat:26g, Saturated Fat:7 g,Total Carbs:274 g, Fiber:20g, Protein:54g, Sugar:254g, Sodium:487mg,Phosphorus: 547mg,Potassium:1971 mg,Cholesterol: 239mg,

Baked Chicken Caprese

Prep time: 5minutes |Cook time: 25 minutes| Serves 4

- Nonstick cooking spray
- 1 pound boneless, skinless chicken breasts
- 2 tablespoons extra-virgin olive oil
- ¼ teaspoon freshly ground black pepper
- ¼ teaspoon kosher or sea salt
- 1 large tomato, sliced thinly
- 1 cup shredded mozzarella or 4 ounces fresh mozzarella cheese, diced
- 1 (14.5-ounce) can low-sodium or no-salt-added crushed tomatoes
- 2 tablespoons fresh torn basil leaves
- 4 teaspoons balsamic vinegar

1. Set one oven rack about 4 inches below the broiler element. Preheat the oven to 450°F. Line a large, rimmed baking sheet with aluminum foil. Place a wire cooling rack on the aluminum foil, and spray the rack with nonstick cooking spray. Set aside.
2. Cut the chicken into 4 pieces (if they aren't already). Put the chicken breasts in a large zip-top plastic bag. with a rolling pin or meat mallet, pound the chicken so it is evenly flattened, about ¼-inch thick. Add the oil, pepper, and salt to the bag. Reseal the bag, and massage the ingredients into the chicken. Take the chicken out of the bag and place it on the prepared wire rack.
3. Cook the chicken for 15 to 18 minutes, or until the internal temperature of the chicken is 165°F on a meat thermometer and the juices run clear. Turn the oven to the high broiler setting. Layer the tomato slices on each chicken breast, and top with the mozzarella. Broil the chicken for another 2 to 3 minutes, or until the cheese is melted (don't let the chicken burn on the edges). Remove the chicken from the oven.
4. While the chicken is cooking, pour the crushed tomatoes into a small, microwave-safe bowl. Cover the bowl with a paper towel, and microwave for about 1 minute on high, until hot. When you're ready to serve, divide the tomatoes among four dinner plates. Place each chicken breast on top of the tomatoes. Top with the basil and a drizzle of balsamic vinegar.

PER SERVING

Calories:258g, Total Fat:10g, Saturated Fat: 2g,Total Carbs:28 g, Fiber:4g, Protein:14g, Sugar:10g, Sodium:573mg,Phosphorus: 169mg,Potassium: 398mg,Cholesterol: 30mg,

Grape Chicken Panzanella

Prep time: 10 minutes |Cook time: 5 minutes| Serves 6

- 3 cups day-old bread (like a baguette, crusty Italian bread, or whole-grain bread), cut into 1-inch cubes
- 5 tablespoons extra-virgin olive oil, divided
- 2 cups chopped cooked chicken breast (about 1 pound)
- 1 cup red seedless grapes, halved
- ½ pint grape or cherry tomatoes, halved (about ¾ cup)
- ½ cup Gorgonzola cheese crumbles (about 2 ounces)
- ⅓ cup chopped walnuts
- ¼ cup diced red onion (about ⅛ onion)
- 3 tablespoons chopped fresh mint leaves
- ¼ teaspoon freshly ground black pepper
- 1 tablespoon balsamic vinegar
- Zest and juice of 1 small lemon
- 1 teaspoon honey

1. Line a large, rimmed baking sheet with aluminum foil. Set aside. Set one oven rack about 4 inches below the broiler element. Preheat the broiler to high.
2. In a large serving bowl, drizzle the cubed bread with 2 tablespoons of oil, and mix gently with your hands to coat. Spread the mixture over the prepared baking sheet. Place the baking sheet under the broiler for 2 minutes. Stir the bread, then broil for another 30 to 60 seconds, watching carefully so the bread pieces are toasted and not burned. Remove from the oven and set aside.
3. In the same (now empty) large serving bowl, mix together the chicken, grapes, tomatoes, Gorgonzola, walnuts, onion, mint, and pepper. Add the toasted bread pieces, and gently mix together.
4. In a small bowl, whisk together the remaining 3 tablespoons of oil, vinegar, zest and juice from the lemon, and honey. Drizzle the dressing over the salad, toss gently to mix, and serve.

PER SERVING

Calories:273g, Total Fat:14g, Saturated Fat: 4g,Total Carbs:16 g, Fiber:2g, Protein:21g, Sugar:7g, Sodium:343mg,Phosphorus: 222mg,Potassium: 288mg,Cholesterol: 52mg,

Balsamic Chicken Breasts with Feta

Prep time: 5 minutes | Cook time: 35 minutes | Serves 4

- 1 lb chicken breasts, cut into strips
- 2 tbsp olive oil
- 1 fennel bulb, chopped
- Salt and black pepper to taste
- 2 tbsp balsamic vinegar
- 2 cups tomatoes, cubed
- 1 tbsp chives, chopped
- ¼ cup feta cheese, crumbled

1. Warm the olive oil in a skillet over medium heat and sear chicken for 5 minutes, stirring often.
2. Mix in fennel, salt, pepper, vinegar, and tomatoes and cook for 20 minutes. Top with feta cheese and chives and serve.

PER SERVING

Calories: 290;Fat: 16g;Protein: 15g;Carbs: 16g.

saucy Turkey with Ricotta Cheese

Prep time: 5 minutes | Cook time: 65 minutes | Serves 4

- 2 tbsp olive oil
- 1 turkey breast, cubed
- 1½ cups salsa verde
- Salt and black pepper to taste
- 4 oz ricotta cheese, crumbled
- 2 tbsp cilantro, chopped

1. Preheat the oven to 380° F. Grease a roasting pan with oil. In a bowl, place turkey, salsa verde, salt, and pepper and toss to coat.
2. Transfer to the roasting pan and bake for 50 minutes. Top with ricotta cheese and cilantro and serve.

PER SERVING

Calories: 340;Fat: 16g;Protein: 35g;Carbs: 23g.

Eggplant & Chicken Skillet

Prep time: 5 minutes | Cook time: 45 minutes | Serves 4

- 2 tbsp olive oil
- 1 lb eggplants, cubed
- Salt and black pepper to taste
- 1 onion, chopped
- 2 garlic cloves, minced
- 1 tsp hot paprika
- 1 tbsp oregano, chopped
- 1 cup chicken stock
- 1 lb chicken breasts, cubed
- 1 cup half-and-half
- 3 tsp toasted chopped almonds

1. Warm the olive oil in a skillet over medium heat and sauté chicken for 8 minutes, stirring often. Mix in eggplants, onion, and garlic and cook for

another 5 minutes.
2. Season with salt, pepper, hot paprika, and oregano and pour in the stock. Bring to a boil and simmer for 16 minutes. Stir in half and half for 2 minutes. Serve topped with almonds.

PER SERVING

Calories: 400;Fat: 13g;Protein: 26g;Carbs: 22g.

Herb-Marinated Chicken Skewers

Prep time: 10 minutes, plus 30 minutes to marinate | Cook time: 15 minutes | Serves 4

- ¼ cup extra-virgin olive oil
- Grated zest of 1 lemon
- Juice of 2 lemons, about ½ cup
- 1 tablespoon dried oregano
- ½ tablespoon dried thyme
- 3 garlic cloves, minced
- ½ teaspoon salt
- ¼ teaspoon freshly ground black pepper
- 3 pounds boneless, skinless chicken breasts, cut into 2-inch cubes
- Stainless steel skewers

1. In a large bowl with a resealable lid, mix the oil, lemon zest, lemon juice, oregano, thyme, garlic, salt, and pepper. Add the chicken to the herb marinade and stir to coat. Cover the bowl and refrigerate for 20 to 30 minutes.
2. Remove the chicken from the refrigerator, and thread the chicken pieces onto the skewers, about 4 to 5 pieces per skewer. Discard the marinade.
3. Heat a large cast-iron skillet over medium-high heat. Place 3 to 4 skewers in the skillet, and cook for 5 to 7 minutes, turning until the chicken is cooked through and a food thermometer inserted into the thickest part of the chicken reaches an internal temperature of 165°F. Repeat with the remaining skewers until all are cooked, and serve.

PER SERVING

Calories: 519; Fat: 19g; Protein: 79g; Carbohydrates: 3g; Fiber: 1g; Sugar: 1g; Sodium: 532mg

Tunisian Baharaat Grilled Chicken

Prep time: 5 minutes | Cook time: 25 minutes | Serves 4

- 2 tbsp olive oil
- ¼ cup apple cider vinegar
- 1 lemon, zested and juiced
- 4 cloves garlic, minced
- 2 tsp sea salt
- ½ tsp chili powder
- 1 tsp Arabic 7 spices (baharaat)
- ½ tsp cinnamon
- 1 lb chicken breasts

1. In a shallow dish, whisk the olive oil, vinegar, lemon juice, lemon zest, garlic, salt, baharaat, chili powder, and cinnamon. Add the chicken and toss to coat. Marinate for 1 hour. Next, drain, reserving the marinade.
2. Heat your grill to medium-high. Cook the chicken for 10-14 minutes, brushing them with the marinade every 5 minutes until the chicken is golden brown. Serve and enjoy!

PER SERVING

Calories: 516;Fat: 33g;Protein: 49g;Carbs: 2.5g.

Herby Turkey Stew

Prep time: 5 minutes | Cook time: 65 minutes | Serves 4

- 1 skinless, boneless turkey breast, cubed
- 2 tbsp olive oil
- Salt and black pepper to taste
- 1 tbsp sweet paprika
- ½ cup chicken stock
- 1 lb pearl onions
- 2 garlic cloves, minced
- 1 carrot, sliced
- 1 tsp cumin, ground
- 1 tbsp basil, chopped
- 1 tbsp cilantro, chopped

1. Warm the olive oil in a pot over medium heat and sear turkey for 8 minutes, stirring occasionally.
2. Stir in pearl onions, carrot, and garlic and cook for another 3 minutes. Season with salt, pepper, cumin, and paprika.
3. Pour in the stock and bring to a boil; cook for 40 minutes. Top with basil and cilantro.

PER SERVING

Calories: 260;Fat: 12g;Protein: 19g;Carbs: 24g.

Portuguese-style Chicken Breasts

Prep time: 5 minutes | Cook time: 45 minutes | Serves 4

- 2 tbsp avocado oil
- 1 lb chicken breasts, cubed
- Salt and black pepper to taste
- 1 red onion, chopped
- 15 oz canned chickpeas
- 15 oz canned tomatoes, diced
- 1 cup Kalamata olives, pitted and halved
- 2 tbsp lime juice
- 1 tsp cilantro, chopped

1. Warm the olive oil in a pot over medium heat and sauté chicken and onion for 5 minutes.
2. Put in salt, pepper, chickpeas, tomatoes, olives, lime juice, cilantro, and 2 cups of water. Cover with lid and bring to a boil, then reduce the heat and simmer for 30 minutes. Serve warm.

PER SERVING

Calories: 360;Fat: 16g;Protein: 28g;Carbs: 26g.

Za'atar Roasted Chicken Thighs

Prep time: 5 minutes | Cook time: 20 minutes | Serves 6

- 6 boneless, skinless chicken thighs
- 1 tablespoon extra-virgin olive oil
- 1 tablespoon za'atar seasoning
- 1 teaspoon garlic powder

1. Preheat the oven to 375°F. Line a baking sheet with aluminum foil or parchment paper.
2. Arrange the chicken thighs on the baking sheet and coat each with oil.
3. In a small bowl, mix the za'atar seasoning and garlic powder.
4. Sprinkle the seasoning mixture onto the chicken thighs and press it down into the meat with clean hands, so it adheres.
5. Bake for 15 to 20 minutes, or until a food thermometer inserted into the thickest part of each chicken thigh registers 165°F. Let rest for 2 to 3 minutes before serving.

PER SERVING (1 SEASONED CHICKEN THIGH)

Calories: 193; Fat: 8g; Protein: 28g; Carbohydrates: 0g; Fiber: 0g; Sugar: 0g; Sodium: 135mg

Harissa-Spiced Turkey Burgers with Tzatziki

Prep time: 10 minutes | Cook time: 10 minutes | Serves 4

- 1 pound lean ground turkey
- ½ yellow onion, chopped
- 2 garlic cloves, minced
- 1 teaspoon ground cumin
- 1 tablespoon harissa seasoning
- 1 teaspoon salt
- 2 teaspoons extra-virgin olive oil
- 4 whole wheat hamburger buns, for serving
- 1 batch Easy Tzatziki, or store-bought tzatziki
- arugula

1. In a large mixing bowl, combine the ground turkey, onion, garlic, cumin, harissa seasoning, and salt. Using clean hands, form the turkey mixture into four patties.
2. In a large skillet, heat the oil over medium heat. Place the turkey patties into the hot skillet, and cook them for 4 to 5 minutes per side, or until browned and a thermometer inserted into the thickest part of each patty registers 165°F.
3. Serve in hamburger buns and top the patties with Easy Tzatziki and arugula.

PER SERVING (1 TURKEY BURGER WITH TZATZIKI AND ARUGULA)

Calories: 390; Fat: 18g; Protein: 29g; Carbohydrates: 30g; Fiber: 4g; Sugar: 7g; Sodium: 934mg

Bulgur and Turkey Stuffed Zucchini

Prep time: 10 minutes | Cook time: 30 minutes | Serves 6

- 6 medium zucchini
- 1 pound lean ground turkey
- 1 yellow onion, chopped
- 1 red bell pepper, seeded and finely chopped
- 1 cup low-sodium chicken broth
- ½ cup bulgur
- 1 teaspoon dried oregano
- ½ teaspoon salt
- ½ teaspoon dried dill

1. Preheat the oven to 400°F.
2. Halve each zucchini lengthwise. Scoop out and reserve the flesh in a small bowl, leaving a ¼-inch-thick border around the edge to maintain the shape of the zucchini.
3. Arrange the zucchini halves cut-side down in an 11-by-13-inch baking dish. Bake the zucchini halves for 10 to 15 minutes or until tender. Remove the zucchini from the oven and set it aside.
4. While the zucchini is baking, heat a large skillet or sauté pan over medium heat. Add the ground turkey, and cook for 5 minutes, or until fully browned.
5. Stir in the onion, bell pepper, and reserved zucchini flesh, and cook for another 3 minutes, or until softened.

6. Add the chicken broth to the pan and bring it to a boil. Stir in the bulgur, oregano, salt, and dill. Reduce the heat to low and simmer for 12 to 15 minutes, or until the bulgur is tender.
7. Spoon the turkey mixture into the baked zucchini halves, cover with aluminum foil,
1. and bake for an additional 10 minutes. Remove from the oven and serve.

PER SERVING

Calories: 201; Fat: 7g; Protein: 18g; Carbohydrates: 18g; Fiber: 4g; Sugar: 7g; Sodium: 265mg

Sun-Dried Tomato and Arugula Stuffed Chicken Breasts

Prep time: 10 minutes | Cook time: 20 minutes | Serves 4

- 4 boneless, skinless chicken breasts
- 1½ cups arugula, finely chopped
- ½ cup sun-dried tomatoes packed in oil, chopped
- ¼ cup plus 2 tablespoons grated Parmesan cheese
- 2 garlic cloves, minced
- ½ cup Italian bread crumbs
- 1 tablespoon extra-virgin olive oil

1. Preheat the oven to 350°F. Line a baking sheet with aluminum foil or parchment paper and set it aside.
2. Cut a deep pocket into the side of each chicken breast.
3. In a medium bowl, mix the arugula, sun-dried tomatoes, ¼ cup of Parmesan cheese, and the garlic.
4. Stuff each chicken breast with the arugula mixture. Use toothpicks to seal each pocket, then transfer the stuffed chicken breasts to the prepared baking sheet.
5. In a small bowl, mix the bread crumbs and the remaining 2 tablespoons of Parmesan cheese.
6. Coat each chicken breast with oil and coat each with the bread crumb mixture, pressing to make the bread crumbs adhere.
7. Bake for 20 minutes, or until a food thermometer inserted into the thickest part of each chicken breast registers 165°F.
8. Let the chicken rest for 2 minutes. Remove the toothpicks before serving.

PER SERVING (1 STUFFED CHICKEN BREAST)

Calories: 251; Fat: 10g; Protein: 30g; Carbohydrates: 10g; Fiber: 1g; Sugar: 1g; Sodium: 301mg

Turkey Burgers with Mango Salsa

Prep time: 15 minutes | Cook time: 10 minutes | Serves 6

- 1½ pounds ground turkey breast
- 1 teaspoon sea salt, divided
- ¼ teaspoon freshly ground black pepper
- 2 tablespoons extra-virgin olive oil
- 2 mangos, peeled, pitted, and cubed
- ½ red onion, finely chopped
- Juice of 1 lime
- 1 garlic clove, minced
- ½ jalapeño pepper, seeded and finely minced
- 2 tablespoons chopped fresh cilantro leaves

1. Form the turkey breast into 4 patties and season with ½ teaspoon of sea salt and the pepper.
2. In a large nonstick skillet over medium-high heat, heat the olive oil until it shimmers.
3. Add the turkey patties and cook for about 5 minutes per side until browned.
4. While the patties cook, mix together the mango, red onion, lime juice, garlic, jalapeño, cilantro, and remaining ½ teaspoon of sea salt in a small bowl. Spoon the salsa over the turkey patties and serve.

PER SERVING

Calories: 384; Protein: 34g; Total Carbohydrates: 27g; Sugars: 24g; Fiber: 3g; Total Fat: 16g; Saturated Fat: 3g; Cholesterol: 84mg; Sodium: 543mg

Herb-Roasted Turkey Breast

Prep time: 15 minutes | Cook time: 1½ hours (plus 20 minutes to rest) | Serves 6

2 tablespoons extra-virgin olive oil
4 garlic cloves, minced
Zest of 1 lemon
1 tablespoon chopped fresh thyme leaves
1 tablespoon chopped fresh rosemary leaves
2 tablespoons chopped fresh Italian parsley leaves
1 teaspoon ground mustard
1 teaspoon sea salt
¼ teaspoon freshly ground black pepper
1 (6-pound) bone-in, skin-on turkey breast
1 cup dry white wine

1. Preheat the oven to 325°F.
2. In a small bowl, whisk the olive oil, garlic, lemon zest, thyme, rosemary, parsley, mustard, sea salt, and pepper.
3. Spread the herb mixture evenly over the surface of the turkey breast, and loosen the skin and rub underneath as well. Place the turkey breast in a roasting pan on a rack, skin-side up.
4. Pour the wine in the pan. Roast for 1 to 1½ hours until the turkey reaches an internal temperature of 165°F. Remove from the oven and let rest for 20 minutes, tented with aluminum foil to keep it warm, before carving.

PER SERVING

Calories: 392; Protein: 84g; Total Carbohydrates: 2g; Sugars: <1g; Fiber: <1g; Total Fat: 6g; Saturated Fat: <1g; Cholesterol: 210mg; Sodium: 479mg

Chicken Sausage and Peppers

Prep time: 10 minutes | Cook time: 20 minutes | Serves 6

- 2 tablespoons extra-virgin olive oil
- 6 Italian chicken sausage links
- 1 onion, thinly sliced
- 1 red bell pepper, seeded and thinly sliced
- 1 green bell pepper, seeded and thinly sliced
- 3 garlic cloves, minced
- ½ cup dry white wine
- ½ teaspoon sea salt
- ¼ teaspoon freshly ground black pepper
- Pinch red pepper flakes

1. In a large skillet over medium-high heat, heat the olive oil until it shimmers.
2. Add the sausages and cook for 5 to 7 minutes, turning occasionally, until browned, and they reach an internal temperature of 165°F. With tongs, remove the sausage from the pan and set aside on a platter, tented with aluminum foil to keep warm.
3. Return the skillet to the heat and add the onion, red bell pepper, and green bell pepper. Cook for 5 to 7 minutes, stirring occasionally, until the vegetables begin to brown.
4. Add the garlic and cook for 30 seconds, stirring constantly.
5. Stir in the wine, sea salt, pepper, and red pepper flakes. Use the side of a spoon to scrape and fold in any browned bits from the bottom of the pan. Simmer for about 4 minutes more, stirring, until the liquid reduces by half. Spoon the peppers over the sausages and serve.

PER SERVING

Calories: 173; Protein: 22g; Total Carbohydrates: 6g; Sugars: 2g; Fiber: <1g; Total Fat: 5g; Saturated Fat: 1g; Cholesterol: 85mg; Sodium: 1,199mg

Chicken Piccata

Prep time: 10 minutes | Cook time: 15 minutes | Serves 6

- ½ cup whole-wheat flour
- ½ teaspoon sea salt
- ⅛ teaspoon freshly ground black pepper
- 1½ pounds boneless, skinless chicken breasts, cut into 6 pieces and pounded ½-inch thick
- 3 tablespoons extra-virgin olive oil
- 1 cup unsalted chicken broth
- ½ cup dry white wine
- Juice of 1 lemon
- Zest of 1 lemon
- ¼ cup capers, drained and rinsed
- ¼ cup chopped fresh parsley leaves

1. In a shallow dish, whisk the flour, sea salt, and pepper. Dredge the chicken in the flour and tap off any excess.
2. In a large skillet over medium-high heat, heat the olive oil until it shimmers.
3. Add the chicken and cook for about 4 minutes per side until browned. Remove the chicken from the pan and set aside, tented with aluminum foil to keep warm.
4. Return the skillet to the heat and add the broth, wine, lemon juice, and lemon zest, and capers. Use the side of a spoon to scrape and fold in any browned bits from the bottom of the pan. Simmer for 3 to 4 minutes, stirring, until the liquid thickens. Remove the skillet from the heat and return the chicken to the pan. Turn to coat. Stir in the parsley and serve.

PER SERVING

Calories: 153; Protein: 8g; Total Carbohydrates: 9g; Sugars: <1g; Fiber: <1g; Total Fat: 9g; Saturated Fat: 1g; Cholesterol: 19mg; Sodium: 352mg

One-Pan Tuscan Chicken

Prep time: 10 minutes | Cook time: 25 minutes | Serves 6

- ¼ cup extra-virgin olive oil, divided
- 1 pound boneless, skinless chicken breasts, cut into ¾-inch pieces
- 1 onion, chopped
- 1 red bell pepper, chopped
- 3 garlic cloves, minced
- ½ cup dry white wine
- 1 (14-ounce) can crushed tomatoes, undrained
- ½ teaspoon sea salt
- ⅛ teaspoon freshly ground black pepper
- ⅛ teaspoon red pepper flakes
- ¼ cup chopped fresh basil leaves

1. In a large skillet over medium-high heat, heat 2 tablespoons of olive oil until it shimmers.
2. Add the chicken and cook for about 6 minutes, stirring, until browned. Remove the chicken from the skillet and set aside on a platter, tented with aluminum foil to keep warm.
3. Return the skillet to the heat and heat the remaining 2 tablespoons of olive oil until it shimmers.
4. Add the onion and red bell pepper. Cook for about 5 minutes, stirring occasionally, until the vegetables are soft.
5. Add the garlic and cook for 30 seconds, stirring constantly.
6. Stir in the wine, and use the side of the spoon to scrape and fold in any browned bits from the bottom of the pan. Cook for 1 minute, stirring.
7. Add the crushed and chopped tomatoes, white beans, Italian seasoning, sea salt, pepper, and red pepper flakes. Bring to a simmer and reduce the heat to medium. Cook for 5 minutes, stirring occasionally.
8. Return the chicken and any juices that have collected to the skillet. Cook for 1 to 2 minutes until the chicken heats through. Remove from the heat and stir in the basil before serving.

PER SERVING

Calories: 271; Protein: 14g; Total Carbohydrates: 29g; Sugars: 8g; Fiber: 8g; Total Fat: 0g; Saturated Fat: 1g; Cholesterol: 14mg; Sodium: 306mg

Chicken Kapama

Prep time: 10 minutes | Cook time: 2 hours | Serves 4

- 1 (32-ounce) can chopped tomatoes, drained
- ¼ cup dry white wine
- 2 tablespoons tomato paste
- 3 tablespoons extra-virgin olive oil
- ¼ teaspoon red pepper flakes
- 1 teaspoon ground allspice
- ½ teaspoon dried oregano
- 2 whole cloves
- 1 cinnamon stick
- ½ teaspoon sea salt
- ⅛ teaspoon freshly ground black pepper
- 4 boneless, skinless chicken breast halves

1. In a large pot over medium-high heat, combine the tomatoes, wine, tomato paste, olive oil, red pepper flakes, allspice, oregano, cloves, cinnamon stick, sea salt, and pepper. Bring to a simmer, stirring occasionally.
2. Reduce the heat to medium-low and simmer for 30 minutes, stirring occasionally. Remove and discard the whole cloves and cinnamon stick from the sauce and let the sauce cool.
3. Preheat the oven to 350°F.
4. Place the chicken in a 9-by-13-inch baking dish. Pour the sauce over the chicken and cover the pan with aluminum foil. Bake for 40 to 45 minutes, or until the chicken reaches an internal temperature of 165°F.

PER SERVING

Calories: 220; Protein: 8g; Total Carbohydrates: 11g; Sugars: 7g; Fiber: 3g; Total Fat: 14g; Saturated Fat: 3g; Cholesterol: 19mg; Sodium: 273mg

Spinach and Feta Stuffed Chicken Breasts

Prep time: 10 minutes | Cook time: 45 minutes| Serves 4

- 2 tablespoons extra-virgin olive oil
- 1 pound fresh baby spinach
- 3 garlic cloves, minced
- Zest of 1 lemon
- ½ teaspoon sea salt
- ⅛ teaspoon freshly ground black pepper
- ½ cup crumbled feta cheese
- 4 boneless, skinless chicken breast halves, pounded to ½-inch thickness

1. Preheat the oven to 350°F.
2. In a large skillet over medium-high heat, heat the olive oil until it shimmers.
3. Add the spinach. Cook for 3 to 4 minutes, stirring, until wilted.
4. Add the garlic, lemon zest, sea salt, and pepper. Cook for 30 seconds, stirring constantly. Cool slightly and mix in the cheese.
5. Spread the spinach and cheese mixture in an even layer over the chicken pieces and roll the breast around the filling. Hold closed with toothpicks or butcher's twine.
6. Place the breasts in a 9-by-13-inch baking dish and bake for 30 to 40 minutes, or until the chicken reaches an internal temperature of 165°F. Remove from the oven and let rest for 5 minutes before slicing and serving.

PER SERVING

Calories: 263; Protein: 17g; Total Carbohydrates: 7g; Sugars: 3g; Fiber: 3g; Total Fat: 20g; Saturated Fat: 9g; Cholesterol: 63mg; Sodium: 901mg

Rosemary Baked Chicken Drumsticks

Prep time: 5 minutes | Cook time: 1 hour| Serves 6

- 2 tablespoons chopped fresh rosemary leaves
- 1 teaspoon garlic powder
- ½ teaspoon sea salt
- ⅛ teaspoon freshly ground black pepper
- Zest of 1 lemon
- 12 chicken drumsticks

1. Preheat the oven to 350°F.
2. In a small bowl, combine the rosemary, garlic powder, sea salt, pepper, and lemon zest.
3. Place the drumsticks in a 9-by-13-inch baking dish and sprinkle with the rosemary mixture. Bake for about 1 hour, or until the chicken reaches an internal temperature of 165°F.

PER SERVING

Calories: 163; Protein: 26g; Total Carbohydrates: 2g; Sugars: <1g; Fiber: <1g; Total Fat: 6g; Saturated Fat: 2g; Cholesterol: 81mg; Sodium: 309mg

Chicken with Onions, Potatoes, Figs, and Carrots

Prep time: 5 minutes | Cook time: 45 minutes| Serves 4

- 2 cups fingerling potatoes, halved
- 4 fresh figs, quartered
- 2 carrots, julienned
- 2 tablespoons extra-virgin olive oil
- 1 teaspoon sea salt, divided
- ¼ teaspoon freshly ground black pepper
- 4 chicken leg-thigh quarters
- 2 tablespoons chopped fresh parsley leaves

1. Preheat the oven to 425°F.
2. In a small bowl, toss the potatoes, figs, and carrots with the olive oil, ½ teaspoon of sea salt, and the pepper. Spread in a 9-by-13-inch baking dish.
3. Season the chicken with the remaining ½ teaspoon of sea salt. Place it on top of the vegetables. Bake for 35 to 45 minutes, or until the vegetables are soft and the chicken reaches an internal temperature of 165°F.
4. Sprinkle with the parsley and serve.

PER SERVING

Calories: 429; Protein: 52g; Total Carbohydrates: 27g; Sugars: 12g; Fiber: 4g; Total Fat: 12g; Saturated Fat: 3g; Cholesterol: 131mg; Sodium: 603mg

Chicken Gyros with Tzatziki

Prep time: 10 minutes | Cook time: 1 hour (plus 20 minutes to rest) | Serves 6

1 pound ground chicken breast
1 onion, grated with excess water wrung out (see tip)
2 tablespoons dried rosemary
1 tablespoon dried marjoram
6 garlic cloves, minced
½ teaspoon sea salt
¼ teaspoon freshly ground black pepper
tzatziki sauce

1. Preheat the oven to 350°F.
2. In a stand mixer or food processor, combine the chicken, onion, rosemary, marjoram, garlic, sea salt, and pepper. Blend for about 2 minutes until the mixture forms a paste. Alternatively, mix these ingredients in a bowl until well combined (see preparation tip).
3. Press the mixture into a loaf pan. Bake for about 1 hour until it reaches an internal temperature of 165°F. Remove from the oven and let rest for 20 minutes before slicing.
4. Slice the gyro and spoon the tzatziki sauce over the top.

PER SERVING

Calories: 289; Protein: 50g; Total Carbohydrates: 20g; Sugars: 10g; Fiber: 1g; Total Fat: 1g; Saturated Fat: <1g; Cholesterol: 67mg; Sodium: 494mg

Chapter 5
Beef, Pork, and Lamb

Spicy Lamb Burgers with Harissa Mayo

Prep Time: 15 minutes | Cook Time: 10 minutes | Serves 2

- ½ small onion, minced
- 1 garlic clove, minced
- 2 teaspoons minced fresh parsley
- 2 teaspoons minced fresh mint
- ¼ teaspoon salt
- Pinch freshly ground black pepper
- 1 teaspoon cumin
- 1 teaspoon smoked paprika
- ¼ teaspoon coriander
- 8 ounces lean ground lamb
- 2 tablespoons olive oil mayonnaise
- ½ teaspoon harissa paste (more or less to taste)
- 2 hamburger buns or pitas, fresh greens, tomato slices (optional, for serving)

1. Preheat the grill to medium-high (350–400°F) and oil the grill grate. Alternatively, you can cook these in a heavy pan (cast iron is best) on the stovetop.
2. In a large bowl, combine the onion, garlic, parsley, mint, salt, pepper, cumin, paprika, and coriander. Add the lamb and, using your hands, combine the meat with the spices so they are evenly distributed. Form meat mixture into 2 patties.
3. Grill the burgers for 4 minutes per side, or until the internal temperature registers 160°F for medium.
4. If cooking on the stovetop, heat the pan to medium-high and oil the pan. Cook the burgers for 5 to 6 minutes per side, or until the internal temperature registers 160°F.
5. While the burgers are cooking, combine the mayonnaise and harissa in a small bowl.
6. Serve the burgers with the harissa mayonnaise and slices of tomato and fresh greens on a bun or pita—or skip the bun altogether.

PER SERVING

Calories: 381; Total fat: 20g; Total carbs: 27g; Fiber: 2g; Sugar: 4g; Protein: 22g; Sodium: 653mg; Cholesterol: 68mg

Slow Cooker Mediterranean Beef Stew

Prep Time: 20 minutes | Cook Time: 8 hours (slow cooker) or 3 hours (stovetop) | Serves 2, with leftovers for lunch

- 1 (15-ounce) can diced or crushed tomatoes with basil
- 1 teaspoon beef base or 1 beef bouillon cube
- 2 tablespoons olive oil, divided
- 8 ounces baby bella (cremini) mushrooms, quartered
- ½ large onion, diced
- 2 garlic cloves, minced
- 1 pound cubed beef stew meat
- 3 tablespoons flour
- ¼ teaspoon salt
- Pinch freshly ground black pepper
- ¾ cup dry red wine
- ¼ cup minced brined olives
- 1 fresh rosemary sprig
- 1 (15-ounce) can white cannellini beans, drained and rinsed
- 1 medium zucchini, cut in half lengthwise and then cut into 1-inch pieces.

1. Pour the can of tomatoes into a slow cooker and set it to low heat. Add the beef base and stir to combine.
2. Heat 1 tablespoon of olive oil in a large sauté pan over medium heat. Add the mushrooms and onion and sauté for 10 minutes, or until they're golden. Add the garlic and cook for another 30 seconds. Transfer the vegetables to the slow cooker.
3. In a plastic food storage bag, combine the stew meat with the flour, salt, and pepper. Seal the bag and shake well to combine.
4. Heat the remining 1 tablespoon of oil in the sauté pan over high heat. Add the floured meat and sear to get a crust on the outside edges. Deglaze the pan by adding about half of the red wine and scraping up any browned bits on the bottom. Stir so the wine thickens a bit and transfer to the slow cooker along with any remaining wine.
5. Stir the stew to combine the ingredients. Add the olives and rosemary, cover, and cook for 6 to 8 hours on low.
6. About 30 minutes before the stew is finished, add the beans and zucchini to let them warm through.

PER SERVING

Calories: 388; Total fat: 15g; Total carbs: 25g; Fiber: 8g; Sugar: 6g; Protein: 31g; Sodium: 583mg; Cholesterol: 51mg

Greek-style Lamb Burgers

Prep time: 5 minutes | Cook time: 15 minutes | Serves 4

- 1 pound ground lamb
- ½ teaspoon salt
- ½ teaspoon freshly ground black pepper
- 4 tablespoons crumbled feta cheese
- Buns, toppings, and tzatziki, for serving (optional)

1. Preheat the grill to high heat.
2. In a large bowl, using your hands, combine the lamb with the salt and pepper.
3. Divide the meat into 4 portions. Divide each portion in half to make a top and a bottom. Flatten each half into a 3-inch circle.
4. Make a dent in the center of one of the halves and place 1 tablespoon of the feta cheese in the center. Place the second half of the patty on top of the feta cheese and press down to close the 2 halves together, making it resemble a round burger.
5. Grill each side for 3 minutes, for medium-well. Serve on a bun with your favorite toppings and tzatziki sauce, if desired.

PER SERVING

Calories: 345;Fat: 29.0g;Protein: 20.0g;Carbs: 1.0g.

Slow Cooker Beef Stew

Prep time: 5 minutes | Cook time: 8 Hours 10 Minutes | Serves 4

- 2 tbsp canola oil
- 2 lb beef stew meat, cubed
- Salt and black pepper to taste
- 2 cups beef stock
- 2 shallots, chopped
- 2 tbsp thyme, chopped
- 2 garlic cloves, minced
- 1 carrot, chopped
- 3 celery stalks, chopped
- 28 oz canned tomatoes, diced
- 2 tbsp parsley, chopped

1. Place the beef meat, salt, pepper, beef stock, canola oil, shallots, thyme, garlic, carrot, celery, and tomatoes in your slow cooker.
2. Put the lid and cook for 8 hours on Low. Sprinkle with parsley and serve warm.

PER SERVING

Calories: 370;Fat: 17g;Protein: 35g;Carbs: 28g

Pork Chops In Tomato Olive Sauce

Prep time: 5 minutes | Cook time: 25 minutes | Serves 4

- 2 tbsp olive oil
- 4 pork loin chops, boneless
- 6 tomatoes, crushed
- 3 tbsp basil, chopped
- 10 black olives, halved
- 1 yellow onion, chopped
- 1 garlic clove, minced

1. Warm the olive oil in a skillet over medium heat and brown pork chops for 6 minutes on all sides.
2. Share into plates. In the same skillet, stir tomatoes, basil, olives, onion, and garlic and simmer for 4 minutes. Drizzle tomato sauce over.

PER SERVING

Calories: 340;Fat: 18g;Protein: 35g;Carbs: 13g.

Greek-Style Ground Beef Pita Sandwiches

Prep Time: 15 minutes | Cook Time: 10 minutes | Serves 2

FOR THE BEEF

- 1 tablespoon olive oil
- ½ medium onion, minced
- 2 garlic cloves, minced
- 6 ounces lean ground beef
- 1 teaspoon dried oregano
- For the yogurt sauce
- ⅓ cup plain Greek yogurt
- 1 ounce crumbled feta cheese (about 3 tablespoons)
- 1 tablespoon minced fresh parsley
- 1 tablespoon minced scallion
- 1 tablespoon freshly squeezed lemon juice
- Pinch salt
- For the sandwiches
- 2 large Greek-style pitas
- ½ cup cherry tomatoes, halved
- 1 cup diced cucumber
- Salt
- Freshly ground black pepper

TO MAKE THE BEEF

- Heat the olive oil in a sauté pan over medium high-heat. Add the onion, garlic, and ground beef and sauté for 7 minutes, breaking up the meat well. When the meat is no longer pink, drain off any fat and stir in the oregano. Turn off the heat.
- To make the yogurt sauce
- In a small bowl, combine the yogurt, feta, parsley, scallion, lemon juice, and salt.

TO ASSEMBLE THE SANDWICHES

1. Warm the pitas in the microwave for 20 seconds each.
2. To serve, spread some of the yogurt sauce over each warm pita. Top with the ground beef, cherry tomatoes, and diced cucumber. Season with salt and pepper. Add additional yogurt sauce if desired.

PER SERVING

Calories: 541; Total fat: 21g; Total carbs: 57g; Fiber: 4g; Sugar: 9g; Protein: 29g; Sodium: 694mg; Cholesterol: 73mg

Tender Pork Shoulder

Prep time: 5 minutes | Cook time: 2 hours 15 minutes| Serves 4

- 3 tbsp olive oil
- 2 lb pork shoulder
- 1 onion, chopped
- 2 tbsp garlic, minced
- 1 tbsp hot paprika
- 1 tbsp basil, chopped
- 1 cup chicken broth
- Salt and black pepper to taste

1. Preheat oven to 350° F. Heat olive oil in a skillet and brown the pork on all sides for about 8-10 minutes; remove to a baking dish. Add onion and garlic to the skillet and sauté for 3 minutes until softened.
2. Stir in hot paprika, salt, and pepper for 1 minute and pour in chicken broth. Transfer to the baking dish, cover with aluminium foil and bake for 90 minutes.
3. Then remove the foil and continue baking for another 20 minutes until browned on top. Let the pork cool for a few minutes, slice, and sprinkle with basil. Serve topped with the cooking juices.

PER SERVING

Calories: 310;Fat: 15g;Protein: 18g;Carbs: 21g.

Lemon Herb-Crusted Pork Tenderloin

Prep Time: 10 minutes| Cook Time: 20 minutes | Serves 2

- 1 (8-ounce) pork tenderloin
- Zest of 1 lemon
- ½ teaspoon dried thyme
- ¼ teaspoon garlic powder
- ¼ teaspoon za'atar seasoning
- ¼ teaspoon salt
- 1 tablespoon olive oil

1. Preheat the oven to 425°F and set the rack to the middle position.
2. Trim away any of the silver skin from the pork tenderloin, to prevent it from curling while it cooks.
3. Combine the lemon zest, thyme, garlic powder, za'atar, and salt in a small bowl. Rub it evenly over the pork tenderloin.
4. Heat the olive oil in a sauté pan over medium-high heat. Add the pork and sauté for 3 minutes, turning often, until it's golden on all sides.
5. Place the tenderloin in an oven-safe baking dish and roast for 15 minutes, or until the internal temperature registers 145°F. Remove it from the oven and let it rest for 3 minutes before serving.

PER SERVING

Calories: 182; Total fat: 11g; Total carbs: 1g; Fiber: 0g; Sugar: 0g; Protein: 20g; Sodium: 356mg; Cholesterol: 65mg

One-Pan Creamy Italian Sausage Orecchiette

Prep Time: 5 minutes | Cook Time: 25 minutes | Serves 2

- 1 tablespoon olive oil
- ½ medium onion, diced
- 2 garlic cloves, minced
- 2 ounces baby bella (cremini) mushrooms, sliced
- 4 ounces hot or sweet Italian sausage
- ½ teaspoon Italian herb seasoning
- 1½ cups dry orecchiette pasta (about 6 ounces)
- 2 cups low-sodium chicken stock
- 2 cups packed baby spinach
- ¼ cup heavy cream
- Salt

1. Heat the olive oil in a sauté pan over medium-high heat. Add the onion, garlic, and mushrooms and sauté for 5 minutes.
2. Remove the sausage from its casing and add it to the pan, breaking it up well. Cook for another 5 minutes, or until the sausage is no longer pink.
3. Add the Italian herb seasoning, pasta, and chicken stock. Bring the mixture to a boil.
4. Cover the pan, reduce the heat to medium-low, and let it simmer for 10 to 15 minutes, or until the pasta is cooked. Remove from the heat.
5. Add the spinach and stir it in to let it wilt.
6. Add the cream and season with salt. The sauce will tighten up as it cools. If it seems too thick, add additional chicken stock or water.

PER SERVING

Calories: 531; Total fat: 19g; Total carbs: 69g; Fiber: 5g; Sugar: 5g; Protein: 23g; Sodium: 569mg; Cholesterol: 38mg

Pork Tenderloin with Chermoula Sauce

Prep Time: 15 minutes | Cook Time: 20 minutes | Serves 2

- ½ cup fresh parsley
- ½ cup fresh cilantro
- 6 small garlic cloves
- 3 tablespoons olive oil, divided
- 3 tablespoons freshly squeezed lemon juice
- 1 teaspoon smoked paprika
- 2 teaspoons cumin
- ½ teaspoon salt, divided
- 1 (8-ounce) pork tenderloin

1. Preheat the oven to 425°F and set the rack to the middle position.
2. In the bowl of a food processor, combine the parsley, cilantro, garlic, 2 tablespoons of olive oil, the lemon juice, paprika, cumin, and ¼ teaspoon of salt. Pulse 15 to 20 times, or until the mixture is fairly smooth. Scrape the sides down as needed to incorporate all of the ingredients. Transfer the sauce to a small bowl and set aside.
3. Season the pork tenderloin on all sides with the remaining ¼ teaspoon of salt and a generous pinch of pepper.
4. Heat the remaining 1 tablespoon of olive oil in a sauté pan. Add the pork and sear for 3 minutes, turning often, until it's golden on all sides.
5. Transfer the pork to an oven-safe baking dish and roast for 15 minutes, or until the internal temperature registers 145°F.

PER SERVING

Calories: 168; Total fat: 13g; Total carbs: 3g; Fiber: 1g; Sugar: 0g; Protein: 11g; Sodium: 333mg; Cholesterol: 33mg

Grilled Filet Mignon with Red Wine Mushroom Sauce

Prep Time: 20 minutes, plus 30 minutes for meat to come to room temperature | Cook Time: 20 minutes, plus 5 minutes to rest | Serves 2

- 2 (3-ounce) pieces filet mignon
- 2 tablespoons olive oil, divided
- 8 ounces baby bella (cremini) mushrooms, quartered
- 1 large shallot, minced (about ⅓ cup)
- 2 teaspoons flour
- 2 teaspoons tomato paste
- ½ cup red wine
- 1 cup low-sodium chicken stock
- ½ teaspoon dried thyme
- 1 sprig fresh rosemary
- 1 teaspoon herbes de Provence
- ¼ teaspoon salt
- ¼ teaspoon garlic powder
- ¼ teaspoon onion powder
- Pinch freshly ground black pepper

1. Preheat the oven to 425°F and set the oven rack to the middle position.
2. Remove the filets from the refrigerator about 30 minutes before you're ready to cook them. Pat them dry with a paper towel and let them rest while you prepare the mushroom sauce.
3. In a sauté pan, heat 1 tablespoon of olive oil over medium-high heat. Add the mushrooms and shallot and sauté for 10 minutes.
4. Add the flour and tomato paste and cook for another 30 seconds. Add the wine and scrape up any browned bits from the sauté pan. Add the chicken stock, thyme, and rosemary.
5. In a small bowl, combine the herbes de Provence, salt, garlic powder, onion powder, and pepper.
6. Rub the beef with the remaining 1 tablespoon of olive oil and season it on both sides with the herb mixture.
7. Heat an oven-safe sauté pan over medium-high heat. Add the beef and sear for 2½ minutes on each side. Then, transfer the pan to the oven for 5 more minutes to finish cooking. Use a meat thermometer to check the internal temperature and remove it at 130°F for medium-rare.
8. Tent the meat with foil and let it rest for 5 minutes before serving topped with the mushroom sauce.

PER SERVING

Calories: 385; Total fat: 20g; Total carbs: 15g; Fiber: 0g; Sugar: 5g; Protein: 25g; Sodium: 330mg; Cholesterol: 59mg

Baked Lamb Kofta Meatballs

Prep Time: 15 minutes | Cook Time: 30 minutes | Serves 2

- ¼ cup walnuts
- ½ small onion
- 1 garlic clove
- 1 roasted piquillo pepper
- 2 tablespoons fresh parsley
- 2 tablespoons fresh mint
- ¼ teaspoon salt
- ¼ teaspoon cumin
- ¼ teaspoon allspice
- Pinch cayenne pepper
- 8 ounces lean ground lamb

1. Preheat the oven to 350°F and set the rack to the middle position. Line a baking sheet with foil.
2. In the bowl of a food processor, combine the walnuts, onion, garlic, roasted pepper, parsley, mint, salt, cumin, allspice, and cayenne pepper. Pulse about 10 times to combine everything.
3. Transfer the spice mixture to the bowl and add the lamb. with your hands or a spatula, mix the spices into the lamb.
4. Roll into 1½-inch balls (about the size of golf balls).
5. Place the meatballs on the foil-lined baking sheet and bake for 30 minutes, or until cooked to an internal temperature of 160°F.

PER SERVING

Calories: 408; Total fat: 23g; Total carbs: 7g; Fiber: 3g; Sugar: 1g; Protein: 22g; Sodium: 429mg; Cholesterol: 80mg

Roast Pork Tenderloin with Cherry-Balsamic Sauce

Prep Time: 20 minutes | Cook Time: 20 minutes, plus 5 minutes to rest | Serves 2

- 1 cup frozen cherries, thawed
- ⅓ cup balsamic vinegar
- 1 fresh rosemary sprig
- 1 (8-ounce) pork tenderloin
- ¼ teaspoon salt
- ⅛ teaspoon freshly ground black pepper
- 1 tablespoon olive oil

1. Combine the cherries and vinegar in a blender and purée until smooth.
2. Pour into a saucepan, add the rosemary sprig, and bring the mixture to a boil. Reduce the heat to medium-low and simmer for 15 minutes, or until it's reduced by half.
3. While the sauce is simmering, preheat the oven to 425°F and set the rack in the middle position.
4. Season the pork on all sides with the salt and pepper.
5. Heat the oil in a sauté pan over medium-high heat. Add the pork and sear for 3 minutes, turning often, until it's golden on all sides.
6. Transfer the pork to an oven-safe baking dish and roast for 15 minutes, or until the internal temperature is 145°F.
7. Let the pork rest for 5 minutes before serving. Serve sliced and topped with the cherry-balsamic sauce.

PER SERVING

Calories: 328; Total fat: 11g; Total carbs: 30g; Fiber: 1g; Sugar: 26g; Protein: 21g; Sodium: 386mg; Cholesterol: 65mg

Greek-Inspired Beef Kebabs

Prep Time: 15 minutes, plus 4 hours to marinate | Cook Time: 15 minutes | Serves 2

- 6 ounces beef sirloin tip, trimmed of fat and cut into 2-inch pieces
- 3 cups of any mixture of vegetables: mushrooms, zucchini, summer squash, onions, cherry tomatoes, red peppers
- ½ cup olive oil
- ¼ cup freshly squeezed lemon juice
- 2 tablespoons balsamic vinegar
- 2 teaspoons dried oregano
- 1 teaspoon garlic powder
- 1 teaspoon minced fresh rosemary
- 1 teaspoon salt

1. Place the meat in a large shallow container or in a plastic freezer bag.
2. Cut the vegetables into similar-size pieces and place them in a second shallow container or freezer bag.

3. For the marinade, combine the olive oil, lemon juice, balsamic vinegar, oregano, garlic powder, rosemary, and salt in a measuring cup. Whisk well to combine. Pour half of the marinade over the meat, and the other half over the vegetables.
4. Place the meat and vegetables in the refrigerator to marinate for 4 hours.
5. When you are ready to cook, preheat the grill to medium-high (350–400°F) and grease the grill grate.
6. Thread the meat onto skewers and the vegetables onto separate skewers.
7. Grill the meat for 3 minutes on each side. They should only take 10 to 12 minutes to cook, but it will depend on how thick the meat is.
8. Grill the vegetables for about 3 minutes on each side or until they have grill marks and are softened.

PER SERVING

Calories: 285; Total fat: 18g; Total carbs: 9g; Fiber: 4g; Sugar: 4g; Protein: 21g; Sodium: 123mg; Cholesterol: 77mg

Herbed Lamb Chops with Lemon-Rosemary Dressing

Prep time: 5 minutes, plus 1 hour to marinate and 15 minutes to rest | Cook time: 10 minutes | Serves 6

- 1 cup freshly squeezed lemon juice
- ¾ cup extra-virgin olive oil
- ¼ cup fresh rosemary
- 3 garlic cloves
- 1 teaspoon salt
- ½ teaspoon freshly ground black pepper
- 6 lamb chops, 1 inch thick

1. In a food processor, blend the lemon juice, oil, rosemary, garlic, salt, and pepper for 15 seconds. Set aside.
2. Put the lamb chops in a large plastic zip-top bag or container with a resealable lid. Cover the lamb with two-thirds of the dressing, ensuring that all the lamb chops are fully coated. Let the lamb marinate in the refrigerator for at least 1 hour.
3. Remove the lamb chops from the refrigerator and let them sit at room temperature for 15 minutes. Heat a grill, grill pan, or cast-iron skillet to high heat.
4. Cook the lamb chops for 2 minutes on each side for medium-rare or 3 minutes per side for medium. Let rest 5 minutes before serving.
5. Serve by drizzling the reserved dressing over the lamb.

PER SERVING

Calories: 505; Fat: 46g; Protein: 22g; Carbohydrates: 1g; Fiber: 0g; Sugar: 0g; Sodium: 219mg

Lamb and Mushroom Meatballs with Yogurt Sauce

Prep time: 10 minutes | Cook time: 25 minutes | Serves 4

FOR THE MEATBALLS

- ½ pound button mushrooms
- ½ small yellow onion
- 1 garlic clove
- 1 pound ground lamb
- ½ cup whole wheat bread crumbs
- 1 large egg
- ½ teaspoon ground cumin
- ½ teaspoon paprika
- ½ teaspoon ground cinnamon

FOR THE YOGURT SAUCE

- 1 cup low-fat plain Greek yogurt
- ½ cup chopped fresh mint
- 1 tablespoon freshly squeezed lemon juice

1. To make the meatballs: In a food processor, pulse the mushrooms until finely chopped.
2. Heat a large oven-safe or cast-iron skillet over medium-high heat. Put the mushrooms into the hot skillet and cook until all water is released, 2 to 3 minutes. Remove the mushrooms from the heat and let cool.
3. Preheat the oven to 400°F.
4. Put the onion and garlic into the food processor and pulse until they are finely chopped. Transfer the onion and garlic mixture to a large bowl. Add the ground lamb, bread crumbs, egg, cumin, paprika, cinnamon, and cooled mushrooms to the onion and garlic.
5. Heat the same cast-iron skillet on medium heat. Using clean hands, form the lamb mixture into 12 meatballs. Put the meatballs into the hot skillet and brown each side for 1 to 2 minutes.
6. Cover the skillet with aluminum foil and transfer it to the oven. Bake for 20 minutes, or until cooked through, and a food thermometer inserted into the largest meatball registers 165°F. Let cool for 5 minutes before serving.
7. To make the yogurt sauce: In a small bowl, mix the yogurt, mint, and lemon juice. Serve the sauce alongside the cooked meatballs.

PER SERVING (3 MEATBALLS WITH YOGURT SAUCE)

Calories: 328; Fat: 17g; Protein: 31g; Carbohydrates: 14g; Fiber: 2g; Sugar: 6g; Sodium: 183mg

Dijon and Herb Pork Tenderloin

Prep time: 10 minutes | Cook time: 20 minutes (plus 10 minutes to rest) | Serves 6

- ½ cup fresh Italian parsley leaves, chopped
- 3 tablespoons fresh rosemary leaves, chopped
- 3 tablespoons fresh thyme leaves, chopped
- 3 tablespoons Dijon mustard
- 1 tablespoon extra-virgin olive oil
- 4 garlic cloves, minced
- ½ teaspoon sea salt
- ¼ teaspoon freshly ground black pepper
- 1 (1½-pound) pork tenderloin

1. Preheat the oven to 400°F.
2. In a blender or food processor, combine the parsley, rosemary, thyme, mustard, olive oil, garlic, sea salt, and pepper. Process for about 30 seconds until smooth. Spread the mixture evenly over the pork and place it on a rimmed baking sheet.
3. Bake for about 20 minutes, or until the meat reaches an internal temperature of 140°F. Remove from the oven and let rest for 10 minutes before slicing and serving.

PER SERVING

Calories: 393; Protein: 74g; Total Carbohydrates: 5g; Sugars: <1g; Fiber: 3g; Total Fat: 12g; Saturated Fat: 4g; Cholesterol: 167mg; Sodium: 617mg

Lamb with String Beans (Arni me Fasolakia)

Prep time: 10 minutes | Cook time: 1 hour | Serves 6

- ¼ cup extra-virgin olive oil, divided
- 6 lamb chops, trimmed of extra fat
- 1 teaspoon sea salt, divided
- ½ teaspoon freshly ground black pepper
- 2 tablespoons tomato paste
- 1½ cups hot water
- 1 pound green beans, trimmed and halved crosswise
- 1 onion, chopped
- 2 tomatoes, chopped

1. In a large skillet over medium-high heat, heat 2 tablespoons of olive oil until it shimmers.
2. Season the lamb chops with ½ teaspoon of sea salt and ⅛ teaspoon of pepper. Cook the lamb in the hot oil for about 4 minutes per side until browned on both sides. Transfer the meat to a platter and set aside.
3. Return the skillet to the heat and add the remaining 2 tablespoons of olive oil. Heat until it shimmers.
4. In a bowl, dissolve the tomato paste in the hot water. Add it to the hot skillet along with the green beans, onion, tomatoes, and the remaining ½ teaspoon of sea salt and ¼ teaspoon of pepper. Bring to a simmer, using the side of a spoon to scrape and fold in any browned bits from the bottom of the pan.
5. Return the lamb chops to the pan. Bring to a boil and reduce the heat to medium-low. Simmer for 45 minutes until the beans are soft, adding additional water as needed to adjust the thickness of the sauce.

PER SERVING

Calories: 439; Protein: 50g; Total Carbohydrates: 10g; Sugars: 4g; Fiber: 4g; Total Fat: 22g; Saturated Fat: 6g; Cholesterol: 153mg; Sodium: 456mg

Moussaka

Prep time: 10 minutes | Cook time: 45 minutes | Serves 8

- 5 tablespoons extra-virgin olive oil, divided
- 1 eggplant, sliced (unpeeled)
- 1 onion, chopped
- 1 green bell pepper, seeded and chopped
- 1 pound ground turkey
- 3 garlic cloves, minced
- 2 tablespoons tomato paste
- 1 (14-ounce) can chopped tomatoes, drained
- 1 tablespoon Italian seasoning
- 2 teaspoons Worcestershire sauce
- 1 teaspoon dried oregano
- ½ teaspoon ground cinnamon
- 1 cup unsweetened nonfat plain Greek yogurt
- 1 egg, beaten
- ¼ teaspoon freshly ground black pepper
- ¼ teaspoon ground nutmeg
- ¼ cup grated Parmesan cheese
- 2 tablespoons chopped fresh parsley leaves

1. Preheat the oven to 400°F.
2. In a large skillet over medium-high heat, heat 3 tablespoons of olive oil until it shimmers.
3. Add the eggplant slices and brown for 3 to 4 minutes per side. Transfer to paper towels to drain.
4. Return the skillet to the heat and add the remaining 2 tablespoons of olive oil. Add the onion and green bell pepper. Cook for about 5 minutes, stirring, until the vegetables are soft. Remove from the pan and set aside.
5. Return the skillet to the heat and add the turkey. Cook for about 5 minutes, crumbling with a spoon, until browned.
6. Add the garlic and cook for 30 seconds, stirring constantly.
7. Stir in the tomato paste, tomatoes, Italian seasoning, Worcestershire sauce, oregano, and cinnamon. Return the onion and bell pepper to the pan. Cook for 5 minutes, stirring.
8. In a small bowl, whisk the yogurt, egg, pepper, nutmeg, and cheese.
9. In a 9-by-13-inch baking dish, spread half the meat mixture. Layer with half the eggplant. Add the remaining meat mixture and the remaining eggplant. Spread with the yogurt mixture. Bake for about 20 minutes until golden brown.
10. Garnish with the parsley and serve.

PER SERVING

Calories: 338; Protein: 28g; Total Carbohydrates: 16g; Sugars: 10g; Fiber: 5g; Total Fat: 20g; Saturated Fat: 4g; Cholesterol: 110mg; Sodium: 194mg

Tzatziki Pork Chops

Prep time: 10 minutes, plus 30 minutes to marinate | Cook time: 25 minutes | Serves 6

- 6 (5-ounce) boneless pork chops
- 1 cup Easy Tzatziki, or store-bought tzatziki

1. Place the pork chops in a resealable container and smother them with the tzatziki. Toss to coat the meat evenly. Refrigerate for 30 minutes to 1 hour.
2. Arrange the marinated pork chops on the prepared baking sheet, then bake them for 15 to 20 minutes, or until a food thermometer inserted into the thickest part of the pork registers 145°F. Let rest for 5 minutes before serving.

PER SERVING (1 MARINATED PORK CHOP)

Calories: 298; Fat: 14g; Protein: 35g; Carbohydrates: 6g; Sugar: 6g; Sodium: 412mg

Marinated Pork Loin with Olive Tapenade

Prep time: 10 minutes, plus 1 hour to marinate | Cook time: 20 minutes | Serves 4

FOR THE PORK

- 4 (4-ounce) boneless pork loins
- 1 cup Greek salad dressing

FOR THE TAPENADE

- 1 cup sliced black olives
- 1 cup pitted kalamata olives
- ¼ cup extra-virgin olive oil
- 2 garlic cloves
- 1 tablespoon capers
- 1 tablespoon freshly squeezed lemon juice
- ½ cup chopped fresh basil, divided

1. To make the pork: Put the pork loins and Greek dressing in a resealable zip-top bag or a bowl with a lid. Toss to coat the pork with dressing, and refrigerate for at least 1 hour, or up to overnight.
2. To make the tapenade: In a food processor, combine the black olives, kalamata olives, oil, garlic, capers, lemon juice, and ¼ cup basil. Pulse until finely chopped or it is the desired texture. Refrigerate the tapenade in a resealable container until ready to use.
3. Arrange the marinated pork loins on the prepared baking sheet, brushing each with more marinade. Discard the rest of the marinade. Bake the pork for 20 minutes, or until cooked through, and a food thermometer inserted into the thickest part of the pork registers 145°F. Let the pork rest for 5 minutes.
4. Top each pork chop with olive tapenade and the remaining ¼ cup of basil and serve.

PER SERVING (1 PORK CHOP WITH OLIVE TAPENADE)

Calories: 460; Fat: 36g; Protein: 25g; Carbohydrates: 9g; Fiber: 2g; Sugar: 3g; Sodium: 780mg

Greek-Inspired Beef Pitas

Prep time: 12 minutes | Cook time: 15 minutes | Serves 4

- 1 tablespoon extra-virgin olive oil
- 1 small yellow onion, chopped
- 2 garlic cloves, minced
- 1 pound lean ground beef
- 1 teaspoon dried oregano
- ½ teaspoon salt
- 4 (8-inch) whole wheat pita rounds
- 1 batch Easy Tzatziki, or store-bought tzatziki
- ½ English cucumber, sliced
- 1 large tomato, chopped
- ¼ cup crumbled feta cheese

1. In a large skillet, heat the oil over medium heat. Add the onion, and cook for 3 minutes, or until the onion has softened. Add the garlic and cook for an additional 30 seconds, or until fragrant.
2. Add the ground beef to the skillet and cook for 5 to 7 minutes, or until it is cooked through and browned. Stir in the oregano and salt, then remove the pan from the heat.
3. Put the cooked beef into each pita round. Top with the tzatziki, cucumber, tomato, and feta before serving.

PER SERVING (1 PITA SANDWICH)

Calories: 522; Fat: 22g; Protein: 35g; Carbohydrates: 47g; Fiber: 6g; Sugar: 10g; Sodium: 934mg

Steak with Red Wine-Mushroom Sauce

Prep time: 10 minutes (plus 4 to 8 hours to marinate) | Cook time: 20 minutes | Serves 4

FOR THE MARINADE AND STEAK

- 1 cup dry red wine
- 3 garlic cloves, minced
- 2 tablespoons extra-virgin olive oil
- 1 tablespoon low-sodium soy sauce
- 1 tablespoon dried thyme
- 1 teaspoon Dijon mustard
- 2 tablespoons extra-virgin olive oil
- 1 to 1½ pounds skirt steak, flat iron steak, or tri-tip steak

FOR THE MUSHROOM SAUCE

- 2 tablespoons extra-virgin olive oil
- 1 pound cremini mushrooms, quartered
- ½ teaspoon sea salt
- 1 teaspoon dried thyme
- ⅛ teaspoon freshly ground black pepper
- 2 garlic cloves, minced
- 1 cup dry red wine

TO MAKE THE MARINADE AND STEAK

1. In a small bowl, whisk the wine, garlic, olive oil, soy sauce, thyme, and mustard. Pour into a resealable bag and add the steak. Refrigerate the steak to marinate for 4 to 8 hours. Remove the steak from the marinade and pat it dry with paper towels.
2. In a large skillet over medium-high heat, heat the olive oil until it shimmers.
3. When the mushroom sauce is ready, slice the steak against the grain into ½-inch-thick slices.

TO MAKE THE MUSHROOM SAUCE

1. In the same skillet over medium-high heat, heat the olive oil until it shimmers.
2. Add the mushrooms, sea salt, thyme, and pepper. Cook for about 6 minutes, stirring very infrequently, until the mushrooms are browned.
3. Add the garlic and cook for 30 seconds, stirring constantly.
4. Stir in the wine, and use the side of a wooden spoon to scrape and fold in any browned bits from the bottom of the skillet. Cook for about 4 minutes, stirring occasionally, until the liquid reduces by half. Serve the mushrooms spooned over the steak.

PER SERVING

Calories: 405; Protein: 33g; Total Carbohydrates: 7g; Sugars: 2g; Fiber: <1g; Total Fat: 22g; Saturated Fat: 5g; Cholesterol: 67mg; Sodium: 430mg

Beef and Tomato Stew

Prep time: 10 minutes | Cook time: 1 hour 30 minutes | Serves 6

- 2 pounds beef chuck roast, cubed
- 1 red bell pepper, seeded and chopped
- 2 carrots, sliced
- 4 garlic cloves, minced
- 2 teaspoons smoked paprika
- 1 teaspoon dried oregano
- ½ teaspoon salt
- 1 (28-ounce) can low-sodium crushed tomatoes
- 1 (28-ounce) can fire-roasted diced tomatoes
- 1 (14-ounce) can low-sodium beef broth
- 2 tablespoons tomato paste
- ½ cup pitted green olives

1. Heat a large pot over medium heat.
2. Put the beef chuck roast into the pot and cook for 5 minutes, or until browned.
3. Add the bell pepper, carrots, and garlic, and cook for 3 minutes or until the vegetables soften. Stir in the paprika, oregano, and salt, and cook for an additional 30 seconds.
4. Add the crushed tomatoes, diced tomatoes, beef broth, and tomato paste, and bring to a boil.
5. Reduce the heat to low, and simmer for 1 hour, 20 minutes, stirring intermittently.
6. Stir in the olives and peas (if using) and cook for an additional minute. Remove from the heat and serve.

PER SERVING

Calories: 384; Fat: 21g; Protein: 33g; Carbohydrates: 20g; Fiber: 7g; Sugar: 12g; Sodium: 810mg

Steak and Swiss Chard Sandwiches with Roasted Garlic Sauce

Prep time: 10 minutes, plus 10 minutes to chill | Cook time: 10 minutes | Serves 6

- ½ cup low-fat milk
- 3 tablespoons freshly squeezed lemon juice
- 2 cloves roasted garlic
- 1 teaspoon Dijon mustard
- ½ teaspoon salt, divided
- ½ cup extra-virgin olive oil
- 1½ pounds sirloin tip roast, thinly sliced
- ¼ teaspoon freshly ground black pepper
- 3 cups chopped Swiss chard, stems removed
- 6 whole wheat hamburger buns

1. In a high-powered blender or food processor, combine the milk, lemon juice, garlic, mustard, and ¼ teaspoon of salt. Blend on low until mixed.
2. While the sauce is still blending, stream in the oil very slowly until the sauce starts to thicken. Pour it into a jar with a lid, cover, and refrigerate for at least 10 minutes.
3. While the sauce is chilling, heat a large skillet over medium heat. Add the sliced sirloin, the remaining ¼ teaspoon of salt, the black pepper, and the Swiss chard. Cook for 5 to 7 minutes, or until the beef is cooked through and the chard is wilted.
4. Divide the mixture evenly between the six hamburger bun bottoms. Drizzle garlic sauce over each one, then top with tops of the hamburger buns before serving.

PER SERVING (1 SANDWICH)

Calories: 467; Fat: 29g; Protein: 28g; Carbohydrates: 25g; Fiber: 4g; Sugar: 5g; Sodium: 535mg

Greek Meatballs (Keftedes)

Prep time: 20 minutes | Cook time: 25 minutes | Serves 4

- 2 whole-wheat bread slices
- 1¼ pounds ground turkey
- 1 egg
- ¼ cup seasoned whole-wheat bread crumbs
- 3 garlic cloves, minced
- ¼ red onion, grated
- ¼ cup chopped fresh Italian parsley leaves
- 2 tablespoons chopped fresh mint leaves
- 2 tablespoons chopped fresh oregano leaves
- ½ teaspoon sea salt
- ¼ teaspoon freshly ground black pepper

1. Preheat the oven to 350°F.
2. Line a baking sheet with parchment paper or aluminum foil.
3. Run the bread under water to wet it, and squeeze out any excess. Tear the wet bread into small pieces and place it in a medium bowl.
4. Add the turkey, egg, bread crumbs, garlic, red onion, parsley, mint, oregano, sea salt, and

pepper. Mix well. Form the mixture into ¼-cup-size balls. Place the meatballs on the prepared sheet and bake for about 25 minutes, or until the internal temperature reaches 165°F.

PER SERVING

Calories: 350; Protein: 42g; Total Carbohydrates: 10g; Sugars: 1g; Fiber: 3g; Total Fat: 18g; Saturated Fat: 3g; Cholesterol: 186mg; Sodium: 493mg

Spiced Ground Beef and Eggplant Couscous Bowls

Prep time: 10 minutes | Cook time: 20 minutes | Serves 4

- 2 cups low-sodium chicken broth, divided
- 1½ cups uncooked couscous
- 1 tablespoon extra-virgin olive oil
- 1 yellow onion, chopped
- 1 red bell pepper, seeded and chopped
- 3 garlic cloves, minced
- 1 pound lean ground beef
- 1 medium eggplant, peeled and chopped
- 2 teaspoons ground cumin
- 1 teaspoon smoked paprika
- 2 tablespoons tomato paste
- 2 tablespoons red wine vinegar
- Salt (optional)
- ½ cup chopped fresh parsley (optional)

1. In a large saucepan set over high heat, bring 1¾ cups of the chicken broth to a boil. Stir in the couscous, cover, and remove from the heat. Let the couscous sit for 5 minutes, then fluff it with a fork.
2. Meanwhile, in a large skillet, heat the oil over medium heat. Add the onion and bell pepper, and cook, stirring occasionally, for 4 to 5 minutes, or until the vegetables have softened.
3. Stir in the garlic and cook for an additional 30 seconds before adding the ground beef. Cook the beef until browned and cooked through, about 4 minutes.
4. Stir in the eggplant, cumin, and paprika and cook for 3 minutes more, or until the eggplant starts to soften.
5. Reduce the heat to medium-low, and stir in the tomato paste, vinegar, and the remaining ¼ cup of chicken broth. Simmer for 5 minutes, then remove the skillet from the heat. Taste and adjust the seasonings as needed.
6. Divide the couscous evenly between four bowls. Top with the beef mixture and the parsley (if using) before serving.

PER SERVING

Calories: 525; Fat: 16g; Protein: 34g; Carbohydrates: 66g; Fiber: 9g; Sugar: 8g; Sodium: 194mg

Chapter 6
Fish and Seafood

Shrimp over Black Bean Linguine

Prep time: 15 minutes | Cook time: 20 minutes | Serves 4

- 1 pound black bean linguine or spaghetti
- 1 pound fresh shrimp, peeled and deveined
- 4 tablespoons extra-virgin olive oil
- 1 onion, finely chopped
- 3 garlic cloves, minced
- ¼ cup basil, cut into strips

1. Bring a large pot of water to a boil and cook the pasta according to the package instructions.
2. In the last 5 minutes of cooking the pasta, add the shrimp to the hot water and allow them to cook for 3 to 5 minutes. Once they turn pink, take them out of the hot water, and, if you think you may have overcooked them, run them under cool water. Set aside.
3. Reserve 1 cup of the pasta cooking water and drain the noodles. In the same pan, heat the oil over medium-high heat and cook the onion and garlic for 7 to 10 minutes. Once the onion is translucent, add the pasta back in and toss well.
4. Plate the pasta, then top with shrimp and garnish with basil.

PER SERVING

Calories: 668; Protein: 57g; Total Carbohydrates: 73g; Sugars: 1g; Fiber: 31g; Total Fat: 19g; Saturated Fat: 2g; Cholesterol: 227mg; Sodium: 615mg

Easy Shrimp and Orzo Salad

Prep time: 15 minutes | Cook time: 10 minutes | Serves 4

- 1 cup orzo
- 1 hothouse cucumber, seeded and chopped
- ½ cup finely diced red onion
- 2 tablespoons extra-virgin olive oil
- 2 pounds (16- to 18-count) shrimp, peeled and deveined
- 3 lemons, juiced
- Salt
- Freshly ground black pepper
- ¾ cup crumbled feta cheese
- 2 tablespoons dried dill
- 1 cup chopped fresh flat-leaf parsley

1. Bring a large pot of water to a boil, then add the orzo. Cover, reduce heat, and simmer for 15 to 18 minutes, until the orzo is tender. Drain in a colander and set aside to cool.
2. In a separate bowl, combine the cucumber and red onion and set aside.
3. In a medium pan, heat the olive oil over medium heat. Add the shrimp. Reduce the heat and cook for 2 minutes on each side, or until fully cooked and pink.
4. Add the cooked shrimp to the bowl with the cucumber and onion, along with the lemon juice, and toss. Season with salt and pepper. Top with feta and dill, toss gently, and finish with parsley.

PER SERVING

Calories: 567; Protein: 63g; Total Carbohydrates: 44g; Sugars: 5g; Fiber: 4g; Total Fat: 18g; Saturated Fat: 6g; Cholesterol: 505mg; Sodium: 2,226mg

Quick Seafood Paella

Prep time: 15 minutes | Cook time: 20 minutes | Serves 4

- ¼ cup plus 1 tablespoon extra-virgin olive oil
- 1 large onion, finely chopped
- 2 tomatoes, peeled and chopped
- 1½ tablespoons garlic powder
- 1½ cups medium-grain Spanish paella rice or arborio rice
- 2 carrots, finely diced
- Salt
- 1 tablespoon sweet paprika
- 8 ounces lobster meat or canned crab
- ½ cup frozen peas
- 3 cups chicken stock, plus more if needed
- 1 cup dry white wine
- 6 jumbo shrimp, unpeeled
- ⅓ pound calamari rings
- 1 lemon, halved

1. In a large sauté pan or skillet (16-inch is ideal), heat the oil over medium heat until small bubbles start to escape from oil. Add the onion and cook for about 3 minutes, until fragrant, then add tomatoes and garlic powder. Cook for 5 to 10 minutes, until the tomatoes are reduced by half and the consistency is sticky.
2. Stir in the rice, carrots, salt, paprika, lobster, and peas and mix well. In a pot or microwave-safe bowl, heat the chicken stock to almost boiling, then add it to the rice mixture. Bring to a simmer, then add the wine.
3. Smooth out the rice in the bottom of the pan. Cover and cook on low for 10 minutes, mixing occasionally, to prevent burning.
4. Top the rice with the shrimp, cover, and cook for 5 more minutes. Add additional broth to the pan if the rice looks dried out.
5. Right before removing the skillet from the heat, add the calamari rings. Toss the ingredients frequently. In about 2 minutes, the rings will look opaque. Remove the pan from the heat immediately—you don't want the paella to overcook). Squeeze fresh lemon juice over the dish.

PER SERVING

Calories: 632; Protein: 34g; Total Carbohydrates: 71g; Sugars: 6g; Fiber: 5g; Total Fat: 20g; Saturated Fat: 3g; Cholesterol: 224mg; Sodium: 920mg

Fire-Roasted Salmon à l'Orange

Prep time: 15 minutes | Cook time: 30 minutes| Serves 4

- ½ cup extra-virgin olive oil, divided
- 2 tablespoons balsamic vinegar
- 2 tablespoons garlic powder, divided
- 1 tablespoon cumin seeds
- 1 teaspoon sea salt, divided
- 1 teaspoon freshly ground black pepper, divided
- 2 teaspoons smoked paprika
- 4 (8-ounce) salmon fillets, skinless
- 2 small red onion, thinly sliced
- ½ cup halved Campari tomatoes
- 1 small fennel bulb, thinly sliced lengthwise
- 1 large carrot, thinly sliced
- 8 medium portobello mushrooms
- 8 medium radishes, sliced ⅛ inch thick
- ½ cup dry white wine
- ½ lime, zested
- Handful cilantro leaves
- ½ cup halved pitted kalamata olives
- 1 orange, thinly sliced
- 4 roasted sweet potatoes, cut in wedges lengthwise

1. Preheat the oven to 375°F.
2. In a medium bowl, mix 6 tablespoons of olive oil, the balsamic vinegar, 1 tablespoon of garlic powder, the cumin seeds, ¼ teaspoon of sea salt, ¼ teaspoon of pepper, and the paprika. Put the salmon in the bowl and marinate while preparing the vegetables, about 10 minutes.
3. Heat an oven-safe sauté pan or skillet on medium-high heat and sear the top of the salmon for about 2 minutes, or until lightly brown. Set aside.
4. Add the remaining 2 tablespoons of olive oil to the same skillet. Once it's hot, add the onion, tomatoes, fennel, carrot, mushrooms, radishes, the remaining 1 teaspoon of garlic powder, ¾ teaspoon of salt, and ¾ teaspoon of pepper. Mix well and cook for 5 to 7 minutes, until fragrant. Add wine and mix well.
5. Place the salmon on top of the vegetable mixture, browned-side up. Sprinkle the fish with lime zest and cilantro and place the olives around the fish. Put orange slices over the fish and cook for about 7 additional minutes. While this is baking, add the sliced sweet potato wedges on a baking sheet and bake this alongside the skillet.
6. Remove from the oven, cover the skillet tightly, and let rest for about 3 minutes.

PER SERVING

Calories: 841; Protein: 59g; Total Carbohydrates: 60g; Sugars: 15g; Fiber: 15g; Total Fat: 41g; Saturated Fat: 6g; Cholesterol: 170mg; Sodium: 908mg

Spicy Trout over Sautéed Mediterranean Salad

Prep time: 15 minutes | Cook time: 30 minutes| Serves 4

- 2 pounds rainbow trout fillets (about 6 fillets)
- Salt
- Ground white pepper
- 1 tablespoon extra-virgin olive oil
- 1 pound asparagus
- 4 medium golden potatoes, thinly sliced
- 1 scallion, thinly sliced, green and white parts separated
- 1 garlic clove, finely minced
- 1 large carrot, thinly sliced
- 2 Roma tomatoes, chopped
- 8 pitted kalamata olives, chopped
- ¼ cup ground cumin
- 2 tablespoons dried parsley
- 2 tablespoons paprika
- 1 tablespoon vegetable bouillon seasoning
- ½ cup dry white wine

1. Lightly season the fish with salt and white pepper and set aside.
2. In a large sauté pan or skillet, heat the oil over medium heat. Add and stir in the asparagus, potatoes, the white part of the scallions, and garlic to the hot oil. Cook and stir for 5 minutes, until fragrant. Add the carrot, tomatoes, and olives; continue to cook for 5 to 7 minutes, until the carrots are slightly tender.
3. Sprinkle the cumin, parsley, paprika, and vegetable bouillon seasoning over the pan. Season with salt. Stir to incorporate. Put the trout on top of the vegetables and add the wine to cover the vegetables.
4. Reduce the heat to low, cover, and cook for 5 to 7 minutes, until the fish flakes easily with a fork and juices run clear. Top with scallion greens and serve.

PER SERVING

Calories: 493; Protein: 40g; Total Carbohydrates: 41g; Sugars: 8g; Fiber: 7g; Total Fat: 19g; Saturated Fat: 5g; Cholesterol: 110mg; Sodium: 736mg

Rosemary and Lemon Roasted Branzino

Prep time: 15 minutes | Cook time: 30 minutes | Serves 4

- 4 tablespoons extra-virgin olive oil, divided
- 2 (8-ounce) branzino fillets, preferably at least 1 inch thick
- 1 garlic clove, minced
- 1 bunch scallions, white part only, thinly sliced
- ½ cup sliced pitted kalamata or other good-quality black olives
- 1 large carrot, cut into ¼-inch rounds
- 10 to 12 small cherry tomatoes, halved
- ½ cup dry white wine
- 2 tablespoons paprika
- 2 teaspoons kosher salt
- ½ tablespoon ground chili pepper, preferably Turkish or Aleppo
- 2 rosemary sprigs or 1 tablespoon dried rosemary
- 1 small lemon, very thinly sliced

1. Warm a large, oven-safe sauté pan or skillet over high heat until hot, about 2 minutes. Carefully add 1 tablespoon of olive oil and heat until it shimmers, 10 to 15 seconds. Brown the branzino fillets for 2 minutes, skin-side up. Carefully flip the fillets skin-side down and cook for another 2 minutes, until browned. Set aside.
2. Swirl 2 tablespoons of olive oil around the skillet to coat evenly. Add the garlic, scallions, kalamata olives, carrot, and tomatoes, and let the vegetables sauté for 5 minutes, until softened. Add the wine, stirring until all ingredients are well integrated. Carefully place the fish over the sauce.
3. Preheat the oven to 450°F.
4. While the oven is heating, brush the fillets with 1 tablespoon of olive oil and season with paprika, salt, and chili pepper. Top each fillet with a rosemary sprig and several slices of lemon. Scatter the olives over fish and around the pan.
5. Roast until lemon slices are browned or singed, about 10 minutes.

PER SERVING

Calories: 725; Protein: 58g; Total Carbohydrates: 25g; Sugars: 6g; Fiber: 10g; Total Fat: 43g; Saturated Fat: 7g; Cholesterol: 120mg; Sodium: 2,954mg

Crushed Marcona Almond Swordfish

Prep time: 15 minutes | Cook time: 20 minutes | Serves 4

- ½ cup almond flour
- ¼ cup crushed Marcona almonds
- ½ to 1 teaspoon salt, divided
- 2 pounds Swordfish, preferably 1 inch thick
- 1 large egg, beaten (optional)
- ¼ cup pure apple cider
- ¼ cup extra-virgin olive oil, plus more for frying
- 3 to 4 sprigs flat-leaf parsley, chopped
- 1 lemon, juiced
- 1 tablespoon Spanish paprika
- 5 medium baby portobello mushrooms, chopped (optional)
- 4 or 5 chopped scallions, both green and white parts
- 3 to 4 garlic cloves, peeled
- ¼ cup chopped pitted kalamata olives

1. On a dinner plate, spread the flour and crushed Marcona almonds and mix in the salt. Alternately, pour the flour, almonds, and ¼ teaspoon of salt into a large plastic food storage bag. Add the fish and coat it with the flour mixture. If a thicker coat is desired, repeat this step after dipping the fish in the egg (if using).
2. In a measuring cup, combine the apple cider, ¼ cup of olive oil, parsley, lemon juice, paprika, and ¼ teaspoon of salt. Mix well and set aside.
3. In a large, heavy-bottom sauté pan or skillet, pour the olive oil to a depth of ⅛ inch and heat on medium heat. Once the oil is hot, add the fish and brown for 3 to 5 minutes, then turn the fish over and add the mushrooms (If using), scallions, garlic, and olives. Cook for an additional 3 minutes. Once the other side of the fish is brown, remove the fish from the pan and set aside.
4. Pour the cider mixture into the skillet and mix well with the vegetables. Put the fried fish into the skillet on top of the mixture and cook with sauce on medium-low heat for 10 minutes, until the fish flakes easily with a fork. Carefully remove the fish from the pan and plate. Spoon the sauce over the fish. Serve with white rice or home-fried potatoes.

PER SERVING

Calories: 620; Protein: 63g; Total Carbohydrates: 10g; Sugars: 1g; Fiber: 5g; Total Fat: 37g; Saturated Fat: 6g; Cholesterol: 113mg; Sodium: 644mg

Cod à la Romana

Prep time: 15 minutes | Cook time: 30 minutes| Serves 4

- 1-pound thick cod fillet, cut in 4 portions
- ¼ teaspoon paprika
- ¼ teaspoon onion powder (optional)
- 3 tablespoons extra-virgin olive oil
- 4 medium scallions
- ½ cup fresh chopped basil, divided
- 3 tablespoons minced garlic (optional)
- 2 teaspoons salt
- 2 teaspoons freshly ground black pepper
- ¼ teaspoon dry marjoram (optional)
- 6 sun-dried tomato slices
- ½ cup dry white wine
- ½ cup crumbled feta cheese
- 1 (15-ounce) can oil-packed artichoke hearts, drained
- 1 lemon, sliced
- 1 cup pitted kalamata olives
- 1 teaspoon capers (optional)
- 4 small red potatoes, quartered

1. Preheat the oven to 375°F.
2. Season the fish with paprika and onion powder (if using).
3. Heat an oven-safe sauté pan or skillet over medium heat and sear the top side of the cod for about 1 minute, or until golden. Set aside.
4. Pour the olive oil into the same skillet and heat over medium heat. Add the scallions, ¼ cup basil, garlic (if using), salt, pepper, marjoram (if using), tomatoes, and white wine and mix well. Bring to a boil and remove from heat.
5. Spread the sauce evenly on the bottom of pan. Then, evenly arrange the fish on top of the tomato basil sauce and sprinkle with feta cheese. Put the artichokes in the pan and top with lemon slices.
6. Sprinkle with olives, capers (if using), and the remaining ¼ cup of fresh basil. Remove from the stovetop and put in the preheated oven; bake the fish for 15 to 20 minutes, until it flakes easily with a fork.
7. Meanwhile, on a baking sheet or wrapped in aluminum foil, put the quartered potatoes in the oven and bake for 15 minutes, until fork-tender.

PER SERVING

Calories: 1,175; Protein: 64g; Total Carbohydrates: 94g; Sugars: 8g; Fiber: 13g; Total Fat: 60g; Saturated Fat: 11g; Cholesterol: 158mg; Sodium: 4,622mg

Braised Branzino over Scallions and Kalamata Olives

Prep time: 15 minutes | Cook time: 20 minutes| Serves 4

- ¾ cup dry white wine
- 2 tablespoons white wine vinegar
- 1 tablespoon honey
- 2 tablespoons corn starch, divided
- 1 large branzino, butterflied
- 2 tablespoons paprika
- 2 tablespoons onion powder
- ½ tablespoon salt
- 6 tablespoons extra-virgin olive oil, divided
- 1 large tomato, cut into ¼-inch cubes
- 4 scallions, both green and white parts, thinly sliced
- 4 kalamata olives, pitted and chopped
- 4 garlic cloves, thinly sliced

1. In a bowl, combine the wine, vinegar, honey, and 2 teaspoons cornstarch, stirring until the honey has dissolved. Set aside.
2. Pat the fish very dry and put the fish skin-side down on a work surface. Sprinkle the fish with paprika, onion powder, and salt. Drizzle with 2 tablespoons of olive oil.
3. Preheat a large sauté pan or skillet over high heat until hot, about 2 minutes. Carefully add 2 tablespoons of olive oil and wait until it shimmers, 10 to 15 seconds. Brown the branzino, skin-side up, for about 2 minutes. Carefully flip it skin-side down and cook for another 2 minutes; set aside.
4. Swirl the remaining 2 tablespoons oil around skillet to evenly coat. Add the tomato, scallions, olives, and garlic and sauté for 5 minutes. Add the wine and vinegar mixture, stirring until all ingredients are well integrated. Carefully place the fish (skin-side down) over the sauce, reduce heat to medium-low, and cook for another 5 minutes. Transfer to a plate with a fork or slotted spoon.

PER SERVING

Calories: 1,060; Protein: 46g; Total Carbohydrates: 56g; Sugars: 14g; Fiber: 5g; Total Fat: 72g; Saturated Fat: 7g; Cholesterol: 90mg; Sodium: 2,808mg

Moroccan Crusted Sea Bass

Prep time: 15 minutes | Cook time: 40 minutes| Serves 4

- 1½ teaspoons ground turmeric, divided
- ¾ teaspoon saffron
- ½ teaspoon ground cumin
- ¼ teaspoon kosher salt
- ¼ teaspoon freshly ground black pepper
- 1½ pound sea bass fillets, about ½ inch thick
- 8 tablespoons extra-virgin olive oil, divided
- 8 garlic cloves, divided (4 minced cloves and 4 sliced)
- 6 medium baby portobello mushrooms, chopped
- 1 large carrot, sliced on an angle
- 2 sun-dried tomatoes, thinly sliced (optional)
- 2 tablespoons tomato paste
- 1 (15-ounce) can chickpeas, drained and rinsed
- 1½ cups low-sodium vegetable broth
- ¼ cup white wine
- 1 tablespoon ground coriander (optional)
- 1 cup sliced artichoke hearts marinated in olive oil
- ½ cup pitted kalamata olives
- ½ lemon, juiced
- ½ lemon, cut into thin rounds
- 4 to 5 rosemary sprigs or 2 tablespoons dried rosemary
- Fresh cilantro, for garnish

1. In a small mixing bowl, combine 1 teaspoon turmeric and the saffron and cumin. Season with salt and pepper. Season both sides of the fish with the spice mixture. Add 3 tablespoons of olive oil and work the fish to make sure it's well coated with the spices and the olive oil.
2. In a large sauté pan or skillet, heat 2 tablespoons of olive oil over medium heat until shimmering but not smoking. Sear the top side of the sea bass for about 1 minute, or until golden. Remove and set aside.
3. In the same skillet, add the minced garlic and cook very briefly, tossing regularly, until fragrant. Add the mushrooms, carrot, sun-dried tomatoes (if using), and tomato paste. Cook for 3 to 4 minutes over medium heat, tossing frequently, until fragrant. Add the chickpeas, broth, wine, coriander (if using), and the sliced garlic. Stir in the remaining ½ teaspoon ground turmeric. Raise the heat, if needed, and bring to a boil, then lower heat to simmer. Cover part of the way and let the sauce simmer for about 20 minutes, until thickened.
4. Carefully add the seared fish to the skillet. Ladle a bit of the sauce on top of the fish. Add the artichokes, olives, lemon juice and slices, and rosemary sprigs. Cook another 10 minutes or until the fish is fully cooked and flaky. Garnish with fresh cilantro.

PER SERVING

Calories: 696; Protein: 48g; Total Carbohydrates: 37g; Sugars: 3g; Fiber: 9g; Total Fat: 41g; Saturated Fat: 6g; Cholesterol: 90mg; Sodium: 810mg

Salmon Patties à la Puttanesca

Prep time: 15 minutes | Cook time: 20 minutes| Serves 4

- 2 scallions, both white and green parts, thinly sliced
- ¼ cup light mayonnaise
- 3 tablespoons Dijon mustard
- 1 large egg, beaten
- 1 tablespoon freshly squeezed lemon juice
- 1 tablespoon dried parsley
- 1 teaspoon paprika
- 1 teaspoon red pepper flakes
- ½ tablespoon kosher salt
- ¼ teaspoon freshly ground black pepper
- ½ cup panko bread crumbs
- 2 tablespoons extra-virgin olive oil, plus more as needed

1. In a large bowl, combine the scallions, mayonnaise, mustard, egg, lemon juice, parsley, paprika, red pepper flakes, salt, and pepper and mix until well incorporated.
2. Add the salmon and panko bread crumbs to the bowl and combine. Form into 2 equal-size patties.
3. In a large sauté pan or skillet, heat the oil over medium heat. Cook the patties until golden and crispy, 3 to 4 minutes per side. Drain on paper towels.
4. Serve over spinach with lemon wedges, or stuff everything into a pita and enjoy!

PER SERVING

Calories: 413; Protein: 18g; Total Carbohydrates: 25g; Sugars: 3g; Fiber: 2g; Total Fat: 25g; Saturated Fat: 3g; Cholesterol: 136mg; Sodium: 2559mg

Pesto Shrimp with Wild Rice Pilaf

Prep time: 5 minutes | Cook time: 5 minutes| Serves 4

- 1 pound medium shrimp, peeled and deveined
- ¼ cup pesto sauce
- 1 lemon, sliced
- 2 cups cooked wild rice pilaf

1. Preheat the air fryer to 360°F.
2. In a medium bowl, toss the shrimp with the pesto sauce until well coated.
3. Place the shrimp in a single layer in the air fryer basket. Put the lemon slices over the shrimp and roast for 5 minutes.
4. Remove the lemons and discard. Serve a quarter of the shrimp over ½ cup wild rice with some favorite steamed vegetables.

PER SERVING

Calories: 249; Total Fat: 10g; Saturated Fat: 2g; Protein: 20g; Total Carbohydrates: 20g; Fiber: 2g; Sugar: 1g; Cholesterol: 145mg

Baked Spanish Salmon

Prep time: 15 minutes | Cook time: 20 minutes | Serves 4

- 2 small red onions, thinly sliced
- 1 cup shaved fennel bulbs
- 1 cup cherry tomatoes
- 15 green pimiento-stuffed olives
- Salt
- Freshly ground black pepper
- ½ teaspoon smoked paprika
- 4 (8-ounce) salmon fillets
- ½ cup low-sodium chicken broth
- 2 to 4 tablespoons extra-virgin olive oil
- 2 cups cooked couscous

1. Put the oven racks in the middle of the oven and preheat the oven to 375°F.
2. On 2 baking sheets, spread out the onions, fennel, tomatoes, and olives. Season them with salt, pepper, cumin, and paprika.
3. Place the fish over the vegetables, season with salt, and gently pour the broth over the 2 baking sheets. Drizzle a light stream of olive oil over baking sheets before popping them in the oven.
4. Bake the vegetables and fish for 20 minutes, checking halfway to ensure nothing is burning. Serve over couscous.

PER SERVING

Calories: 476; Protein: 50g; Total Carbohydrates: 26g; Sugars: 3g; Fiber: 3g; Total Fat: 18g; Saturated Fat: 3g; Cholesterol: 170mg; Sodium: 299mg

Baked Salmon with Tomatoes and Olives

Prep time: 5 minutes | Cook time: 8 minutes | Serves 4

- 2 tablespoons olive oil
- 4 (1½-inch-thick) salmon fillets
- ½ teaspoon salt
- ¼ teaspoon cayenne
- 1 teaspoon chopped fresh dill
- 2 Roma tomatoes, diced
- ¼ cup sliced Kalamata olives
- 4 lemon slices

1. Preheat the air fryer to 380°F.
2. Brush the olive oil on both sides of the salmon fillets, and then season them lightly with salt, cayenne, and dill.
3. Place the fillets in a single layer in the basket of the air fryer, then layer the tomatoes and olives over the top. Top each fillet with a lemon slice.
4. Bake for 8 minutes, or until the salmon has reached an internal temperature of 145°F.

PER SERVING

Calories: 241; Total Fat: 15g; Saturated Fat: 2g; Protein: 23g; Total Carbohydrates: 3g; Fiber: 1g; Sugar: 2g; Cholesterol: 62mg

Lemon-Pepper Trout

Prep time: 5 minutes | Cook time: 15 minutes | Serves 4

- 4 trout fillets
- 2 tablespoons olive oil
- ½ teaspoon salt
- 1 teaspoon black pepper
- 2 garlic cloves, sliced
- 1 lemon, sliced, plus additional wedges for serving

1. Preheat the air fryer to 380°F.
2. Brush each fillet with olive oil on both sides and season with salt and pepper. Place the fillets in an even layer in the air fryer basket.
3. Place the sliced garlic over the tops of the trout fillets, then top the garlic with lemon slices and cook for 12 to 15 minutes, or until it has reached an internal temperature of 145°F.
4. Serve with fresh lemon wedges.

PER SERVING

Calories: 231; Total Fat: 12g; Saturated Fat: 2g; Protein: 29g; Total Carbohydrates: 1g; Fiber: 0g; Sugar: 0g; Cholesterol: 84mg

Herbed Shrimp Pita

Prep time: 5 minutes | Cook time: 8 minutes | Serves 4

- 1 pound medium shrimp, peeled and deveined
- 2 tablespoons olive oil
- 1 teaspoon dried oregano
- ½ teaspoon dried thyme
- ½ teaspoon garlic powder
- ¼ teaspoon onion powder
- ½ teaspoon salt
- ¼ teaspoon black pepper
- 4 whole wheat pitas
- 4 ounces feta cheese, crumbled
- 1 cup shredded lettuce
- 1 tomato, diced
- ¼ cup black olives, sliced
- 1 lemon

1. Preheat the oven to 380°F.
2. In a medium bowl, combine the shrimp with the olive oil, oregano, thyme, garlic powder, onion powder, salt, and black pepper.
3. Pour shrimp in a single layer in the air fryer basket and cook for 6 to 8 minutes, or until cooked through.
4. Remove from the air fryer and divide into warmed pitas with feta, lettuce, tomato, olives, and a squeeze of lemon.

PER SERVING

Calories: 395; Total Fat: 16g; Saturated Fat: 6g; Protein: 26g; Total Carbohydrates: 40g; Fiber: 5g; Sugar: 3g; Cholesterol: 168mg

Sea Bass with Roasted Root Vegetables

Prep time: 5 minutes | Cook time: 15 minutes| Serves 4

- 1 carrot, diced small
- 1 parsnip, diced small
- 1 rutabaga, diced small
- ¼ cup olive oil
- 2 teaspoons salt, divided
- 4 sea bass fillets
- ½ teaspoon onion powder
- 2 garlic cloves, minced
- 1 lemon, sliced, plus additional wedges for serving

1. Preheat the air fryer to 380°F.
2. In a small bowl, toss the carrot, parsnip, and rutabaga with olive oil and 1 teaspoon salt.
3. Lightly season the sea bass with the remaining 1 teaspoon of salt and the onion powder, then place it into the air fryer basket in a single layer.
4. Spread the garlic over the top of each fillet, then cover with lemon slices.
5. Pour the prepared vegetables into the basket around and on top of the fish. Roast for 15 minutes.
6. Serve with additional lemon wedges if desired.

PER SERVING

Calories: 299; Total Fat: 16g; Saturated Fat: 3g; Protein: 25g; Total Carbohydrates: 13g; Fiber: 3g; Sugar: 5g; Cholesterol: 53mg

Steamed Cod with Garlic and Swiss Chard

Prep time: 5 minutes | Cook time: 15 minutes| Serves 4

- 1 teaspoon salt
- ½ teaspoon dried oregano
- ½ teaspoon dried thyme
- ½ teaspoon garlic powder
- 4 cod fillets
- ½ white onion, thinly sliced
- 2 cups Swiss chard, washed, stemmed, and torn into pieces
- ¼ cup olive oil
- 1 lemon, quartered

1. Preheat the air fryer to 380°F.
2. In a small bowl, whisk together the salt, oregano, thyme, and garlic powder.
3. Tear off four pieces of aluminum foil, with each sheet being large enough to envelop one cod fillet and a quarter of the vegetables.
4. Place a cod fillet in the middle of each sheet of foil, then sprinkle on all sides with the spice mixture.
5. In each foil packet, place a quarter of the onion slices and ½ cup Swiss chard, then drizzle 1 tablespoon olive oil and squeeze ¼ lemon over the contents of each foil packet.
6. Fold and seal the sides of the foil packets and then place them into the air fryer basket. Steam for 12 minutes.
7. Remove from the basket, and carefully open each packet to avoid a steam burn.

PER SERVING

Calories: 252; Total Fat: 14g; Saturated Fat: 2g; Protein: 26g; Total Carbohydrates: 4g; Fiber: 1g; Sugar: 1g; Cholesterol: 61mg

Greek Fish Pitas

Prep time: 5 minutes | Cook time: 15 minutes| Serves 4

- 1 pound pollock, cut into 1-inch pieces
- ¼ cup olive oil
- 1 teaspoon salt
- ½ teaspoon dried oregano
- ½ teaspoon dried thyme
- ½ teaspoon garlic powder
- ¼ teaspoon cayenne
- 4 whole wheat pitas
- 1 cup shredded lettuce
- 2 Roma tomatoes, diced
- Nonfat plain Greek yogurt
- lemon, quartered

1. Preheat the air fryer to 380°F.
2. In a medium bowl, combine the pollock with olive oil, salt, oregano, thyme, garlic powder, and cayenne.
3. Put the pollock into the air fryer basket and cook for 15 minutes.
4. Serve inside pitas with lettuce, tomato, and Greek yogurt with a lemon wedge on the side.

PER SERVING

Calories: 368; Total Fat: 16g; Saturated Fat: 2g; Protein: 21g; Total Carbohydrates: 38g; Fiber: 6g; Sugar: 2g; Cholesterol: 52mg

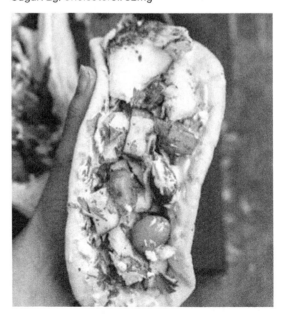

Roasted Whole Red Snapper

Prep time: 5 minutes | Cook time: 35 minutes| Serves 4

- 1 teaspoon salt
- ½ teaspoon black pepper
- ½ teaspoon ground cumin
- ¼ teaspoon cayenne
- 1 (1- to 1½-pound) whole red snapper, cleaned and patted dry
- 2 tablespoons olive oil
- 2 garlic cloves, minced
- ¼ cup fresh dill
- lemon wedges, for serving

1. Preheat the air fryer to 360°F
2. In a small bowl, mix together the salt, pepper, cumin, and cayenne.
3. Coat the outside of the fish with olive oil, then sprinkle the seasoning blend over the outside of the fish. Stuff the minced garlic and dill inside the cavity of the fish.
4. Place the snapper into the basket of the air fryer and roast for 20 minutes. Flip the snapper over, and roast for 15 minutes more, or until the snapper reaches an internal temperature of 145°F.

PER SERVING

Calories: 125; Total Fat: 2g; Saturated Fat: 0g; Protein: 23g; Total Carbohydrates: 2g; Fiber: 0g; Sugar: 0g; Cholesterol: 42mg

Shrimp Quinoa Bowl with Black Olives

Prep time: 5 minutes | Cook time: 25 minutes| Serves 4

- 10 black olives, pitted and halved
- ¼ cup olive oil
- 1 cup quinoa
- 1 lemon, cut in wedges
- 1 lb shrimp, peeled and cooked
- 2 tomatoes, sliced
- 2 bell peppers, thinly sliced
- 1 red onion, chopped
- 1 tsp dried dill
- 1 tbsp fresh parsley, chopped
- Salt and black pepper to taste

1. Place the quinoa in a pot and cover with 2 cups of water over medium heat. Bring to a boil, reduce the heat, and simmer for 12-15 minutes or until tender. Remove from heat and fluff it with a fork.
2. Mix in the quinoa with olive oil, dill, parsley, salt, and black pepper. Stir in tomatoes, bell peppers, olives, and onion. Serve decorated with shrimp and lemon wedges.

PER SERVING

Calories: 662;Fat: 21g;Protein: 79g;Carbs: 38g

Pan-fried Chili Sea Scallops

Prep time: 5 minutes | Cook time: 25 minutes| Serves 4

- 1½ lb large sea scallops, tendons removed
- 3 tbsp olive oil
- 1 garlic clove, finely chopped
- ½ red pepper flakes
- 2 tbsp chili sauce
- ¼ cup tomato sauce
- 1 small shallot, minced
- 1 tbsp minced fresh cilantro
- Salt and black pepper to taste

1. Warm the olive oil in a skillet over medium heat. Add the scallops and cook for 2 minutes without moving them. Flip them and continue to cook for 2 more minutes, without moving them, until golden browned. Set aside.
2. Add the shallot and garlic to the skillet and sauté for 3-5 minutes until softened. Pour in the chili sauce, tomato sauce, and red pepper flakes and stir for 3-4 minutes.
3. Add the scallops back and warm through. Adjust the taste and top with cilantro

PER SERVING

Calories: 204;Fat: 14.1g;Protein: 14g;Carbs: 5g

Spicy Grilled Shrimp with Lemon Wedges

Prep time: 5 minutes | Cook time: 8 minutes| Serves 6

- 1 large clove garlic, crushed
- 1 teaspoon coarse salt
- 1 teaspoon paprika
- ½ teaspoon cayenne pepper
- 2 teaspoons lemon juice
- 2 tablespoons plus 1 teaspoon olive oil, divided
- 2 pounds large shrimp, peeled and deveined
- 8 wedges lemon, for garnish

1. Preheat the grill to medium heat.
2. Stir together the garlic, salt, paprika, cayenne pepper, lemon juice, and 2 tablespoons of olive oil in a small bowl until a paste forms. Add the shrimp and toss until well coated.
3. Grease the grill grates lightly with remaining 1 teaspoon of olive oil.
4. Grill the shrimp for 4 to 6 minutes, flipping the shrimp halfway through, or until the shrimp is totally pink and opaque.
5. Garnish the shrimp with lemon wedges and serve hot.

PER SERVING

Calories: 163;Fat: 5.8g;Protein: 25.2g;Carbs: 2.8g

Hake Fillet In Herby Tomato Sauce

Prep time: 5 minutes | Cook time: 35 minutes| Serves 4

- 2 tbsp olive oil
- 1 onion, sliced thin
- 1 fennel bulb, sliced
- Salt and black pepper to taste
- 4 garlic cloves, minced
- 1 tsp fresh thyme, chopped
- 1 can diced tomatoes,
- ½ cup dry white wine
- 4 skinless hake fillets
- 2 tbsp fresh basil, chopped

1. Warm the olive oil in a skillet over medium heat. Sauté the onion and fennel for about 5 minutes until softened. Stir in garlic and thyme and cook for about 30 seconds until fragrant. Pour in tomatoes and wine and bring to simmer.
2. Season the hake with salt and pepper. Nestle hake skinned side down into the tomato sauce and spoon some sauce over the top. Bring to simmer. Cook for 10-12 minutes until hake easily flakes with a fork. Sprinkle with basil and serve.

PER SERVING

Calories: 452;Fat: 9.9g;Protein: 78g;Carbs: 9.7g

Crispy Sole Fillets

Prep time: 5 minutes | Cook time: 15 minutes| Serves 4

- ¼ cup olive oil
- ½ cup flour
- ½ tsp paprika
- 8 skinless sole fillets
- Salt and black pepper to taste
- 4 lemon wedges

1. Warm the olive oil in a skillet over medium heat. Mix the flour with paprika in a shallow dish. Coat the fish with the flour, shaking off any excess.
2. Sear the sole fillets for 2-3 minutes per side until lightly browned. Serve with lemon wedges.

PER SERVING

Calories: 219;Fat: 15g;Protein: 8.7g;Carbs: 13g

Roasted Red Snapper with Citrus Topping

Prep time: 5 minutes | Cook time: 35 minutes| Serves 2

- 2 tbsp olive oil
- 1 tsp fresh cilantro, chopped
- ½ tsp grated lemon zest
- ½ tbsp lemon juice
- ½ tsp grated grapefruit zest
- ½ tbsp grapefruit juice
- ½ tsp grated orange zest
- ½ tbsp orange juice
- ½ shallot, minced
- ¼ tsp red pepper flakes
- Salt and black pepper to taste
- 1 whole red snapper, cleaned

1. Preheat oven to 380°F. Whisk the olive oil, cilantro, lemon juice, orange juice, grapefruit juice, shallot, and pepper flakes together in a bowl. Season with salt and pepper. Set aside the citrus topping until ready to serve.
2. In a separate bowl, combine lemon zest, orange zest, grapefruit zest, salt, and pepper. with a sharp knife, make 3-4 shallow slashes, about 2 inches apart, on both sides of the snapper.
3. Spoon the citrus mixture into the fish cavity and transfer to a greased baking sheet. Roast for 25 minutes until the fish flakes. Serve drizzled with citrus topping, and enjoy!

PER SERVING

Calories: 257;Fat: 21g;Protein: 16g;Carbs: 1.6g

Bell Pepper & Scallop Skillet

Prep time: 5 minutes | Cook time: 25 minutes| Serves 4

- 3 tbsp olive oil
- 2 celery stalks, sliced
- 2 lb sea scallops, halved
- 3 garlic cloves, minced
- Juice of 1 lime
- 1 red bell pepper, chopped
- 1 tbsp capers, chopped
- 1 tbsp mayonnaise
- 1 tbsp rosemary, chopped
- 1 cup chicken stock

1. Warm olive oil in a skillet over medium heat and cook celery and garlic for 2 minutes.
2. Stir in bell pepper, lime juice, capers, rosemary, and stock and bring to a boil. Simmer for 8 minutes. Mix in scallops and mayonnaise and cook for 5 minutes.

PER SERVING

Calories: 310;Fat: 16g;Protein: 9g;Carbs: 33g

Crispy Herb Crusted Halibut

Prep time: 5 minutes | Cook time: 25 minutes | Serves 4

- 4 halibut fillets, patted dry
- Extra-virgin olive oil, for brushing
- ½ cup coarsely ground unsalted pistachios
- 1 tablespoon chopped fresh parsley
- 1 teaspoon chopped fresh basil
- 1 teaspoon chopped fresh thyme
- Pinch sea salt
- Pinch freshly ground black pepper

1. Preheat the oven to 350°F. Line a baking sheet with parchment paper.
2. Place the fillets on the baking sheet and brush them generously with olive oil.
3. In a small bowl, stir together the pistachios, parsley, basil, thyme, salt, and pepper.
4. Spoon the nut mixture evenly on the fish, spreading it out so the tops of the fillets are covered.
5. Bake in the preheated oven until it flakes when pressed with a fork, about 20 minutes.
6. Serve immediately.

PER SERVING

Calories: 262;Fat: 11.0g;Protein: 32.0g;Carbs: 4.0g.

Lemon Rosemary Roasted Branzino

Prep time: 5 minutes | Cook time: 35 minutes | Serves 2

- 4 tablespoons extra-virgin olive oil, divided
- 2 branzino fillets, preferably at least 1 inch thick
- 1 garlic clove, minced
- 1 bunch scallions (white part only), thinly sliced
- 10 to 12 small cherry tomatoes, halved
- 1 large carrot, cut into ¼-inch rounds
- ½ cup dry white wine
- 2 tablespoons paprika
- 2 teaspoons kosher salt
- ½ tablespoon ground chili pepper
- 2 rosemary sprigs or 1 tablespoon dried rosemary
- 1 small lemon, thinly sliced
- ½ cup sliced pitted kalamata olives

1. Heat a large ovenproof skillet over high heat until hot, about 2 minutes. Add 1 tablespoon of olive oil and heat for 10 to 15 seconds until it shimmers.
2. Add the branzino fillets, skin-side up, and sear for 2 minutes. Flip the fillets and cook for an additional 2 minutes. Set aside.
3. Swirl 2 tablespoons of olive oil around the skillet to coat evenly.
4. Add the garlic, scallions, tomatoes, and carrot, and sauté for 5 minutes, or until softened.
5. Add the wine, stirring until all ingredients are well combined. Carefully place the fish over the sauce.
6. Preheat the oven to 450°F.
7. Brush the fillets with the remaining 1 tablespoon of olive oil and season with paprika, salt, and chili pepper. Top each fillet with a rosemary sprig

and lemon slices. Scatter the olives over fish and around the skillet.
8. Roast for about 10 minutes until the lemon slices are browned. Serve hot.

PER SERVING

Calories: 724;Fat: 43.0g;Protein: 57.7g;Carbs: 25.0g

Tuna Gyros with Tzatziki

Prep time: 5 minutes | Cook time: 15 minutes | Serves 4

- 4 oz tzatziki
- ½ lb canned tuna, drained
- ½ cup tahini
- 4 sundried tomatoes, diced
- 2 tbsp warm water
- 2 garlic cloves, minced
- 1 tbsp lemon juice
- 4 pita wraps
- 5 black olives, chopped
- Salt and black pepper to taste

1. In a bowl, combine the tahini, water, garlic, lemon juice, salt, and black pepper. Warm the pita wraps in a grilled pan for a few minutes, turning once.
2. Spread the tahini and tzatziki sauces over the warmed pitas and top with tuna, sundried tomatoes, and olives. Fold in half and serve immediately.

PER SERVING

Calories: 334;Fat: 24g;Protein: 21.3g;Carbs: 9g.

Salmon In Cream Sauce

Prep Time: 10 minutes| Cook Time: 13 minutes| Serves 4

- ¾ tsp. lemon-pepper seasoning
- 1 tsp. dried thyme
- 1 tsp. dried parsley
- 4 (5-oz.) salmon fillets
- 5 tbsp. fresh lemon juice, divided
- 4 tbsp. olive oil, divided
- 1 shallot, minced
- 5 tbsp. white wine, divided
- 1 tbsp. white wine vinegar
- 1 C. half-and-half
- Salt and ground white pepper, as required

1. In a small-sized bowl, blend together the lemon pepper seasoning and dried herbs.
2. In a shallow dish, place the salmon filets and rub with 3 tbsp. of lemon juice.
3. Season the non-skin side with herb mixture. Set aside.
4. In a wok, melt 2 tbsp. of olive oil over medium heat and sauté the shallot for about 2 minutes.
5. Stir in the remaining lemon juice, ¼ C. of wine and vinegar and simmer for about 2-3 minutes.
6. Stir in half-and-half, salt and white pepper and cook for about 2-3 minutes.
7. Remove from heat and set aside, covered to keep warm.
8. In a wok, heat remaining butter over medium heat.
9. Place the salmon in the wok, herb side down and cook for about 1-2 minutes.
10. Transfer the salmon fillets onto a plate, herb side up.
11. In the wok, add the remaining wine, scraping up the browned bits from bottom.
12. Place the salmon fillets into the wok, herb side up and cook for about 8 minutes.
13. Transfer the salmon fillets onto serving plates.
14. Top with pan sauce and serve.

PER SERVING

Calories: 333; Fat: 22.9g;Carbs: 2.1g;Fiber: 0.3g;Protein: 27.8g

Walnut-Crusted Salmon

Prep Time: 15 minutes| Cook Time: 20 minutes| Serves 2

1 C. walnuts
1 tbsp. fresh dill, chopped
2 tbsp. fresh lemon rind, grated
½ tsp. garlic salt
Ground black pepper, as required
1 tbsp. unsalted butter, melted
3-4 tbsp. Dijon mustard
4 (3-oz.) salmon fillets
4 tsp. fresh lemon juice

1. Preheat your oven to 350 °F. Line a large-sized baking sheet with parchment paper.
2. In a food processor, place the walnuts and pulse until roughly chopped.

3. Add the dill, lemon rind, garlic salt, black pepper, and butter and pulse until a crumbly mixture forms.
4. Place the salmon fillets onto the prepared baking sheet in a single layer, skin-side down.
5. Coat the top of each salmon fillet with Dijon mustard.
6. Place the walnut mixture over each fillet and gently press into the surface of salmon.
7. Bake for approximately 15-20 minutes.
8. Remove the salmon fillets from oven and transfer onto the serving plates.
9. Drizzle with the lemon juice and serve.

PER SERVING

Calories: 396; Fat: 26.5g;Carbs: 6g;Fiber: 2.4g;Protein: 36.9g

Salmon with Avocado Cream

Prep Time: 15 minutes| Cook Time: 8 minutes| Serves 4

FOR AVOCADO CREAM

- 2 avocados, peeled, pitted and chopped
- 1 C. plain Greek yogurt
- 2 garlic cloves, chopped
- 3-4 tbsp. fresh lime juice
- Salt and ground black pepper, as required

FOR SALMON

- 2 tsp. ground cumin
- 2 tsp. red chili powder
- 2 tsp. paprika
- 2 tsp. garlic powder
- Salt and ground black pepper, as required
- 4 (6-oz.) skinless salmon fillet
- 2 tbsp. olive oil

1. For avocado cream: in a food processor, add all the ingredients and pulse until smooth.
2. In a small-sized bowl, blend together the spices.
3. Coat the salmon fillets with spice mixture evenly.
4. In a non-stick wok, heat olive oil over medium-high heat and cook salmon fillets for about 3 minutes.
5. Flip and cook for about 4-5 minutes or until desired doneness.
6. Transfer the salmon fillets onto serving plates.
7. Top with avocado cream and serve.

PER SERVING

Calories: 527; Fat: 36.2g;Carbs: 12.3g;Fiber: 4.9g;Protein: 38.4g

Halibut & Veggie Parcel

Prep Time: 15 minutes| Cook Time: 40 minutes| Serves 4

- 1 onion, chopped
- 1 large tomato, chopped
- 1 (5-oz.) jar pitted olives
- ¼ C. capers
- ¼ C. olive oil
- 1 tbsp. fresh lemon juice
- Salt and ground black pepper, as required
- 4 (6-oz.) halibut fillets
- 1 tbsp. Greek seasoning

1. Preheat your oven to 350 °F.
2. In a bowl, add the onion, tomato, onion, olives, capers, oil, lemon juice, salt and black pepper and mix well.
3. Season the halibut fillets with the Greek seasoning and arrange onto a large-sized piece of foil
4. Top the fillets with the tomato mixture.
5. Carefully fold all the edges of to create a large-sized packet.
6. Arrange the packet onto a baking sheet.
7. Bake for approximately 30-40 minutes.
8. Serve hot.

PER SERVING

Calories: 365; Fat: 20.7g;Carbs: 8.2g;Fiber: 2.6g;Protein: 37.2g

Tuna In Wine Sauce

Prep Time: 15 minutes| Cook Time: 10 minutes| Serves 4

- Olive oil cooking spray
- 4 (6-oz.) (1-inch thick) tuna steak
- 2 tbsp. olive oil, divided
- Salt and ground black pepper, as required
- 2 garlic cloves, mince
- 1 C. fresh tomatoes, chopped
- 1 C. dry white wine
- 2/3 C. olives, pitted and sliced
- ¼ C. capers, drained
- 2 tbsp. fresh thyme, chopped
- 1½ tbsp. fresh lemon zest, grated
- 2 tbsp. fresh lemon juice
- 3 tbsp. fresh parsley, chopped

1. Preheat the grill to high heat. Grease the grill grate with cooking spray.
2. Coat the tuna steaks with 1 tbsp. of the olive oil and sprinkle with salt and black pepper.
3. Set aside for about 5 minutes.
4. For sauce: in a small-sized wok, heat the remaining oil over medium heat and sauté the garlic for about 1 minute.
5. Add the tomatoes and cook for about 2 minutes.
6. Stir in the wine and cook until boiling.
7. Add the remaining ingredients except for parsley and cook, uncovered for about 5 minutes.
8. Stir in the parsley, salt and black pepper and

remove from heat.
9. Meanwhile, place the tuna steaks onto the grill over direct heat and cook for about 1-2 minutes per side.
10. Serve the tuna steaks hot with the topping of sauce.

PER SERVING

Calories: 468; Fat: 10.7g;Carbs: 7.3g;Fiber: 2.3g;Protein: 52.1g

Tilapia Piccata

Prep Time: 10 minutes| Cook Time: 8 minutes| Serves 4

- Olive oil cooking spray
- 3 tbsp. fresh lemon juice
- 2 tbsp. olive oil
- 2 garlic cloves, minced
- ½ tsp. lemon zest, grated
- 2 tsp. capers, drained
- 3 tbsp. fresh basil, minced and divided
- 4 (6-oz.) tilapia fillets
- Salt and ground black pepper, as required

1. Preheat the broiler of the oven. Arrange an oven rack about 4-inch from the heating element.
2. Grease a broiler pan with cooking spray.
3. In a small-sized bowl, add the lemon juice, oil, garlic and lemon zest and whisk until well blended.
4. Add the capers and 2 tbsp. of basil and stir to combine.
5. Reserve 2 tbsp. of mixture in a small-sized bowl.
6. Coat the fish fillets with remaining capers mixture and sprinkle with salt and black pepper.
7. Place the tilapia fillets onto the broiler pan and broil for about 3-4 minutes per side.
8. Remove from oven and place the fish fillets onto serving plates.
9. Drizzle with reserved capers mixture and serve with the garnishing of remaining basil.

PER SERVING

Calories: 206; Fat: 8.7g;Carbs: 0.9g;Fiber: 0.2g;Protein: 31.9g

Tilapia Casserole

Prep Time: 10 minutes| Cook Time: 14 minutes| Serves 4

- 2 (14-oz.) cans diced tomatoes with basil and garlic with juice
- 1/3 C. fresh parsley, chopped and divided
- ¼ tsp. dried oregano
- ½ tsp. red pepper flakes, crushed
- 4 (6-oz.) tilapia fillets
- 2 tbsp. fresh lemon juice
- 2/3 C. feta cheese, crumbled

1. Preheat your oven to 400 °F.
2. In a shallow baking dish, add the tomatoes, ¼ C. of the parsley, oregano, and red pepper flakes, and mix until well blended.
3. Arrange the tilapia fillets over the tomato mixture in a single layer and drizzle with the lemon juice.
4. Place some tomato mixture over the tilapia fillets and sprinkle with the feta cheese evenly.
5. Bake for approximately 12-14 minutes.
6. Serve hot with the garnishing of remaining parsley.

PER SERVING

Calories: 246; Fat: 7.4g;Carbs: 9.4g;Fiber: 2.7g;Protein: 37.2g

Tilapia with Beans & Veggies

Prep Time: 15 minutes| Cook Time: 50 minutes| Serves 12

- 1 tbsp. olive oil
- 1 onion, chopped
- 1 garlic clove, finely chopped
- 1 (15-oz.) can chickpeas, drained and rinsed
- 3 tomatoes, chopped
- 4 olives, pitted and chopped
- ¼ C. fresh parsley, chopped
- 2 tbsp. chicken bouillon granules
- 2 tbsp. ground cumin
- 2 tbsp. paprika
- 1 tsp. cayenne pepper
- Salt, as required
- 3 lb. tilapia fillets

1. In a wok, heat the oil over medium heat and sauté the onion and garlic for about 5 minutes.
2. Add the chickpeas, carrot, bell peppers, tomatoes and olives and cook for about 5 minutes, stirring occasionally.
3. Add the parsley, chicken bouillon granules and spices and stir to combine.
4. Arrange the tilapia fillets on top in a single layer and place enough water to cover the veggies.
5. Now, adjust the heat to low and simmer, covered for about 40 minutes.
6. Serve hot.

PER SERVING

Calories: 261; Fat: 5g;Carbs: 27.1g;Fiber: 7.8g;Protein: 29g

Cod In Tomato Sauce

Prep Time: 15 minutes| Cook Time: 32 minutes| Serves 5

- 1 tsp. dried dill weed
- 2 tsp. sumac
- 2 tsp. ground coriander
- 1½ tsp. ground cumin
- 1 tsp. ground turmeric
- 2 tbsp. olive oil
- 1 large sweet onion, chopped
- 8 garlic cloves, chopped
- 2 jalapeño peppers, chopped
- 5 medium tomatoes, chopped
- 3 tbsp. tomato paste
- 2 tbsp. fresh lime juice
- ½ C. water
- Salt and ground black pepper, as required
- 5 (6-oz.) cod fillets

1. For spice mixture: in a small-sized bowl, add the dill weed and spices and mix well.
2. In a large-sized, deep wok, heat the oil over medium-high heat and sauté the onion for about 2-3 minutes.
3. Add the garlic and jalapeño and sauté for about 2 minutes.
4. Stir in the tomatoes, tomato paste, lime juice, water, half of the spice mixture, salt and pepper and cook until boiling.
5. Now, adjust the heat to medium-low and cook, covered for about 10 minutes, stirring occasionally.
6. Meanwhile, season the cod fillets with the remaining spice mixture, salt and pepper evenly.
7. Place the fish fillets into the wok and gently press into the tomato mixture.
8. Now, adjust the heat to medium-high and cook for about 2 minutes.
9. Now, adjust the heat to medium and cook, covered for about 10-15 minutes or until desired doneness of the fish.
10. Serve hot.

PER SERVING

Calories: 248; Fat: 8.1g;Carbs: 12.9g;Fiber: 3.2g;Protein: 33.1g

White Fish with Raisins

Prep Time: 15 minutes| Cook Time: 38 minutes| Serves 6

- 1/3 C. olive oil
- 1 small red onion, finely chopped
- 2 large tomatoes, chopped
- 1/3 C. golden raisins
- 10 garlic cloves, chopped
- 1½ tbsp. capers
- 1½ tsp. ground coriander
- 1 tsp. ground cumin
- 1 tsp. paprika
- ½ tsp. cayenne pepper
- Salt and ground black pepper, as required
- 1½ lb. white fish fillets
- 1 tbsp. fresh lemon juice
- 1 tsp. lemon zest, grated
- 3 tbsp. fresh parsley, chopped

1. Preheat your oven to 400 °F.
2. In a medium-sized pan, heat the oil over medium-high heat and sauté the onion for about 3 minutes.
3. Add the tomatoes, raisins, garlic, capers, spices, Pinch of salt and black pepper and cook until boiling.
4. Now, adjust the heat to medium-low and simmer for about 15 minutes.
5. Meanwhile, season the fish fillets with salt and black pepper evenly.
6. Remove the pan from heat and place about ½ of the cooked tomato sauce in the bottom of a
7. 9½x13-inch baking dish evenly.
8. Place the fish fillets over the sauce and top with the lemon juice, lemon zest and remaining tomato sauce.
9. Bake for approximately 15-18 minutes or until fish is done completely.
10. Serve hot with the garnishing of parsley.

PER SERVING

Calories: 343; Fat: 21.1g;Carbs: 12.2g;Fiber: 1.8g;Protein: 29.3g

Garlicky Shrimp

Prep Time: 15 minutes| Cook Time: 6 minutes| Serves 3

- 2 tbsp. olive oil
- 3 garlic cloves, sliced
- 1 lb. shrimp, peeled and deveined
- 1 tbsp. fresh rosemary, chopped
- ½ tsp. red pepper flakes, crushed
- Salt and ground black pepper, as required
- 1 tbsp. fresh lemon juice

1. In a large-sized wok, heat the oil over medium heat and sauté the garlic slices or about 2 minutes or until golden brown.
2. with a slotted spoon, transfer the garlic slices into a bowl.

3. In the same wok, add the shrimp, rosemary, red pepper flakes, salt and black pepper and cook for about 3-4 minutes, stirring frequently.
4. Stir in the lemon juice and remove from heat.
5. Serve hot with a topping of the garlic slices.

PER SERVING

Calories: 270; Fat: 12.2g;Carbs: 4.3g;Fiber: 0.6g;Protein: 34.8g

Scallops with Spinach

Prep Time: 15 minutes| Cook Time: 10 minutes| Serves 4

- 20 oz. sea scallops, side muscle removed
- Salt and ground black pepper, as required
- 3 tsp. olive oil, divided
- 6 oz. fresh baby spinach
- 2 garlic cloves, minced
- 1 tbsp. fresh lemon juice

1. Season the scallops with salt and black pepper evenly.
2. In a large-sized cast-iron wok, heat 1 tsp. of oil over medium heat and cook the scallops for about 2-3 minutes per side.
3. with a slotted spoon, transfer the scallops onto a plate.
4. In the same wok, heat the oil over medium heat and cook the spinach and garlic for about 3-4 minutes.
5. Stir in the salt and black pepper and remove from heat.
6. Transfer the spinach onto serving plates and top with scallops.
7. Drizzle with lemon juice and serve.

PER SERVING

Calories: 165; Fat: 4.4g;Carbs: 5.5g;Fiber: 1g;Protein: 25.2g

Mussels with Tomatoes

Prep Time: 15 minutes| Cook Time: 15 minutes| Serves 6

- 1 tbsp. olive oil
- 2 celery stalks, chopped
- 1 onion, chopped
- 4 garlic cloves, minced
- ½ tsp. dried oregano, crushed
- 1 (15-oz.) can diced tomatoes
- 1 tsp. honey
- 1 tsp. red pepper flakes, crushed
- 2 lb. mussels, cleaned
- 2 C. dry white wine
- Salt and ground black pepper, as required
- ¼ C. fresh basil, chopped

In a large-sized wok, heat the oil over medium heat and sauté the celery, onion and garlic for about 5 minutes.

1. Add the tomato, honey and red pepper flakes and cook for about 10 minutes.
2. Meanwhile, in a large-sized saucepan, add mussels and wine and cook until boiling.
3. Simmer, covered for about 10 minutes.
4. Transfer the mussel mixture into tomato mixture and stir to combine.
5. Season with salt and black pepper and remove from heat.
6. Serve hot with the garnishing of basil.

PER SERVING

Calories: 244; Fat: 6g;Carbs: 14.3g;Fiber: 1.5g;Protein: 19.1g

Octopus In Tomato Sauce

Prep Time: 20 minutes| Cook Time: 1 hr. 25 minutes| Serves 8

2¼ lb. fresh octopus, washed
1 bay leaf
1/3 C. water
4 tbsp. olive oil
2 onions, finely chopped
Pinch of saffron threads, crushed
1 garlic clove, finely chopped
1 tbsp. tomato paste
1 (14-oz.) can diced tomatoes
1 tbsp. honey
¾ C. dry red wine
Salt and ground black pepper, as required
¼ C. fresh basil leaves, chopped

1. Remove the eyes of the octopus and cut out the beak.
2. Then, clean the head thoroughly.
3. In a deep pan, add the octopus, bay leaf and water over medium heat and cook for about 20 minutes.
4. Add the wine and simmer for about 50 minutes.
5. Meanwhile, for sauce: in a wok, heat the oil over medium heat and sauté the onions and saffron

for about 3-4 minutes.
6. Add the garlic and tomato paste and sauté for about 1-2 minutes.
7. Stir in the tomatoes and honey and simmer for about 10 minutes.
8. Transfer the sauce into the pan of octopus and cooking for about 15 minutes.
9. Serve hot with the garnishing of basil.

PER SERVING

Calories: 215; Fat: 8.4g;Carbs: 7.8g;Fiber: 1.3g;Protein: 22.6g

Seafood Stew

Prep Time: 20 minutes| Cook Time: 25 minutes| Serves 6

- 2 tbsp. olive oil
- 1 medium onion, finely chopped
- 2 garlic cloves, minced
- ¼ tsp. red pepper flakes, crushed
- ½ lb. tomatoes, seeded and chopped
- 1/3 C. dry white wine
- 1 C. clam juice
- 1 tbsp. tomato paste
- Salt, as required
- 1 lb. large shrimp, peeled and deveined
- 1 lb. snapper fillets, cubed into 1-inch size
- ½ lb. sea scallops
- 1 tbsp. dried parsley, crushed
- 2 tsp. fresh lemon zest, finely grated

1. In a large-sized Dutch oven, heat oil over medium heat and sauté the onion for about 3-4 minutes.
2. Add garlic and red pepper flakes and sauté for about 1 minute.
3. Add tomatoes and cook for about 2 minutes.
4. Add wine, clam juice, tomato paste and salt and cook until boiling.
5. Now, adjust the heat to low and simmer, covered for about 10 minutes.
6. Stir in seafood and simmer, covered for about 6-8 minutes.
7. Stir in parsley and lemon zest and remove from heat.
8. Serve hot.

PER SERVING

Calories: 310; Fat: 7.8g;Carbs: 11.1g;Fiber: 1.2g;Protein: 44.1g

Chapter 7
Salads, Soups, and Sandwiches

Powerhouse Arugula Salad

Prep time: 5 minutes | Cook time: 15 minutes | Serves 4

- 4 tablespoons extra-virgin olive oil
- Zest and juice of 2 clementines or 1 orange (2 to 3 tablespoons)
- 1 tablespoon red wine vinegar
- ½ teaspoon salt
- ¼ teaspoon freshly ground black pepper
- 8 cups baby arugula
- 1 cup coarsely chopped walnuts
- 1 cup crumbled goat cheese
- ½ cup pomegranate seeds

1. In a small bowl, whisk together the olive oil, zest and juice, vinegar, salt, and pepper and set aside.
2. To assemble the salad for serving, in a large bowl, combine the arugula, walnuts, goat cheese, and pomegranate seeds. Drizzle with the dressing and toss to coat.

PER SERVING

Calories: 444, Total Fat: 40g, Total Carbs: 11g, Net Carbs: 8g, Fiber: 3g, Protein: 10g; Sodium: 412mg

Cream of Cauliflower Gazpacho

Prep time: 15 minutes | Cook time: 25 minutes | Serves 4

- 1 cup raw almonds
- ½ teaspoon salt
- ½ cup extra-virgin olive oil, plus 1 tablespoon, divided
- 1 small white onion, minced
- 1 small head cauliflower, stalk removed and broken into florets (about 3 cups)
- 2 garlic cloves, finely minced
- 2 cups chicken or vegetable stock or broth, plus more if needed
- 1 tablespoon red wine vinegar
- ¼ teaspoon freshly ground black pepper

1. Bring a small pot of water to a boil. Add the almonds to the water and boil for 1 minute, being careful to not boil longer or the almonds will become soggy. Drain in a colander and run under cold water. Pat dry and, using your fingers, squeeze the meat of each almond out of its skin. Discard the skins.
2. In a food processor or blender, blend together the almonds and salt. with the processor running, drizzle in ½ cup extra-virgin olive oil, scraping down the sides as needed. Set the almond paste aside.
3. In a large stockpot, heat the remaining 1 tablespoon olive oil over medium-high heat. Add the onion and sauté until golden, 3 to 4 minutes. Add the cauliflower florets and sauté for another 3 to 4 minutes. Add the garlic and sauté for 1 minute more.
4. Add 2 cups stock and bring to a boil. Cover, reduce the heat to medium-low, and simmer the vegetables until tender, 8 to 10 minutes. Remove from the heat and allow to cool slightly.
5. Add the vinegar and pepper. Using an immersion blender, blend until smooth. Alternatively, you can blend in a stand blender, but you may need to divide the mixture into two or three batches. with the blender running, add the almond paste and blend until smooth, adding extra stock if the soup is too thick.
6. Serve warm, or chill in refrigerator at least 4 to 6 hours to serve a cold gazpacho.

PER SERVING

Calories: 505, Total Fat: 45g, Total Carbs: 15g, Net Carbs: 10g, Fiber: 5g, Protein: 10g; Sodium: 484mg

Avocado Gazpacho

Prep time: 5 minutes | Cook time: 15 minutes | Serves 4

- 2 cups chopped tomatoes
- 2 large ripe avocados, halved and pitted
- 1 large cucumber, peeled and seeded
- 1 medium bell pepper (red, orange or yellow), chopped
- 1 cup plain whole-milk Greek yogurt
- ¼ cup extra-virgin olive oil
- ¼ cup chopped fresh cilantro
- ¼ cup chopped scallions, green part only
- 2 tablespoons red wine vinegar
- Juice of 2 limes or 1 lemon
- ½ to 1 teaspoon salt
- ¼ teaspoon freshly ground black pepper

1. In a blender or in a large bowl, if using an immersion blender, combine the tomatoes, avocados, cucumber, bell pepper, yogurt, olive oil, cilantro, scallions, vinegar, and lime juice. Blend until smooth. If using a stand blender, you may need to blend in two or three batches.
2. Season with salt and pepper and blend to combine the flavors.
3. Chill in the refrigerator for 1 to 2 hours before serving. Serve cold.

PER SERVING

Calories: 392, Total Fat: 32g, Total Carbs: 20g, Net Carbs: 11g, Fiber: 9g, Protein: 6g; Sodium: 335mg

Tuscan Kale Salad with Anchovies

Prep Time: 15 minutes, plus 30 minutes to rest | Cook time: 5 minutes| Serves 4

- 1 large bunch lacinato or dinosaur kale
- ¼ cup toasted pine nuts
- 1 cup shaved or coarsely shredded fresh Parmesan cheese
- ¼ cup extra-virgin olive oil
- 8 anchovy fillets, roughly chopped
- 2 to 3 tablespoons freshly squeezed lemon juice (from 1 large lemon)
- 2 teaspoons red pepper flakes (optional)

1. Remove the rough center stems from the kale leaves and roughly tear each leaf into about 4-by-1-inch strips. Place the torn kale in a large bowl and add the pine nuts and cheese.
2. In a small bowl, whisk together the olive oil, anchovies, lemon juice, and red pepper flakes (if using). Drizzle over the salad and toss to coat well. Let sit at room temperature 30 minutes before serving, tossing again just prior to serving.

PER SERVING

Calories: 337, Total Fat: 25g, Total Carbs: 12g, Net Carbs: 10g, Fiber: 2g, Protein: 16g; Sodium: 603mg

Traditional Greek Salad

Prep time: 5 minutes | Cook time: 15 minutes| Serves 4

- 2 large English cucumbers
- 4 Roma tomatoes, quartered
- 1 green bell pepper, cut into 1- to 1½-inch chunks
- ¼ small red onion, thinly sliced
- 4 ounces pitted Kalamata olives
- ¼ cup extra-virgin olive oil
- 2 tablespoons freshly squeezed lemon juice
- 1 tablespoon red wine vinegar
- 1 tablespoon chopped fresh oregano or 1 teaspoon dried oregano
- ¼ teaspoon freshly ground black pepper
- 4 ounces crumbled traditional feta cheese

1. Cut the cucumbers in half lengthwise and then into ½-inch-thick half-moons. Place in a large bowl.
2. Add the quartered tomatoes, bell pepper, red onion, and olives.
3. In a small bowl, whisk together the olive oil, lemon juice, vinegar, oregano, and pepper. Drizzle over the vegetables and toss to coat.
4. Divide between salad plates and top each with 1 ounce of feta.

PER SERVING

Calories: 278, Total Fat: 22g, Total Carbs: 12g, Net Carbs: 8g, Fiber: 4g, Protein: 8g; Sodium: 572mg

Crab Cake Lettuce Cups

Prep Time: 25 minutes, plus 15 minutes to marinate | Cook time: 25 minutes| Serves 4

- 1 pound jumbo lump crab
- 1 large egg
- 6 tablespoons roasted garlic aioli or avocado oil mayonnaise, divided
- 2 tablespoons Dijon mustard
- ½ cup almond flour
- 1 teaspoon celery salt
- 1 teaspoon garlic powder
- 1 teaspoon dried dill (optional)
- ½ teaspoon freshly ground black pepper
- ¼ cup extra-virgin olive oil
- 4 large Bibb lettuce leaves, thick spine removed

1. Place the crabmeat in a large bowl and pick out any visible shells, then break apart the meat with a fork.
2. In a small bowl, whisk together the egg, 2 tablespoons aioli, and Dijon mustard. Add to the crabmeat and blend with a fork. Add the almond flour, red onion, paprika, celery salt, garlic powder, dill (if using), and pepper and combine well. Let sit at room temperature for 10 to 15 minutes.
3. Form into 8 small cakes, about 2 inches in diameter.
4. In large skillet, heat the olive oil over medium-high heat. Fry the cakes until browned, 2 to 3 minutes per side. Cover the skillet, reduce the heat to low, and cook for another 6 to 8 minutes, or until set in the center. Remove from the skillet.
5. To serve, wrap 2 small crab cakes in each lettuce leaf and top with 1 tablespoon aioli.

PER SERVING (2 CRAB CAKES)

Calories: 344, Total Fat: 24g, Total Carbs: 8g, Net Carbs: 6g, Fiber: 2g, Protein: 24g; Sodium: 615mg

Dilled Tuna Salad Sandwich

Prep time: 5 minutes | Cook time: 15 minutes| Serves 4

- 4 versatile sandwich rounds
- 2 (4-ounce) cans tuna, packed in olive oil
- 2 tablespoons roasted garlic aioli, or avocado oil mayonnaise with 1 to 2 teaspoons freshly squeezed lemon juice and/or zest
- 1 very ripe avocado, peeled, pitted, and mashed
- 1 tablespoon chopped fresh capers (optional)
- 1 teaspoon chopped fresh dill or ½ teaspoon dried dill

1. Make sandwich rounds according to recipe. Cut each round in half and set aside.
2. In a medium bowl, place the tuna and the oil from cans. Add the aioli, avocado, capers (if using), and dill and blend well with a fork.
3. Toast sandwich rounds and fill each with one-quarter of the tuna salad, about ⅓ cup.

PER SERVING (1 SANDWICH)

Calories: 436, Total Fat: 36g, Total Carbs: 5g, Net Carbs: 2g, Fiber: 3g, Protein: 23g; Sodium: 790mg

Orange-Tarragon Chicken Salad Wrap

Prep time: 5 minutes | Cook time: 15 minutes | Serves 4

- ½ cup plain whole-milk Greek yogurt
- 2 tablespoons Dijon mustard
- 2 tablespoons extra-virgin olive oil
- 2 tablespoons chopped fresh tarragon or 1 teaspoon dried tarragon
- ½ teaspoon salt
- ¼ teaspoon freshly ground black pepper
- 2 cups cooked shredded chicken
- ½ cup slivered almonds
- 4 to 8 large Bibb lettuce leaves, tough stem removed
- 2 small ripe avocados, peeled and thinly sliced
- Zest of 1 clementine, or ½ small orange (about 1 tablespoon)

1. In a medium bowl, combine the yogurt, mustard, olive oil, tarragon, orange zest, salt, and pepper and whisk until creamy.
2. Add the shredded chicken and almonds and stir to coat.
3. To assemble the wraps, place about ½ cup chicken salad mixture in the center of each lettuce leaf and top with sliced avocados.

PER SERVING

Calories: 440, Total Fat: 32g, Total Carbs: 12g, Net Carbs: 4g, Fiber: 8g, Protein: 26g; Sodium: 445mg

Caprese Grilled Cheese

Prep time: 5 minutes | Cook time: 15 minutes | Serves 4

- 4 versatile sandwich rounds
- 8 tablespoons jarred pesto
- 4 ounces fresh mozzarella cheese, cut into 4 round slices
- 1 Roma tomato or small slicing tomato, cut into 4 slices
- 4 tablespoons extra-virgin olive oil

1. Slice each sandwich round in half horizontally and place, cut-side up, on a large cutting board.
2. Spread 1 tablespoon pesto over each half. Top 4 of the rounds with a mozzarella slice and tomato slice and close with the remaining sandwich rounds.
3. In a large skillet, heat 2 tablespoons olive oil over medium-high heat. Brush the remaining 2 tablespoons olive oil over the tops of the sandwiches.
4. When the skillet is hot, add each sandwich, unoiled-side down, pressing down with the back of a spatula to grill. Cook 3 to 4 minutes, or until cheese begins to melt, before flipping and pressing down with the back of a spatula. Grill on second side another 3 to 4 minutes, or until golden and cheese is very melted. Serve hot.

PER SERVING (1 SANDWICH)

Calories: 598, Total Fat: 56g, Total Carbs: 8g, Net Carbs: 7g, Fiber: 1g, Protein: 16g; Sodium: 950mg

Fennel and Cod Chowder with Fried Mushrooms

Prep time: 15 minutes | Cook time: 35 minutes | Serves 4

- 1 cup extra-virgin olive oil, divided
- 1 small head cauliflower, core removed and broken into florets (about 2 cups)
- 1 small white onion, thinly sliced
- 1 fennel bulb, white part only, trimmed and thinly sliced
- ½ cup dry white wine (optional)
- 2 garlic cloves, minced
- 1 teaspoon salt
- ¼ teaspoon freshly ground black pepper
- 4 cups fish stock, plus more if needed
- 1 pound thick cod fillet, cut into ¾-inch cubes
- 4 ounces shiitake mushrooms, stems trimmed and thinly sliced (⅛-inch slices)
- ¼ cup chopped Italian parsley, for garnish (optional)
- ¼ cup plain whole-milk Greek yogurt, for garnish (optional)

1. In large stockpot, heat ¼ cup olive oil over medium-high heat. Add the cauliflower florets, onion, and fennel and sauté for 10 to 12 minutes, or until almost tender. Add the white wine (if using), garlic, salt, and pepper and sauté for another 1 to 2 minutes.
2. Add 4 cups fish stock and bring to a boil. Cover, reduce the heat to medium-low, and simmer until vegetables are very tender, another 8 to 10 minutes. Remove from the heat and allow to cool slightly.
3. Using an immersion blender, purée the vegetable mixture, slowly drizzling in ½ cup olive oil, until very smooth and silky, adding additional fish stock if the mixture is too thick.
4. Turn the heat back to medium-high and bring the soup to a low simmer. Add the cod pieces and cook, covered, until the fish is cooked through, about 5 minutes. Remove from the heat and keep covered.
5. In a medium skillet, heat the remaining ¼ cup olive oil over medium-high heat. When very hot, add the mushrooms and fry until crispy. Remove with a slotted spoon and transfer to a plate, reserving the frying oil. Toss the mushrooms with a sprinkle of salt.
6. Serve the chowder hot, topped with fried mushrooms and drizzled with 1 tablespoon reserved frying oil. Garnish with chopped fresh parsley and 1 tablespoon of Greek yogurt (if using).

PER SERVING

Calories: 658, Total Fat: 54g, Total Carbs: 15g, Net Carbs: 10g, Fiber: 5g, Protein: 28g; Sodium: 832mg

Greek Chicken and "Rice" Soup with Artichokes

Prep time: 5 minutes | Cook time: 15 minutes| Serves 4

- 4 cups chicken stock or store-bought chicken stock
- 2 cups riced cauliflower, divided
- 2 large egg yolks
- ¼ cup freshly squeezed lemon juice (about 2 lemons)
- ¾ cup extra-virgin olive oil, divided
- 8 ounces cooked chicken, coarsely chopped
- 1 (13.75-ounce) can artichoke hearts, drained and quartered
- ¼ cup chopped fresh dill

1. In a large saucepan, bring the stock to a low boil. Reduce the heat to low and simmer, covered.
2. Transfer 1 cup of the hot stock to a blender or food processor. Add ½ cup raw riced cauliflower, the egg yolks, and lemon juice and purée. While the processor or blender is running, stream in ½ cup olive oil and blend until smooth.
3. Whisking constantly, pour the purée into the simmering stock until well blended together and smooth. Add the chicken and artichokes and simmer until thickened slightly, 8 to 10 minutes. Stir in the dill and remaining 1½ cups riced cauliflower. Serve warm, drizzled with the remaining ¼ cup olive oil.

PER SERVING

Calories: 566, Total Fat: 46g, Total Carbs: 14g, Net Carbs: 7g, Fiber: 7g, Protein: 24g; Sodium: 754mg

Israeli Salad with Nuts and Seeds

Prep time: 5 minutes | Cook time: 15 minutes| Serves 4

- ¼ cup pine nuts
- ¼ cup shelled pistachios
- ¼ cup coarsely chopped walnuts
- ¼ cup shelled pumpkin seeds
- ¼ cup shelled sunflower seeds
- 2 large English cucumbers, unpeeled and finely chopped
- 1 pint cherry tomatoes, finely chopped
- ½ small red onion, finely chopped
- ½ cup finely chopped fresh flat-leaf Italian parsley
- ¼ cup extra-virgin olive oil
- 2 to 3 tablespoons freshly squeezed lemon juice (from 1 lemon)
- 1 teaspoon salt
- ¼ teaspoon freshly ground black pepper
- 4 cups baby arugula

1. In a large dry skillet, toast the pine nuts, pistachios, walnuts, pumpkin seeds, and sunflower seeds over medium-low heat until golden and fragrant, 5 to 6 minutes, being careful not to burn them. Remove from the heat and set aside.
2. In a large bowl, combine the cucumber, tomatoes, red onion, and parsley.

3. In a small bowl, whisk together olive oil, lemon juice, salt, and pepper. Pour over the chopped vegetables and toss to coat.
4. Add the toasted nuts and seeds and arugula and toss with the salad to blend well. Serve at room temperature or chilled.

PER SERVING

Calories: 414, Total Fat: 34g, Total Carbs: 17g, Net Carbs: 11g, Fiber: 6g, Protein: 10g; Sodium: 642mg

Pistachio-Parmesan Kale-Arugula Salad

Prep time: 20 minutes |Cook time: 0 minutes| Serves 6

- 6 cups raw kale, center ribs removed and discarded, leaves coarsely chopped
- ¼ cup extra-virgin olive oil
- 2 tablespoons freshly squeezed lemon juice (from about 1 small lemon)
- ½ teaspoon smoked paprika
- 2 cups arugula
- ⅓ cup unsalted shelled pistachios
- 6 tablespoons grated Parmesan or Pecorino Romano cheese

1. In a large salad bowl, combine the kale, oil, lemon juice, and smoked paprika. with your hands, gently massage the leaves for about 15 seconds or so, until all are thoroughly coated. Let the kale sit for 10 minutes.
2. When you're ready to serve, gently mix in the arugula and pistachios. Divide the salad among six serving bowls, sprinkle 1 tablespoon of grated cheese over each, and serve.

PER SERVING

Calories:105g, Total Fat:9g, Saturated Fat: 2g,Total Carbs:4 g, Fiber:2g, Protein:4g, Sugar:1g, Sodium:176mg,Phosphorus: 84mg,Potassium: 193mg,Cholesterol: 7mg,

Easy Italian Orange and Celery Salad

Prep time: 15 minutes |Cook time: 0 minutes| Serves 6

- 3 celery stalks, including leaves, sliced diagonally into ½-inch slices
- 2 large oranges, peeled and sliced into rounds
- ½ cup green olives (or any variety)
- 1 tablespoon olive brine
- 1 tablespoon freshly squeezed lemon or orange juice (from ½ small lemon or 1 orange round)
- ¼ teaspoon kosher or sea salt
- ¼ teaspoon freshly ground black pepper

1. Place the celery, oranges, olives, and onion on a large serving platter or in a shallow, wide bowl.
2. In a small bowl, whisk together the oil, olive brine, and lemon juice. Pour over the salad, sprinkle with salt and pepper, and serve.

PER SERVING

Calories:21g, Total Fat:1g, Saturated Fat:0 g,Total Carbs:2 g, Fiber:1g, Protein:1g, Sugar:2g, Sodium:138mg,Phosphorus: 6mg,Potassium: 53mg,Cholesterol: 1mg,

Melon Caprese Salad

Prep time: 20 minutes |Cook time: 0 minutes| Serves 6

- 1 cantaloupe, quartered and seeded
- ½ small seedless watermelon
- 2 cups fresh mozzarella balls (about 8 ounces)
- ⅓ cup fresh basil or mint leaves, torn into small pieces
- 2 tablespoons extra-virgin olive oil
- 1 tablespoon balsamic vinegar
- ¼ teaspoon freshly ground black pepper
- ¼ teaspoon kosher or sea salt

1. Using a melon baller or a metal, teaspoon-size measuring spoon, scoop balls out of the cantaloupe. You should get about 2½ to 3 cups from one cantaloupe. (If you prefer, cut the melon into bite-size pieces instead of making balls.) Put them in a large colander over a large serving bowl.
2. Using the same method, ball or cut the watermelon into bite-size pieces; you should get about 2 cups. Put the watermelon balls in the colander with the cantaloupe.
3. Let the fruit drain for 10 minutes. Pour the juice from the bowl into a container to refrigerate and save for drinking or adding to smoothies. Wipe the bowl dry, and put in the cut fruit.
4. Add the tomatoes, mozzarella, basil, oil, vinegar, pepper, and salt to the fruit mixture. Gently mix until everything is incorporated and serve.

PER SERVING

Calories:58g, Total Fat:2g, Saturated Fat: 1g,Total Carbs:9 g, Fiber:1g, Protein:1g, Sugar:5g, Sodium:156mg,Phosphorus: 14mg,Potassium: 221mg,Cholesterol: 2mg,

Chopped Greek Antipasto Salad

Prep time: 20 minutes |Cook time: 0 minutes| Serves 6

FOR THE SALAD

- 1 head Bibb lettuce or ½ head romaine lettuce, chopped (about 2½ cups)
- ¼ cup loosely packed chopped basil leaves
- 1 (15-ounce) can chickpeas, drained and rinsed
- 1 (14-ounce) can artichoke hearts, drained and halved
- 1 pint grape tomatoes, halved (about 1½ cups)
- 1 seedless cucumber, peeled and chopped (about 1½ cups)
- ½ cup cubed feta cheese (about 2 ounces)
- 1 (2.25-ounce) can sliced black olives (about ½ cup)
- For the dressing
- 3 tablespoons extra-virgin olive oil
- 1 tablespoon red wine vinegar
- 1 tablespoon freshly squeezed lemon juice (from about ½ small lemon)
- 1 tablespoon chopped fresh oregano or ½ teaspoon dried oregano
- 1 teaspoon honey
- ¼ teaspoon freshly ground black pepper

1. In a medium bowl, toss the lettuce and basil together. Spread out on a large serving platter or in a large salad bowl. Arrange the chickpeas, artichoke hearts, tomatoes, cucumber, feta, and olives in piles next to each other on top of the lettuce layer.
2. In a small pitcher or bowl, whisk together the oil, vinegar, lemon juice, oregano, honey, and pepper. Serve on the side with the salad, or drizzle over all the ingredients right before serving.

PER SERVING

Calories:164g, Total Fat:8g, Saturated Fat: 3g,Total Carbs:18 g, Fiber:7g, Protein:7g, Sugar:7g, Sodium:336mg,Phosphorus: 125mg,Potassium: 345mg,Cholesterol: 14mg,

Mediterranean Potato Salad

Prep time: 10 minutes |Cook time: 20 minutes| Serves 6

- 2 pounds Yukon Gold baby potatoes, cut into 1-inch cubes
- 3 tablespoons freshly squeezed lemon juice (from about 1 medium lemon)
- 3 tablespoons extra-virgin olive oil
- 1 tablespoon olive brine
- ¼ teaspoon kosher or sea salt
- 1 (2.25-ounce) can sliced olives (about ½ cup)
- 1 cup sliced celery (about 2 stalks) or fennel
- 2 tablespoons chopped fresh oregano
- 2 tablespoons torn fresh mint

1. In a medium saucepan, cover the potatoes with cold water until the waterline is one inch above the potatoes. Set over high heat, bring the potatoes to a boil, then turn down the heat to medium-low. Simmer for 12 to 15 minutes, until the potatoes are just fork tender.
2. While the potatoes are cooking, in a small bowl, whisk together the lemon juice, oil, olive brine, and salt.
3. Drain the potatoes in a colander and transfer to a serving bowl. Immediately pour about 3 tablespoons of the dressing over the potatoes. Gently mix in the olives and celery.
4. Before serving, gently mix in the oregano, mint, and the remaining dressing.

PER SERVING

Calories:219g, Total Fat:6g, Saturated Fat: 2g,Total Carbs:39 g, Fiber:5g, Protein:4g, Sugar:11g, Sodium:230mg,Phosphorus: 96mg,Potassium:715 mg,Cholesterol: 2mg,

Roasted Broccoli Panzanella Salad

Prep time: 10 minutes |Cook time: 20 minutes| Serves 4

1 pound broccoli (about 3 medium stalks), trimmed, cut into 1-inch florets and ½-inch stem slices
3 tablespoons extra-virgin olive oil, divided
1 pint cherry or grape tomatoes (about 1½ cups)
1½ teaspoons honey, divided
3 cups cubed whole-grain crusty bread
1 tablespoon balsamic vinegar
½ teaspoon freshly ground black pepper
¼ teaspoon kosher or sea salt
Grated Parmesan cheese (or other hard cheese) and chopped fresh oregano leaves, for serving (optional)

1. Place a large, rimmed baking sheet in the oven. Preheat the oven to 450°F with the pan inside.
2. Put the broccoli in a large bowl, and drizzle with 1 tablespoon of the oil. Toss to coat.
3. Carefully remove the hot baking sheet from the oven and spoon the broccoli onto it, leaving some oil in the bottom of the bowl. Add the tomatoes to the same bowl, and toss to coat with the leftover

oil (don't add any more oil). Toss the tomatoes with 1 teaspoon of honey, and scrape them onto the baking sheet with the broccoli.
4. Roast for 15 minutes, stirring halfway through. Remove the sheet from the oven, and add the bread cubes. Roast for 3 more minutes. The broccoli is ready when it appears slightly charred on the tips and is tender-crisp when poked with a fork.
5. Spoon the vegetable mixture onto a serving plate or into a large, flat bowl.
6. In a small bowl, whisk the remaining 2 tablespoons of oil together with the vinegar, the remaining ½ teaspoon of honey, and the pepper and salt. Pour over the salad, and toss gently. Sprinkle with cheese and oregano, if desired, and serve.

PER SERVING

Calories:161g, Total Fat:7g, Saturated Fat:1 g,Total Carbs:19 g, Fiber:6g, Protein:8g, Sugar:6g, Sodium:396mg,Phosphorus:159 mg,Potassium: 309mg,Cholesterol: 4mg,

Pastina Chicken Soup with Kale

Prep time: 5 minutes |Cook time: 25 minutes| Serves 6

- 1 tablespoon extra-virgin olive oil
- 2 garlic cloves, minced (about 1 teaspoon)
- 3 cups packed chopped kale (center ribs removed)
- 1 cup minced carrots (about 2 carrots)
- 8 cups low-sodium or no-salt-added chicken broth
- ¼ teaspoon kosher or sea salt
- ¼ teaspoon freshly ground black pepper
- ¾ cup (6 ounces) uncooked acini de pepe or pastina pasta
- 2 cups shredded cooked chicken (about 12 ounces)
- 3 tablespoons grated Parmesan cheese

1. In a large stockpot over medium heat, heat the oil. Add the garlic and cook for 30 seconds, stirring frequently. Add the kale and carrots and cook for 5 minutes, stirring occasionally.
2. Add the broth, salt, and pepper, and turn the heat to high. Bring the broth to a boil, and add the pasta. Lower the heat to medium and cook for 10 minutes, or until the pasta is cooked through, stirring every few minutes so the pasta doesn't stick to the bottom. Add the chicken, and cook for 2 more minutes to warm through.
3. Ladle the soup into six bowls, top each with ½ tablespoon of cheese, and serve.

PER SERVING

Calories:275g, Total Fat:19g, Saturated Fat: 6g,- Total Carbs:11 g, Fiber:2g, Protein:16g, Sugar:2g, Sodium:298mg,Phosphorus: 187mg,Potassium: 439mg,Cholesterol: 34mg,

Mushroom-Barley Soup

Prep time: 5 minutes |Cook time: 25 minutes| Serves 6

- 2 tablespoons extra-virgin olive oil
- 1 cup chopped onion (about ½ medium onion)
- 1 cup chopped carrots (about 2 carrots)
- 5½ cups chopped mushrooms (about 12 ounces)
- 6 cups low-sodium or no-salt-added vegetable broth
- 1 cup uncooked pearled barley
- ¼ cup red wine
- 2 tablespoons tomato paste
- 4 sprigs fresh thyme or ½ teaspoon dried thyme
- 1 dried bay leaf
- 6 tablespoons grated Parmesan cheese

1. In a large stockpot over medium heat, heat the oil. Add the onion and carrots and cook for 5 minutes, stirring frequently. Turn up the heat to medium-high and add the mushrooms. Cook for 3 minutes, stirring frequently.
2. Add the broth, barley, wine, tomato paste, thyme, and bay leaf. Stir, cover the pot, and bring the soup to a boil. Once it's boiling, stir a few times, reduce the heat to medium-low, cover, and cook for another 12 to 15 minutes, until the barley is cooked through.
3. Remove the bay leaf and serve in soup bowls with 1 tablespoon of cheese sprinkled on top of each.

PER SERVING

Calories:195g, Total Fat:4g, Saturated Fat: 1g,Total Carbs:34 g, Fiber:6g, Protein:7g, Sugar:4g, Sodium:173mg,Phosphorus: 155mg,Potassium: 384mg,Cholesterol: 4mg,

Easy Pasta Fagioli Soup

Prep time: 5 minutes |Cook time: 25 minutes| Serves 6

- 2 tablespoons extra-virgin olive oil
- ½ cup chopped onion (about ¼ onion)
- 3 garlic cloves, minced (about 1½ teaspoons)
- 1 tablespoon minced fresh rosemary or 1 teaspoon dried rosemary
- ¼ teaspoon crushed red pepper
- 4 cups low-sodium or no-salt-added vegetable broth
- 2 (15.5-ounce) cans cannellini, great northern, or light kidney beans, undrained
- 1 (28-ounce) can low-sodium or no-salt-added crushed tomatoes
- 2 tablespoons tomato paste
- 8 ounces uncooked short pasta, such as ditalini, tubetti, or elbows
- 6 tablespoons grated Parmesan cheese (about 1½ ounces)

1. In a large stockpot over medium heat, heat the oil. Add the onion and cook for 4 minutes, stirring frequently. Add the garlic, rosemary, and crushed red pepper. Cook for 1 minute, stirring frequently. Add the broth, canned beans with their liquid, tomatoes, and tomato paste. Simmer

for 5 minutes.
2. To thicken the soup, carefully transfer 2 cups to a blender. Purée, then stir it back into the pot.
3. Bring the soup to a boil over high heat. Mix in the pasta, and lower the heat to a simmer. Cook the pasta for the amount of time recommended on the box, stirring every few minutes to prevent the pasta from sticking to the pot. Taste the pasta to make sure it is cooked through (it could take a few more minutes than the recommended cooking time, since it's cooking with other ingredients).
4. Ladle the soup into bowls, top each with 1 tablespoon of grated cheese, and serve.

PER SERVING

Calories:583g, Total Fat:6g, Saturated Fat: 2g,Total Carbs:103 g, Fiber:29g, Protein:32g, Sugar:8g, Sodium:234mg,Phosphorus: 645mg,Potassium: 2032mg,Cholesterol:6 mg,

Roasted Carrot Soup with Parmesan Croutons

Prep time: 10 minutes |Cook time: 20 minutes| Serves 4

- 2 pounds carrots, unpeeled, cut into ½-inch slices (about 6 cups)
- 2 tablespoons extra-virgin olive oil, divided
- 1 cup chopped onion (about ½ medium onion)
- 2 cups low-sodium or no-salt-added vegetable broth
- 2½ cups water
- 1 teaspoon dried thyme
- ¼ teaspoon crushed red pepper
- ¼ teaspoon kosher or sea salt
- 4 thin slices whole-grain bread
- ⅓ cup freshly grated Parmesan cheese (about 1 ounce)

1. Place one oven rack about four inches below the broiler element. Place two large, rimmed baking sheets in the oven on any oven rack. Preheat the oven to 450°F.
2. In a large bowl, toss the carrots with 1 tablespoon of oil to coat. with oven mitts, carefully remove the baking sheets from the oven and evenly distribute the carrots on both sheets. Bake for 20 minutes, until the carrots are just fork tender, stirring once halfway through. The carrots will still be somewhat firm. Remove the carrots from the oven, and turn the oven to the high broil setting.
3. While the carrots are roasting, in a large stockpot over medium-high heat, heat 1 tablespoon of oil. Add the onion and cook for 5 minutes, stirring occasionally. Add the broth, water, thyme, crushed red pepper, and salt. Bring to a boil, cover, then remove the pan from the heat until the carrots have finished roasting.
4. Add the roasted carrots to the pot, and blend with an immersion blender (or use a regular blender—carefully pour in the hot soup in batches, then return the soup to the pot). Heat the soup for about 1 minute over medium-high heat, until warmed through.
5. Turn the oven to the high broil setting. Place the bread on the baking sheet. Sprinkle the cheese evenly across the slices of bread. Broil the bread 4 inches below the heating element for 1 to 2 minutes, or until the cheese melts, watching carefully to prevent burning.
6. Cut the bread into bite-size croutons. Divide the soup evenly among four bowls, top each with the Parmesan croutons, and serve.

PER SERVING

Calories:312g, Total Fat:6g, Saturated Fat: 1g,Total Carbs:53 g, Fiber:10g, Protein:6g, Sugar:16g, Sodium:650mg,Phosphorus: 245mg,Potassium: 926mg,Cholesterol: 4mg,

Classic Paella Soup

Prep time: 5 minutes |Cook time: 25 minutes| Serves 6

- 1 cup frozen green peas
- 2 tablespoons extra-virgin olive oil
- 1 cup chopped onion (about ½ medium onion)
- 1½ cups coarsely chopped red bell pepper (about 1 large pepper)
- 1½ cups coarsely chopped green bell pepper (about 1 large pepper)
- 2 garlic cloves, chopped (about 1 teaspoon)
- 1 teaspoon ground turmeric
- 1 teaspoon dried thyme
- 2 teaspoons smoked paprika
- 2½ cups uncooked instant brown rice
- 2 cups low-sodium or no-salt-added chicken broth
- 2½ cups water
- 1 (28-ounce) can low-sodium or no-salt-added crushed tomatoes
- 1 pound fresh raw medium shrimp (or frozen raw shrimp completely thawed), shells and tails removed

1. Put the frozen peas on the counter to partially thaw as the soup is being prepared.
2. In a large stockpot over medium-high heat, heat the oil. Add the onion, red and green bell peppers, and garlic. Cook for 8 minutes, stirring occasionally. Add the turmeric, thyme, and smoked paprika, and cook for 2 minutes more, stirring often. Stir in the rice, broth, and water. Bring to a boil over high heat. Cover, reduce the heat to medium-low, and cook for 10 minutes.
3. Stir the peas, tomatoes, and shrimp into the soup. Cook for 4 to 6 minutes, until the shrimp is cooked, turning from gray to pink and white. The soup will be very thick, almost like stew, when ready to serve.

PER SERVING

Calories:275g, Total Fat:5g, Saturated Fat:1 g,Total Carbs:41 g, Fiber:6g, Protein:18g, Sugar:7g, Sodium:644mg,Phosphorus: 393mg,Potassium: 691mg,Cholesterol: 97mg,

Rice Stuffed Bell Peppers

Prep time: 5 minutes | Cook time: 65 minutes| Serves 4

- 4 red bell peppers, tops and seeds removed
- 2 tbsp olive oil
- 1 cup cooked brown rice
- 4 oz crumbled feta cheese
- 4 cups fresh baby spinach
- 3 Roma tomatoes, chopped
- 1 onion, finely chopped
- 1 cup mushrooms, sliced
- 2 garlic cloves, minced
- 1 tsp dried oregano
- Salt and black pepper to taste
- 2 tbsp fresh parsley, chopped

1. Preheat oven to 350° F. Warm olive oil in a skillet over medium heat and sauté onion, garlic, and mushrooms for 5 minutes. Stir in tomatoes, spinach, rice, salt, oregano, parsley, and pepper, cook for 3 minutes until the spinach wilts. Remove from the heat.
2. Stuff the bell peppers with the rice mixture and top with feta cheese. Arrange the peppers on a greased baking pan and pour in 1/4 cup of water. Bake covered with aluminum foil for 30 minutes. Then, bake uncovered for another 10 minutes. Serve and enjoy!

PER SERVING

Calories: 387;Fat: 15g;Protein: 12g;Carbs: 55g.

Green Garden Salad

Prep time: 5 minutes | Cook time: 10 minutes| Serves 4

- ¼ cup extra-virgin olive oil
- 2 green onions, sliced
- ½ tsp fresh lemon zest
- 3 tbsp balsamic vinegar
- Salt to taste
- 2 cups baby spinach
- 1 cup watercress
- 1 cup arugula
- 1 celery stick, sliced

1. In a small bowl, whisk together the lemon zest, balsamic vinegar, olive oil, and salt.
2. Put the remaining ingredients in a large bowl. Pour the dressing over the salad and lightly toss to coat. Serve and enjoy!

PER SERVING

Calories: 172;Fat: 14g;Protein: 4.1g;Carbs: 9.8g.

Italian Spinach & Rice Soup

Prep time: 5 minutes | Cook time: 65 minutes| Serves 6

- 3 tbsp olive oil
- 1 large onion, chopped
- 2 cloves garlic, minced
- 2 lb spinach leaves, chopped
- 6 cups chicken broth
- ½ cup arborio rice
- Salt and black pepper to taste
- 2 oz shaved Parmesan cheese

1. Warm the olive oil in a large pot oven over medium heat and add the onion and garlic. Cook until the onions are soft and translucent, about 5 minutes. Add the spinach and stir.
2. Cover the pot and cook the spinach until wilted, about 3 more minutes. with a slotted spoon, remove the spinach and onions from the pot, leaving the liquid.
3. Transfer the spinach mixture to your food processor and process until smooth, then return to the pot.
4. Add the chicken broth and bring to a boil. Add the rice, reduce heat, and simmer until the rice is tender, about 20 minutes. Adjust the taste. Serve topped with Parmesan shavings.

PER SERVING

Calories: 157;Fat: 3.6g;Protein: 8g;Carbs: 27.1g.

Cheese & Broccoli Quiche

Prep time: 5 minutes | Cook time: 45 minutes| Serves 4

- 1 tsp Mediterranean seasoning
- 3 eggs
- ½ cup heavy cream
- 3 tbsp olive oil
- 1 red onion, chopped
- 2 garlic cloves, minced
- 2 oz mozzarella, shredded
- 1 lb broccoli, cut into florets

1. Preheat oven to 320° F. Warm the oil in a pan over medium heat. Sauté the onion and garlic until just tender and fragrant. Add in the broccoli and continue to cook until crisp-tender for about 4 minutes. Spoon the mixture into a greased casserole dish.
2. Beat the eggs with heavy cream and Mediterranean seasoning. Spoon this mixture over the broccoli layer. Bake for 18-20 minutes. Top with the shredded cheese and broil for 5 to 6 minutes or until hot and bubbly on the top. Serve.

PER SERVING

Calories: 198;Fat: 14g;Protein: 5g;Carbs: 12g.

Paella Soup

Prep time: 5 minutes | Cook time: 25 minutes| Serves 6

- 2 tablespoons extra-virgin olive oil
- 1 cup chopped onion
- 1½ cups coarsely chopped green bell pepper
- 1½ cups coarsely chopped red bell pepper
- 2 garlic cloves, chopped
- 1 teaspoon ground turmeric
- 1 teaspoon dried thyme
- 2 teaspoons smoked paprika
- 2½ cups uncooked instant brown rice
- 2 cups low-sodium or no-salt-added chicken broth
- 2½ cups water
- 1 cup frozen green peas, thawed
- 1 can low-sodium or no-salt-added crushed tomatoes
- 1 pound fresh raw medium shrimp, shells and tails removed

1. In a large stockpot over medium-high heat, heat the oil. Add the onion, bell peppers, and garlic. Cook for 8 minutes, stirring occasionally.
2. Add the turmeric, thyme, and smoked paprika, and cook for 2 minutes more, stirring often. Stir in the rice, broth, and water. Bring to a boil over high heat. Cover, reduce the heat to medium-low, and cook for 10 minutes.
3. Stir the peas, tomatoes, and shrimp into the soup. Cook for 4 minutes, until the shrimp is cooked, turning from gray to pink and white. The soup will be very thick, almost like stew, when ready to serve.
4. Ladle the soup into bowls and serve hot.

PER SERVING

Calories: 431;Fat: 5.7g;Protein: 26.0g;Carbs: 69.1g.

Herby Yogurt Sauce

Prep time: 5 minutes | Cook time: 5 minutes| Serves 4

- ¼ tsp fresh lemon juice
- 1 cup plain yogurt
- 2 tbsp fresh cilantro, minced
- 2 tbsp fresh mint, minced
- 1 garlic clove, minced
- Salt and black pepper to taste

1. Place the lemon juice, yogurt, cilantro, mint, and garlic together in a bowl and mix well. Season with salt and pepper.
2. Let sit for about 30 minutes to blend the flavors. Store in an airtight container in the refrigerator for up to 2-3 days.

PER SERVING

Calories: 46;Fat: 0.8g;Protein: 3.6g;Carbs: 4.8g.

Zesty Spanish Potato Salad

Prep time: 5 minutes | Cook time: 5 minutes| Serves 4

- 4 russet potatoes, peeled and chopped
- 3 large hard-boiled eggs, chopped
- 1 cup frozen mixed vegetables, thawed
- ½ cup plain, unsweetened, full-fat Greek yogurt
- 5 tablespoons pitted Spanish olives
- ½ teaspoon freshly ground black pepper
- ½ teaspoon dried mustard seed
- ½ tablespoon freshly squeezed lemon juice
- ½ teaspoon dried dill
- Salt, to taste

1. Place the potatoes in a large pot of water and boil for 5 to 7 minutes, until just fork-tender, checking periodically for doneness. You don't have to overcook them.
2. Meanwhile, in a large bowl, mix the eggs, vegetables, yogurt, olives, pepper, mustard, lemon juice, and dill. Season with salt to taste. Once the potatoes are cooled somewhat, add them to the large bowl, then toss well and serve.

PER SERVING

Calories: 192;Fat: 5.0g;Protein: 9.0g;Carbs: 30.0g.

Greens, Fennel, and Pear Soup with Cashews

Prep time: 5 minutes | Cook time: 15 minutes| Serves 4

- 2 tablespoons olive oil
- 1 fennel bulb, cut into ¼-inch-thick slices
- 2 leeks, white part only, sliced
- 2 pears, peeled, cored, and cut into ½-inch cubes
- 1 teaspoon sea salt
- ¼ teaspoon freshly ground black pepper
- ½ cup cashews
- 2 cups packed blanched spinach
- 3 cups low-sodium vegetable soup

1. Heat the olive oil in a stockpot over high heat until shimmering.
2. Add the fennel and leeks, then sauté for 5 minutes or until tender.
3. Add the pears and sprinkle with salt and pepper, then sauté for another 3 minutes or until the pears are soft.
4. Add the cashews, spinach, and vegetable soup. Bring to a boil. Reduce the heat to low. Cover and simmer for 5 minutes.
5. Pour the soup in a food processor, then pulse until creamy and smooth.
6. Pour the soup back to the pot and heat over low heat until heated through.
7. Transfer the soup to a large serving bowl and serve immediately.

PER SERVING

Calories: 266;Fat: 15.1g;Protein: 5.2g;Carbs: 32.9g.

Collard Green & Rice Salad

Prep time: 5 minutes | Cook time: 15 minutes | Serves 4

- 1 tbsp olive oil
- 1 cup white rice
- 10 oz collard greens, torn
- 4 tbsp walnuts, chopped
- 2 tbsp balsamic vinegar
- 4 tbsp tahini paste
- Salt and black pepper to taste
- 2 tbsp parsley, chopped

1. Bring to a boil salted water over medium heat. Add in the rice and cook for 15-18 minutes. Drain and rest to cool.
2. Whisk tahini, 4 tbsp of cold water, and vinegar in a bowl. In a separate bowl, combine cooled rice, collard greens, walnuts, salt, pepper, olive oil, and tahini dressing. Serve topped with parsley.

PER SERVING

Calories: 180;Fat: 4g;Protein: 4g;Carbs: 6g.

The Ultimate Chicken Bean Soup

Prep time: 5 minutes | Cook time: 45 minutes | Serves 6

- 3 tbsp olive oil
- 3 garlic cloves, minced
- 1 onion, chopped
- 3 tomatoes, chopped
- 4 cups chicken stock
- 1 lb chicken breasts, cubed
- 1 red chili pepper, chopped
- 1 tbsp fennel seeds, crushed
- 14 oz canned white beans
- 1 lime, zested and juiced
- Salt and black pepper to taste
- 2 tbsp parsley, chopped

1. Warm the olive oil in a pot over medium heat. Cook the onion and garlic, adding a splash of water, for 10 minutes until aromatic.
2. Add in the chicken and chili pepper and sit-fry for another 6-8 minutes.
3. Put in tomatoes, chicken stock, beans, lime zest, lime juice, salt, pepper, and fennel seeds and bring to a boil; cook for 30 minutes. Serve topped with parsley.

PER SERVING

Calories: 670;Fat: 18g;Protein: 56g;Carbs: 74g.

Greek Salad

Prep time: 10 minutes | Cook time: None | Serves 4

FOR THE SALAD

- 1 head romaine lettuce, torn
- ½ cup black olives, pitted and chopped
- 1 red onion, thinly sliced
- 1 tomato, chopped
- 1 cucumber, chopped
- ½ cup crumbled feta cheese

FOR THE DRESSING

- 2 tablespoons extra-virgin olive oil
- 2 tablespoons red wine vinegar
- Juice of 1 lemon
- 1 tablespoon dried oregano (or 2 tablespoons chopped fresh oregano leaves)
- 3 garlic cloves, minced
- ½ teaspoon Dijon mustard
- ½ teaspoon sea salt
- ¼ teaspoon freshly ground black pepper

TO MAKE THE SALAD

1. In a large bowl, mix the lettuce, olives, red onion, tomato, cucumber, and feta.

TO MAKE THE DRESSING

2. In a small bowl, whisk the olive oil, vinegar, lemon juice, oregano, garlic, mustard, sea salt, and pepper.

TO ASSEMBLE

3. Just before serving, toss the salad with the dressing.

PER SERVING

Calories: 203; Protein: 15g; Total Carbohydrates: 13g; Sugars: 5g; Fiber: 3g; Total Fat: 15g; Saturated Fat: 6g; Cholesterol: 25mg; Sodium: 716mg

Caprese Salad

Prep time: 15 minutes | Cook time: None | Serves 4

- 3 large tomatoes, sliced
- 4 ounces part-skim mozzarella cheese, cut into ¼-inch-thick slices
- ¼ cup balsamic vinegar
- 2 tablespoons extra-virgin olive oil
- ½ teaspoon sea salt
- ¼ cup loosely packed basil leaves, torn

1. On a pretty platter, arrange the tomatoes and cheese slices alternating and overlapping in a row.
2. Drizzle with the vinegar and olive oil.
3. Sprinkle with sea salt and basil and serve.

PER SERVING

Calories: 152; Protein: 8g; Total Carbohydrates: 5g; Sugars: 3g; Fiber: 1g; Total Fat: 12g; Saturated Fat: 4g; Cholesterol: 18mg; Sodium: 414mg

Cucumber Salad

Prep time: 15 minutes | Cook time: None | Serves 4

- 4 medium cucumbers, chopped or spiralized into spaghetti noodles
- 1 tomato, chopped
- 3 scallions, white and green parts, chopped
- 2 tablespoons extra-virgin olive oil
- ¼ cup red wine vinegar
- 2 tablespoons chopped fresh dill
- 2 garlic cloves, minced
- 1 teaspoon Dijon mustard
- ½ teaspoon sea salt
- ¼ teaspoon freshly ground black pepper

1. In a large bowl, mix together the cucumber, tomato, and scallions.
2. In a small bowl, whisk the olive oil, vinegar, dill, garlic, mustard, sea salt, and pepper.
3. Toss the dressing with the salad just before serving.

PER SERVING

Calories: 118; Protein: 3g; Total Carbohydrates: 13g; Sugars: 6g; Fiber: 2g; Total Fat: 7g; Saturated Fat: 1g; Cholesterol: 0mg; Sodium: 258mg

Chickpea Salad

Prep time: 10 minutes | Cook time: None | Serves 6

- 2 (14-ounce) cans chickpeas (3 cups), drained
- ½ red onion, finely chopped
- 2 cucumbers, finely chopped
- ¼ cup extra-virgin olive oil
- Juice of 2 lemons
- Zest of 1 lemon
- 1 tablespoon tahini
- 3 garlic cloves, minced
- 2 teaspoons dried oregano
- ½ teaspoon sea salt
- ¼ teaspoon freshly ground black pepper

1. In a medium bowl, combine the chickpeas, red onion, and cucumbers.
2. In a small bowl, whisk the olive oil, lemon juice and zest, tahini, garlic, oregano, sea salt, and pepper.
3. Toss the dressing with the salad and serve.

PER SERVING

Calories: 231; Protein: 12g; Total Carbohydrates: 8g; Sugars: 6g; Fiber: 7g; Total Fat: 12g; Saturated Fat: 2g; Cholesterol: 0mg; Sodium: 170mg

Chop Chop Salad

Prep time: 15 minutes | Cook time: None | Serves 6

- 2 heads romaine lettuce, chopped
- 3 cups chopped skinless cooked chicken breast
- 1 cup canned or jarred (in water) artichoke hearts, drained, rinsed, and chopped
- 2 tomatoes, chopped
- 2 zucchini, chopped
- ½ red onion, finely chopped
- 3 ounces mozzarella cheese, chopped
- ⅓ cup unsweetened nonfat plain Greek yogurt
- 1 tablespoon Dijon mustard
- 2 tablespoons extra-virgin olive oil
- Zest of 1 lemon
- 3 garlic cloves, minced
- 2 tablespoons chopped fresh basil leaves
- 2 tablespoons chopped fresh chives
- ½ teaspoon sea salt
- ⅛ teaspoon freshly ground black pepper

1. In a large bowl, combine the lettuce, chicken, artichoke hearts, tomatoes, zucchini, red onion, and mozzarella.
2. In a small bowl, whisk the yogurt, mustard, olive oil, lemon zest, garlic, basil, chives, sea salt, and pepper.
3. Toss the dressing with the salad before serving.

PER SERVING

Calories: 302; Protein: 29g; Total Carbohydrates: 14g; Sugars: 5g; Fiber: 5g; Total Fat: 15g; Saturated Fat: 4g; Cholesterol: 71mg; Sodium: 480mg

Simple Summer Gazpacho

Prep time: 15 minutes (plus 1 hour to chill) | Cook time: None | Serves 4

- 6 tomatoes, chopped
- 3 garlic cloves, minced
- 2 red bell peppers, finely chopped
- 1 red onion, finely chopped
- 3 cups tomato juice
- ¼ cup red wine vinegar
- ¼ cup extra-virgin olive oil
- ¼ cup basil leaves, torn
- ½ teaspoon sea salt
- ¼ teaspoon freshly ground black pepper

1. In a blender or food processor, combine the tomatoes, garlic, red bell peppers, red onion, tomato juice, vinegar, olive oil, basil, sea salt, and pepper. Pulse for 20 to 30 (1-second) pulses until blended. Chill for 1 hour before serving.

PER SERVING

Calories: 209; Protein: 13g; Total Carbohydrates: 23g; Sugars: 16g; Fiber: 4g; Total Fat: 13g; Saturated Fat: 2g; Cholesterol: 0mg; Sodium: 737mg

Panzanella

Prep time: 15 minutes | Cook time: 8 minutes| Serves 4

- 6 tablespoons extra-virgin olive oil, divided
- 4 whole-grain bread slices, crusts removed, cut into pieces
- 1 cup yellow cherry tomatoes, halved
- 1 cup red cherry tomatoes, halved
- 1 plum tomato, cut into wedges
- ½ red onion, very thinly sliced
- ¼ cup chopped fresh basil leaves
- 1 tablespoon capers, drained and rinsed
- ¼ cup red wine vinegar
- 2 garlic cloves, minced
- ½ teaspoon Dijon mustard
- ½ teaspoon sea salt
- ¼ teaspoon freshly ground black pepper

1. In a large skillet over medium-high heat, heat 2 tablespoons of olive oil until it shimmers.
2. Add the bread and cook for 6 to 8 minutes, stirring occasionally, until crisp and browned. Drain and cool the bread on paper towels.
3. In a large bowl, combine the cooled bread, yellow, red, and plum tomatoes, red onion, basil, and capers.
4. In a small bowl, whisk the remaining 4 tablespoons of olive oil with the vinegar, garlic, mustard, sea salt, and pepper. Toss with the salad and serve.

PER SERVING

Calories: 284; Protein: 5g; Total Carbohydrates: 21g; Sugars: 6g; Fiber: 4g; Total Fat: 22g; Saturated Fat: 3g; Cholesterol: 0mg; Sodium: 399mg

Butternut Squash Soup

Prep time: 15 minutes | Cook time: 35 minutes| Serves 4

- 2 tablespoons extra-virgin olive oil
- 1 onion, chopped
- 1 carrot, chopped
- 1 celery stalk, chopped
- 4 cups unsalted vegetable broth
- 3 cups chopped butternut squash
- 1 teaspoon dried thyme
- ½ teaspoon sea salt
- ¼ teaspoon freshly ground black pepper

1. In a large pot over medium-high heat, heat the olive oil until it shimmers.
2. Add the onion, carrot, and celery. Cook for 5 to 7 minutes, stirring occasionally, until the vegetables begin to brown.
3. Add the broth, squash, thyme, sea salt, and pepper. Bring to a simmer and reduce the heat to medium. Simmer for 20 to 30 minutes until the squash is soft.
4. Purée the soup using an immersion blender, food processor, or blender.

PER SERVING

Calories: 136; Protein: 2g; Total Carbohydrates: 20g; Sugars: 7g; Fiber: 3g; Total Fat: 7g; Saturated Fat: <1g; Cholesterol: 0mg; Sodium: 273mg

White Bean Soup with Kale

Prep time: 15 minutes | Cook time: 20 minutes| Serves 6

- 2 tablespoons extra-virgin olive oil
- 8 ounces Italian chicken sausage (uncooked), sliced
- 1 onion, chopped 1 carrot, chopped
- 1 red bell pepper, seeded and chopped
- 3 garlic cloves, minced
- 6 cups unsalted vegetable broth
- 1 (14-ounce) can white beans, drained
- 4 cups chopped kale
- 1 teaspoon dried thyme
- ½ teaspoon sea salt
- ¼ teaspoon freshly ground black pepper
- Pinch red pepper flakes

1. In a large pot over medium-high heat, heat the olive oil until it shimmers.
2. Add the sausage and cook for about 5 minutes, stirring occasionally, until browned. Remove the sausage from the pot with a slotted spoon and set it aside.
3. Add the onion, carrot, and red bell pepper to the oil remaining in the pot. Cook for about 5 minutes, stirring occasionally, until the vegetables are soft.
4. Add the garlic and cook for 30 seconds, stirring constantly.
5. Stir in the broth, beans, kale, thyme, sea salt, pepper, and red pepper flakes. Bring to a simmer. Reduce the heat to low and simmer for about 5 minutes more until the kale is soft.
6. Return the sausage to the pot. Cook for 1 minute more until the sausage heats through. Serve immediately.

PER SERVING

Calories: 281; Protein: 10g; Total Carbohydrates: 30g; Sugars: 6g; Fiber: 6g; Total Fat: 10g; Saturated Fat: 2g; Cholesterol: 27mg; Sodium: 602mg

Lentil Soup (Faki)

Prep time: 10 minutes | Cook time: 20 minutes| Serves 4

- 2 tablespoons extra-virgin olive oil
- 2 onions, chopped
- 2 celery stalks, chopped
- 2 carrots, chopped
- 4 garlic cloves, minced
- 1 (14-ounce) can lentils, drained
- 2 bay leaves
- 6 cups unsalted vegetable broth
- 1 teaspoon sea salt
- ¼ teaspoon freshly ground black pepper
- Pinch red pepper flakes
- ¼ cup red wine vinegar

1. In a large pot over medium-high heat, heat the olive oil until it shimmers.
2. Add the onions, celery, and carrots. Cook for 5 to 10 minutes, stirring occasionally, until the vegetables are soft.
3. Add the garlic and cook for 30 seconds, stirring constantly.
4. Stir in the lentils, bay leaves, broth, sea salt, pepper, and red pepper flakes. Bring to a simmer. Reduce the heat to medium-low and simmer for 10 minutes, stirring occasionally.
5. Remove and discard the bay leaves. Stir in the vinegar and serve.

PER SERVING

Calories: 288; Protein: 14g; Total Carbohydrates: 43g; Sugars: 10g; Fiber: 17g; Total Fat: 8g; Saturated Fat: 8g; Cholesterol: 0mg; Sodium: 532mg

Chicken and Vegetable Soup

Prep time: 10 minutes | Cook time: 20 minutes| Serves 8

- 2 tablespoons extra-virgin olive oil
- 12 ounces boneless, skinless chicken breast, sliced
- 2 carrots, chopped
- 1 onion, chopped
- 1 red bell pepper, seeded and chopped
- 1 fennel bulb, chopped
- 5 garlic cloves, minced
- 6 cups unsalted chicken broth
- 1 (14-ounce) can crushed tomatoes, undrained
- 2 zucchini, chopped
- 1 tablespoon dried Italian seasoning
- ½ teaspoon sea salt
- ¼ teaspoon freshly ground black pepper

1. In a large pot over medium-high heat, heat the olive oil until it shimmers.
2. Add the chicken and cook for about 5 minutes, stirring occasionally, until browned. Remove the chicken from the pot with a slotted spoon and set it aside.
3. Add the carrots, onion, red bell pepper, and fennel to the oil remaining in the pot. Cook for about 5 minutes, stirring occasionally, until the vegetables are soft.
4. Add the garlic and cook for 30 seconds, stirring constantly.
5. Stir in the broth, tomatoes, zucchini, Italian seasoning, sea salt, and pepper. Bring to a boil, stirring occasionally. Reduce the heat and simmer for about 5 minutes more until the vegetables are soft.
6. Return the chicken to the pot. Cook for 1 minute more until the chicken heats through. Serve immediately.

PER SERVING

Calories: 149; Protein: 15g; Total Carbohydrates: 13g; Sugars: 6g; Fiber: 4g; Total Fat: 5g; Saturated Fat: 1g; Cholesterol: 27mg; Sodium: 370mg

Zucchini and Meatball Soup

Prep time: 20 minutes | Cook time: 25 minutes| Serves 6

- 12 ounces ground turkey
- 1 yellow onion, grated and squeezed of excess water (see tip)
- 1 tablespoon dried Italian seasoning
- 1 teaspoon garlic powder
- 1 teaspoon sea salt, divided
- ½ teaspoon freshly ground black pepper, divided
- 2 tablespoons extra-virgin olive oil
- 1 red onion, chopped
- 5 garlic cloves, minced
- 6 cups unsalted chicken broth
- 1 (14-ounce) can chopped tomatoes, drained
- 3 medium zucchini, chopped or spiralized
- ¼ cup chopped fresh basil leaves

1. In a medium bowl, mix together the turkey, yellow onion, Italian seasoning, garlic powder, ½ teaspoon of sea salt, and ¼ teaspoon of pepper. On a plate, form the mixture into ¾-inch balls and set aside.
2. In a large pot over medium-high heat, heat the olive oil until it shimmers.
3. Add the red onion and cook for about 5 minutes, stirring occasionally, until soft.
4. Add the garlic and cook for 30 seconds, stirring constantly.
5. Stir in the broth, tomatoes, remaining ½ teaspoon of salt, and remaining ¼ teaspoon of pepper. Bring to a boil. Add the meatballs and return to a boil. Reduce the heat to medium-low. Simmer for about 15 minutes, stirring occasionally, until the meatballs are cooked through.
6. Add the zucchini and cook for about 3 minutes more, until soft.
7. Stir in the basil just before serving.

PER SERVING

Calories: 244; Protein: 23g; Total Carbohydrates: 12g; Sugars: 6g; Fiber: 3g; Total Fat: 13g; Saturated Fat: 2g; Cholesterol: 59mg; Sodium: 340mg

Fava and Garbanzo Bean Fül

Prep time: 10 minutes | **Cook time:** 10 minutes | **Serves 6**

- 1 (16-ounce) can garbanzo beans, rinsed and drained
- 1 (15-ounce) can fava beans, rinsed and drained
- 3 cups water
- ½ cup lemon juice
- 3 cloves garlic, peeled and minced
- 1 teaspoon salt
- 3 tablespoons extra-virgin olive oil

1. In a 3-quart pot over medium heat, cook the garbanzo beans, fava beans, and water for 10 minutes.
2. Reserving 1 cup of the liquid from the cooked beans, drain the beans and put them in a bowl.
3. Mix the reserved liquid, lemon juice, minced garlic, and salt together and add to the beans in the bowl. Using a potato masher, mash up about half the beans in the bowl.
4. After mashing half the beans, give the mixture one more stir to make sure the beans are evenly mixed.
5. Drizzle the olive oil over the top.
6. Serve warm.

PER SERVING

Calories: 199; Protein: 10g; Total Carbohydrates: 25g; Sugars: 4g; Fiber: 9g; Total Fat: 9g; Saturated Fat: 1g; Cholesterol: 0mg; Sodium: 395mg

Confetti Couscous

Prep time: 5 minutes | **Cook time:** 20 minutes | **Serves 4**

- 3 tablespoons extra-virgin olive oil
- 1 large onion, chopped
- 2 carrots, chopped
- 1 cup fresh peas
- ½ cup golden raisins
- 1 teaspoon salt
- 2 cups vegetable broth
- 2 cups couscous

1. In a medium pot over medium heat, gently toss the olive oil, onions, carrots, peas, and raisins together and let cook for 5 minutes.
2. Add the salt and broth, and stir to combine. Bring to a boil, and let ingredients boil for 5 minutes.
3. Add the couscous. Stir, turn the heat to low, cover, and let cook for 10 minutes. Fluff with a fork and serve.

PER SERVING

Calories: 511; Protein: 14g; Total Carbohydrates: 92g; Sugars: 17g; Fiber: 7g; Total Fat: 12g; Saturated Fat: 2g; Cholesterol: 0mg; Sodium: 504mg

Lemon Orzo with Fresh Herbs

Prep time: 10 minutes | **Cook time:** 10 minutes | **Serves 4**

- 2 cups orzo
- ½ cup fresh parsley, finely chopped
- ½ cup fresh basil, finely chopped
- 2 tablespoons lemon zest
- ½ cup extra-virgin olive oil
- ⅓ cup lemon juice
- 1 teaspoon salt
- ½ teaspoon freshly ground black pepper

1. Bring a large pot of water to a boil. Add the orzo and cook for 7 minutes. Drain and rinse with cold water. Let the orzo sit in a strainer to completely drain and cool.
2. Once the orzo has cooled, put it in a large bowl and add the parsley, basil, and lemon zest.
3. In a small bowl, whisk together the olive oil, lemon juice, salt, and pepper. Add the dressing to the pasta and toss everything together. Serve at room temperature or chilled.

PER SERVING

Calories: 568; Protein: 11g; Total Carbohydrates: 65g; Sugars: 4g; Fiber: 4g; Total Fat: 29g; Saturated Fat: 4g; Cholesterol: 0mg; Sodium: 586mg

Orzo-Veggie Pilaf

Prep time: 20 minutes | **Cook time:** 10 minutes | **Serves 6**

- 2 cups orzo
- 1 pint (2 cups) cherry tomatoes, cut in half
- 1 cup Kalamata olives
- ½ cup fresh basil, finely chopped
- ½ cup extra-virgin olive oil
- ⅓ cup balsamic vinegar
- 1 teaspoon salt
- ½ teaspoon freshly ground black pepper

1. Bring a large pot of water to a boil. Add the orzo and cook for 7 minutes. Drain and rinse the orzo with cold water in a strainer.
2. Once the orzo has cooled, put it in a large bowl. Add the tomatoes, olives, and basil.
3. In a small bowl, whisk together the olive oil, vinegar, salt, and pepper. Add this dressing to the pasta and toss everything together. Serve at room temperature or chilled.

PER SERVING

Calories: 476; Protein: 8g; Total Carbohydrates: 48g; Sugars: 3g; Fiber: 3g; Total Fat: 28g; Saturated Fat: 4g; Cholesterol: 0mg; Sodium: 851mg

Earthy Lentil and Rice Pilaf

Prep time: 5 minutes | Cook time: 50 minutes | Serves 6

- ¼ cup extra-virgin olive oil
- 1 large onion, chopped
- 6 cups water
- 1 teaspoon ground cumin
- 1 teaspoon salt
- 2 cups brown lentils, picked over and rinsed
- 1 cup basmati rice

1. In a medium pot over medium heat, cook the olive oil and onions for 7 to 10 minutes until the edges are browned.
2. Turn the heat to high, add the water, cumin, and salt, and bring this mixture to a boil, boiling for about 3 minutes.
3. Add the lentils and turn the heat to medium-low. Cover the pot and cook for 20 minutes, stirring occasionally.
4. Stir in the rice and cover; cook for an additional 20 minutes.
5. Fluff the rice with a fork and serve warm.

PER SERVING

Calories: 397; Protein: 18g; Total Carbohydrates: 60g; Sugars: 4g; Fiber: 18g; Total Fat: 11g; Saturated Fat: 1g; Cholesterol: 0mg; Sodium: 396mg

Lentils and Bulgur with Caramelized Onions

Prep time: 10 minutes | Cook time: 50 minutes | Serves 6

- ½ cup extra-virgin olive oil
- 4 large onions, chopped
- 2 teaspoons salt, divided
- 6 cups water
- 2 cups brown lentils, picked over and rinsed
- 1 teaspoon freshly ground black pepper
- 1 cup bulgur wheat

1. In a large pot over medium heat, cook and stir the olive oil, onions, and 1 teaspoon of salt for 12 to 15 minutes, until the onions are a medium brown/golden color.
2. Put half of the cooked onions in a bowl.
3. Add the water, remaining 1 teaspoon of salt, and lentils to the remaining onions. Stir. Cover and cook for 30 minutes.
4. Stir in the black pepper and bulgur, cover, and cook for 5 minutes. Fluff with a fork, cover, and let stand for another 5 minutes.
5. Spoon the lentils and bulgur onto a serving plate and top with the reserved onions. Serve warm.

PER SERVING

Calories: 479; Protein: 20g; Total Carbohydrates: 60g; Sugars: 7g; Fiber: 24g; Total Fat: 20g; Saturated Fat: 3g; Cholesterol: 0mg; Sodium: 789mg

Bulgur and Garbanzo Pilaf

Prep time: 5 minutes | Cook time: 20 minutes | Serves 4

- 3 tablespoons extra-virgin olive oil
- 1 large onion, chopped
- 1 (16-ounce) can garbanzo beans, rinsed and drained
- 2 cups bulgur wheat , rinsed and drained
- 1½ teaspoons salt
- ½ teaspoon cinnamon
- 4 cups water

1. In a large pot over medium heat, cook the olive oil and onion for 5 minutes.
2. Add the garbanzo beans and cook for another 5 minutes.
3. Add the bulgur, salt, cinnamon, and water and stir to combine. Cover the pot, turn the heat to low, and cook for 10 minutes.
4. When the cooking is done, fluff the pilaf with a fork. Cover and let sit for another 5 minutes.

PER SERVING

Calories: 462; Protein: 15g; Total Carbohydrates: 76g; Sugars: 5g; Fiber: 19g; Total Fat: 13g; Saturated Fat: 2g; Cholesterol: 0mg; Sodium: 890mg

Spanish Rice

Prep time: 10 minutes | Cook time: 20 minutes | Serves 4

- 2 tablespoons extra-virgin olive oil
- 1 medium onion, finely chopped
- 1 large tomato, finely diced
- 2 tablespoons tomato paste
- 1 teaspoon smoked paprika
- 1 teaspoon salt
- 1½ cups basmati rice
- 3 cups water

1. In a medium pot over medium heat, cook the olive oil, onion, and tomato for 3 minutes.
2. Stir in the tomato paste, paprika, salt, and rice. Cook for 1 minute.
3. Add the water, cover the pot, and turn the heat to low. Cook for 12 minutes.
4. Gently toss the rice, cover, and cook for another 3 minutes.

PER SERVING

Calories: 328; Protein: 6g; Total Carbohydrates: 60g; Sugars: 3g; Fiber: 2g; Total Fat: 7g; Saturated Fat: 1g; Cholesterol: 0mg; Sodium: 651mg

Garbanzo and Pita No-Bake Casserole

Prep time: 10 minutes | Cook time: 10 minutes | Serves 4

- 4 cups Greek yogurt
- 3 cloves garlic, minced
- 1 teaspoon salt
- 2 (16-ounce) cans garbanzo beans, rinsed and drained
- 2 cups water
- 4 cups pita chips
- 5 tablespoons unsalted butter

1. In a large bowl, whisk together the yogurt, garlic, and salt. Set aside.
2. Put the garbanzo beans and water in a medium pot. Bring to a boil; let beans boil for about 5 minutes.
3. Pour the garbanzo beans and the liquid into a large casserole dish.
4. Top the beans with pita chips. Pour the yogurt sauce over the pita chip layer.
5. In a small saucepan, melt and brown the butter, about 3 minutes. Pour the brown butter over the yogurt sauce.

PER SERVING

Calories: 772; Protein: 39g; Total Carbohydrates: 73g; Sugars: 18g; Fiber: 13g; Total Fat: 36g; Saturated Fat: 15g; Cholesterol: 71mg; Sodium: 1,003mg

Creamy Garlic and Cheese Polenta

Prep time: 5 minutes | Cook time: 30 minutes | Serves 4

- 4 tablespoons (½ stick) unsalted butter, divided
- 1 tablespoon garlic, finely chopped
- 4 cups water
- 1 teaspoon salt
- 1 cup polenta
- ¾ cup Parmesan cheese, divided

1. In a large pot over medium heat, cook 3 tablespoons of butter and the garlic for 2 minutes.
2. Add the water and salt, and bring to a boil. Add the polenta and immediately whisk until it starts to thicken, about 3 minutes. Turn the heat to low, cover, and cook for 25 minutes, whisking every 5 minutes.
3. Using a wooden spoon, stir in ½ cup of the Parmesan cheese.
4. To serve, pour the polenta into a large serving bowl. Sprinkle the top with the remaining 1 tablespoon butter and ¼ cup of remaining Parmesan cheese. Serve warm.

PER SERVING

Calories: 297; Protein: 9g; Total Carbohydrates: 28g; Sugars: 0g; Fiber: 2g; Total Fat: 16g; Saturated Fat: 10g; Cholesterol: 42mg; Sodium: 838mg

Mushroom Risotto

Prep time: 10 minutes | Cook time: 30 minutes | Serves 4

- 6 cups vegetable broth
- 3 tablespoons extra-virgin olive oil, divided
- 1 pound cremini mushrooms, cleaned and sliced
- 1 medium onion, finely chopped
- 2 cloves garlic, minced
- 1½ cups Arborio rice 1 teaspoon salt
- ½ cup freshly grated Parmesan cheese
- ½ teaspoon freshly ground black pepper

1. In a saucepan over medium heat, bring the broth to a low simmer.
2. In a large skillet over medium heat, cook 1 tablespoon olive oil and the sliced mushrooms for 5 to 7 minutes. Set cooked mushrooms aside.
3. In the same skillet over medium heat, add the 2 remaining tablespoons of olive oil, onion, and garlic. Cook for 3 minutes.
4. Add the rice, salt, and 1 cup of broth to the skillet. Stir the ingredients together and cook over low heat until most of the liquid is absorbed. Continue adding ½ cup of broth at a time, stirring until it is absorbed. Repeat until all of the broth is used up.
5. with the final addition of broth, add the cooked mushrooms, Parmesan cheese, and black pepper. Cook for 2 more minutes. Serve immediately.

PER SERVING

Calories: 410; Protein: 11g; Total Carbohydrates: 65g; Sugars: 5g; Fiber: 3g; Total Fat: 12g; Saturated Fat: 3g; Cholesterol: 4mg; Sodium: 2,086mg

Hearty White Bean Stew

Prep time: 10 minutes | Cook time: 30 minutes | Serves 4

- 3 tablespoons extra-virgin olive oil
- 1 large onion, chopped
- 1 (15-ounce) can diced tomatoes
- 2 (15-ounce) cans white cannellini beans
- 1 cup carrots, chopped
- 4 cups vegetable broth
- 1 teaspoon salt
- 1 (1-pound) bag baby spinach, washed

1. In a large pot over medium heat, cook the olive oil and onion for 5 minutes.
2. Add the tomatoes, beans, carrots, broth, and salt. Stir and cook for 20 minutes.
3. Add the spinach, a handful at a time, and cook for 5 minutes, until the spinach has wilted.
4. Serve warm.

PER SERVING

Calories: 356; Protein: 15g; Total Carbohydrates: 47g; Sugars: 10g; Fiber: 16g; Total Fat: 12g; Saturated Fat: 2g; Cholesterol: 0mg; Sodium: 1,832mg

Sweet Potato Black Bean Burgers

Prep time: 5 minutes | Cook time: 15 minutes| Serves 4

- 1 (15-ounce) can black beans, drained and rinsed
- 1 cup mashed sweet potato
- ½ teaspoon dried oregano
- ¼ teaspoon dried thyme
- ¼ teaspoon dried marjoram
- 1 garlic clove, minced
- ¼ teaspoon salt
- ¼ teaspoon black pepper
- 1 tablespoon lemon juice
- 1 cup cooked brown rice
- ¼ to ½ cup whole wheat bread crumbs
- 1 tablespoon olive oil
- For serving:
- Whole wheat buns or whole wheat pitas
- Plain Greek yogurt
- avocado
- lettuce
- tomato
- red onion

1. Preheat the air fryer to 380°F.
2. In a large bowl, use the back of a fork to mash the black beans until there are no large pieces left.
3. Add the mashed sweet potato, oregano, thyme, marjoram, garlic, salt, pepper, and lemon juice, and mix until well combined.
4. Stir in the cooked rice.
5. Add in ¼ cup of the whole wheat bread crumbs and stir. Check to see if the mixture is dry enough to form patties. If it seems too wet and loose, add an additional ¼ cup bread crumbs and stir.
6. Form the dough into 4 patties. Place them into the air fryer basket in a single layer, making sure that they don't touch each other.
7. Brush half of the olive oil onto the patties and bake for 5 minutes.
8. Flip the patties over, brush the other side with the remaining oil, and bake for an additional 4 to 5 minutes.
9. Serve on toasted whole wheat buns or whole wheat pitas with a spoonful of yogurt and avocado, lettuce, tomato, and red onion as desired.

PER SERVING (JUST THE PATTIES)

Calories: 263; Total Fat: 5g; Saturated Fat: 1g; Protein: 9g; Total Carbohydrates: 47g; Fiber: 8g; Sugar: 4g; Cholesterol: 0mg

Spicy Lentil Patties

Prep time: 5 minutes | Cook time: 15 minutes| Serves 4

- 1 cup cooked brown lentils
- ¼ cup fresh parsley leaves
- ½ cup shredded carrots
- ¼ red onion, minced
- ¼ red bell pepper, minced
- 1 jalapeño, seeded and minced
- 2 garlic cloves, minced
- 1 egg
- 2 tablespoons lemon juice
- 2 tablespoons olive oil, divided
- ½ teaspoon onion powder
- ½ teaspoon smoked paprika
- ½ teaspoon dried oregano
- ¼ teaspoon salt
- ¼ teaspoon black pepper
- ½ cup whole wheat bread crumbs
- For serving:
- Whole wheat buns or whole wheat pitas
- Plain Greek yogurt
- tomato
- lettuce
- red onion

1. Preheat the air fryer to 380°F.
2. In a food processor, pulse the lentils and parsley mostly smooth. (You will want some bits of lentils in the mixture.)
3. Pour the lentils into a large bowl, and combine with the carrots, onion, bell pepper, jalapeño, garlic, egg, lemon juice, and 1 tablespoon olive oil.
4. Add the onion powder, paprika, oregano, salt, pepper, and bread crumbs. Stir everything together until the seasonings and bread crumbs are well distributed.
5. Form the dough into 4 patties. Place them into the air fryer basket in a single layer, making sure that they don't touch each other. Brush the remaining 1 tablespoon of olive oil over the patties.
6. Bake for 5 minutes. Flip the patties over and bake for an additional 5 minutes.
7. Serve on toasted whole wheat buns or whole wheat pitas with a spoonful of yogurt and lettuce, tomato, and red onion as desired.

PER SERVING (JUST THE PATTIES)

Calories: 206; Total Fat: 9g; Saturated Fat: 1g; Protein: 8g; Total Carbohydrates: 25g; Fiber: 6g; Sugar: 3g; Cholesterol: 41mg

Red Lentil and Goat Cheese Stuffed Tomatoes

Prep time: 5 minutes | Cook time: 15 minutes | Serves 4

- 4 tomatoes
- ½ cup cooked red lentils
- 1 garlic clove, minced
- 1 tablespoon minced red onion
- 4 basil leaves, minced
- ¼ teaspoon salt
- ¼ teaspoon black pepper
- 4 ounces goat cheese
- 2 tablespoons shredded Parmesan cheese

1. Preheat the air fryer to 380°F.
2. Slice the top off of each tomato.
3. Using a knife and spoon, cut and scoop out half of the flesh inside of the tomato. Place it into a medium bowl.
4. To the bowl with the tomato, add the cooked lentils, garlic, onion, basil, salt, pepper, and goat cheese. Stir until well combined.
5. Spoon the filling into the scooped-out cavity of each of the tomatoes, then top each one with ½ tablespoon of shredded Parmesan cheese.
6. Place the tomatoes in a single layer in the air fryer basket and bake for 15 minutes.

PER SERVING

Calories: 138; Total Fat: 7g; Saturated Fat: 5g; Protein: 9g; Total Carbohydrates: 11g; Fiber: 4g; Sugar: 4g; Cholesterol: 15mg

Herbed Green Lentil Rice Balls

Prep time: 5 minutes | Cook time: 15 minutes | Serves 6

- ½ cup cooked green lentils
- 2 garlic cloves, minced
- ¼ white onion, minced
- ¼ cup parsley leaves
- 5 basil leaves
- 1 cup cooked brown rice
- 1 tablespoon lemon juice
- 1 tablespoon olive oil
- ½ teaspoon salt

1. Preheat the air fryer to 380°F.
2. In a food processor, pulse the cooked lentils with the garlic, onion, parsley, and basil until mostly smooth. (You will want some bits of lentils in the mixture.)
3. Pour the lentil mixture into a large bowl, and stir in brown rice, lemon juice, olive oil, and salt. Stir until well combined.
4. Form the rice mixture into 1-inch balls. Place the rice balls in a single layer in the air fryer basket, making sure that they don't touch each other.
5. Fry for 6 minutes. Turn the rice balls and then fry for an additional 4 to 5 minutes, or until browned on all sides.

PER SERVING

Calories: 80; Total Fat: 3g; Saturated Fat: 0g; Protein: 2g; Total Carbohydrates: 12g; Fiber: 2g; Sugar: 1g; Cholesterol: 0mg

Roasted White Beans with Peppers

Prep time: 5 minutes | Cook time: 15 minutes | Serves 4

- Olive oil cooking spray
- 2 (15-ounce) cans white beans, or cannellini beans, drained and rinsed
- 1 red bell pepper, diced
- ½ red onion, diced
- 3 garlic cloves, minced
- 1 tablespoon olive oil
- ¼ to ½ teaspoon salt
- ½ teaspoon black pepper
- 1 rosemary sprig
- 1 bay leaf

1. Preheat the air fryer to 360°F. Lightly coat the inside of a 5-cup capacity casserole dish with olive oil cooking spray. (The shape of the casserole dish will depend upon the size of the air fryer, but it needs to be able to hold at least 5 cups.)
2. In a large bowl, combine the beans, bell pepper, onion, garlic, olive oil, salt, and pepper.
3. Pour the bean mixture into the prepared casserole dish, place the rosemary and bay leaf on top, and then place the casserole dish into the air fryer.
4. Roast for 15 minutes.
5. Remove the rosemary and bay leaves, then stir well before serving.

PER SERVING

Calories: 196; Total Fat: 5g; Saturated Fat: 0g; Protein: 10g; Total Carbohydrates: 30g; Fiber: 1g; Sugar: 2g; Cholesterol: 0mg

Greek Baked Beans

Prep time: 5 minutes | Cook time: 35 minutes| Serves 4

- Olive oil cooking spray
- 1 (15-ounce) can cannellini beans, drained and rinsed
- 1 (15-ounce) can great northern beans, drained and rinsed
- ½ yellow onion, diced
- 1 (8-ounce) can tomato sauce
- 1½ tablespoons raw honey
- ¼ cup olive oil
- 2 garlic cloves, minced
- 2 tablespoons chopped fresh dill
- ½ teaspoon salt
- ½ teaspoon black pepper
- 1 bay leaf
- 1 tablespoon balsamic vinegar
- 2 ounces feta cheese, crumbled, for serving

1. Preheat the air fryer to 360°F. Lightly coat the inside of a 5-cup capacity casserole dish with olive oil cooking spray. (The shape of the casserole dish will depend upon the size of the air fryer, but it needs to be able to hold at least 5 cups.)
2. In a large bowl, combine all ingredients except the feta cheese and stir until well combined.
3. Pour the bean mixture into the prepared casserole dish.
4. Bake in the air fryer for 30 minutes.
5. Remove from the air fryer and remove and discard the bay leaf. Sprinkle crumbled feta over the top before serving.

PER SERVING

Calories: 397; Total Fat: 18g; Saturated Fat: 4g; Protein: 14g; Total Carbohydrates: 48g; Fiber: 16g; Sugar: 11g; Cholesterol: 13mg

Baked Mushroom Barley Pilaf

Prep time: 5 minutes | Cook time: 40 minutes| Serves 4

- Olive oil cooking spray
- 2 tablespoons olive oil
- 8 ounces button mushrooms, diced
- ½ yellow onion, diced
- 2 garlic cloves, minced
- 1 cup pearl barley
- 2 cups vegetable broth
- 1 tablespoon fresh thyme, chopped
- ½ teaspoon salt
- ¼ teaspoon smoked paprika
- Fresh parsley, for garnish

1. Preheat the air fryer to 380°F. Lightly coat the inside of a 5-cup capacity casserole dish with olive oil cooking spray. (The shape of the casserole dish will depend upon the size of the air fryer, but it needs to be able to hold at least 5 cups.)
2. In a large skillet, heat the olive oil over medium heat. Add the mushrooms and onion and cook, stirring occasionally, for 5 minutes, or until the mushrooms begin to brown.
3. Add the garlic and cook for an additional 2 minutes. Transfer the vegetables to a large bowl.
4. Add the barley, broth, thyme, salt, and paprika.
5. Pour the barley-and-vegetable mixture into the prepared casserole dish, and place the dish into the air fryer. Bake for 15 minutes.
6. Stir the barley mixture. Reduce the heat to 360°F, then return the barley to the air fryer and bake for 15 minutes more.
7. Remove from the air fryer and let sit for 5 minutes before fluffing with a fork and topping with fresh parsley.

PER SERVING

Calories: 263; Total Fat: 8g; Saturated Fat: 1g; Protein: 7g; Total Carbohydrates: 44g; Fiber: 9g; Sugar: 3g; Cholesterol: 0mg

Moroccan-Style Rice and Chickpea Bake

Prep time: 5 minutes | Cook time: 45 minutes| Serves 6

- Olive oil cooking spray
- 1 cup long-grain brown rice
- 2 ¼ cups chicken stock
- 1 (15.5-ounce) can chickpeas, drained and rinsed
- ½ cup diced carrot
- ½ cup green peas
- 1 teaspoon ground cumin
- ½ teaspoon ground turmeric
- ½ teaspoon ground ginger
- ½ teaspoon onion powder
- ½ teaspoon salt
- ¼ teaspoon ground cinnamon
- ¼ teaspoon garlic powder
- ¼ teaspoon black pepper
- Fresh parsley, for garnish

1. Preheat the air fryer to 380°F. Lightly coat the inside of a 5-cup capacity casserole dish with olive oil cooking spray. (The shape of the casserole dish will depend upon the size of the air fryer, but it needs to be able to hold at least 5 cups.)
2. In the casserole dish, combine the rice, stock, chickpeas, carrot, peas, cumin, turmeric, ginger, onion powder, salt, cinnamon, garlic powder, and black pepper. Stir well to combine.
3. Cover loosely with aluminum foil.
4. Place the covered casserole dish into the air fryer and bake for 20 minutes. Remove from the air fryer and stir well.
5. Place the casserole back into the air fryer, uncovered, and bake for 25 minutes more.
6. Fluff with a spoon and sprinkle with fresh chopped parsley before serving.

PER SERVING

Calories: 204; Total Fat: 2g; Saturated Fat: 0g; Protein: 7g; Total Carbohydrates: 40g; Fiber: 5g; Sugar: 4g; Cholesterol: 0mg

Buckwheat Bake with Root Vegetables

Prep time: 15 minutes | Cook time: 35 minutes | Serves 6

- Olive oil cooking spray
- 2 large potatoes, cubed
- 2 carrots, sliced
- 1 small rutabaga, cubed
- 2 celery stalks, chopped
- ½ teaspoon smoked paprika
- ¼ cup plus 1 tablespoon olive oil, divided
- 2 rosemary sprigs
- 1 cup buckwheat groats
- 2 cups vegetable broth
- 2 garlic cloves, minced
- ½ yellow onion, chopped
- 1 teaspoon salt

1. Preheat the air fryer to 380°F. Lightly coat the inside of a 5-cup capacity casserole dish with olive oil cooking spray. (The shape of the casserole dish will depend upon the size of the air fryer, but it needs to be able to hold at least 5 cups.)
2. In a large bowl, toss the potatoes, carrots, rutabaga, and celery with the paprika and ¼ cup olive oil.
3. Pour the vegetable mixture into the prepared casserole dish and top with the rosemary sprigs. Place the casserole dish into the air fryer and bake for 15 minutes.
4. While the vegetables are cooking, rinse and drain the buckwheat groats.
5. In a medium saucepan over medium-high heat, combine the groats, vegetable broth, garlic, onion, and salt with the remaining 1 tablespoon olive oil. Bring the mixture to a boil, then reduce the heat to low, cover, and cook for 10 to 12 minutes.
6. Remove the casserole dish from the air fryer. Remove the rosemary sprigs and discard. Pour the cooked buckwheat into the dish with the vegetables and stir to combine. Cover with aluminum foil and bake for an additional 15 minutes.
7. Stir before serving.

PER SERVING

Calories: 344; Total Fat: 13g; Saturated Fat: 2g; Protein: 8g; Total Carbohydrates: 50g; Fiber: 8g; Sugar: 4g; Cholesterol: 0mg

Savory Gigantes Plaki (Baked Giant White Beans)

Prep time: 5 minutes | Cook time: 35 minutes | Serves 4

- Olive oil cooking spray
- 1 (15-ounce) can cooked butter beans, drained and rinsed
- 1 cup diced fresh tomatoes
- ½ tablespoon tomato paste
- 2 garlic cloves, minced
- ½ yellow onion, diced
- ½ teaspoon salt
- ¼ cup olive oil
- ¼ cup fresh parsley, chopped

1. Preheat the air fryer to 380°F. Lightly coat the inside of a 5-cup capacity casserole dish with olive oil cooking spray. (The shape of the casserole dish will depend upon the size of the air fryer, but it needs to be able to hold at least 5 cups.)
2. In a large bowl, combine the butter beans, tomatoes, tomato paste, garlic, onion, salt, and olive oil, mixing until all ingredients are combined.
3. Pour the mixture into the prepared casserole dish and top with the chopped parsley.
4. Bake in the air fryer for 15 minutes. Stir well, then return to the air fryer and bake for 15 minutes more.

PER SERVING

Calories: 212; Total Fat: 14g; Saturated Fat: 2g; Protein: 5g; Total Carbohydrates: 17g; Fiber: 1g; Sugar: 2g; Cholesterol: 0mg

Mediterranean Creamed Green Peas

Prep time: 5 minutes | Cook time: 25 minutes | Serves 8

- 1 cup cauliflower florets, fresh or frozen
- ½ white onion, roughly chopped
- 2 tablespoons olive oil
- ½ cup unsweetened almond milk
- 3 cups green peas, fresh or frozen
- 3 garlic cloves, minced
- 2 tablespoons fresh thyme leaves, chopped
- 1 teaspoon fresh rosemary leaves, chopped
- ½ teaspoon salt
- ½ teaspoon black pepper
- Shredded Parmesan cheese, for garnish
- Fresh parsley, for garnish

1. Preheat the air fryer to 380°F.
2. In a large bowl, combine the cauliflower florets and onion with the olive oil and toss well to coat.
3. Put the cauliflower-and-onion mixture into the air fryer basket in an even layer and bake for 15 minutes.
4. Transfer the cauliflower and onion to a food processor. Add the almond milk and pulse until smooth.
5. In a medium saucepan, combine the cauliflower puree, peas, garlic, thyme, rosemary, salt, and pepper and mix well. Cook over medium heat for an additional 10 minutes, stirring regularly.
6. Serve with a sprinkle of Parmesan cheese and chopped fresh parsley.

PER SERVING

Calories: 87; Total Fat: 4g; Saturated Fat: 1g; Protein: 4g; Total Carbohydrates: 10g; Fiber: 3g; Sugar: 4g; Cholesterol: 0mg

Baked Farro Risotto with Sage

Prep time: 5 minutes | Cook time: 35 minutes| Serves 6

- Olive oil cooking spray
- 1½ cups uncooked farro
- 2 ½ cups chicken broth
- 1 cup tomato sauce
- 1 yellow onion, diced
- 3 garlic cloves, minced
- 1 tablespoon fresh sage, chopped
- ½ teaspoon salt
- 2 tablespoons olive oil
- 1 cup Parmesan cheese, grated, divided

1. Preheat the air fryer to 380°F. Lightly coat the inside of a 5-cup capacity casserole dish with olive oil cooking spray. (The shape of the casserole dish will depend upon the size of the air fryer, but it needs to be able to hold at least 5 cups.)
2. In a large bowl, combine the farro, broth, tomato sauce, onion, garlic, sage, salt, olive oil, and ½ cup of the Parmesan.
3. Pour the farro mixture into the prepared casserole dish and cover with aluminum foil.
4. Bake for 20 minutes, then uncover and stir. Sprinkle the remaining ½ cup Parmesan over the top and bake for 15 minutes more.
5. Stir well before serving.

PER SERVING

Calories: 284; Total Fat: 10g; Saturated Fat: 3g; Protein: 12g; Total Carbohydrates: 40g; Fiber: 4g; Sugar: 3g; Cholesterol: 14mg

---

Black-eyed Pea and Vegetable Stew

Prep time: 5 minutes | Cook time: 45 minutes| Serves 2

- ½ cup black-eyed peas, soaked in water overnight
- 3 cups water, plus more as needed
- ¼ teaspoon turmeric
- ¼ teaspoon cayenne pepper
- ¼ teaspoon ground cumin seeds, toasted
- ¼ cup finely chopped parsley
- ¼ teaspoon salt (optional)
- ½ teaspoon fresh lime juice

1. Pour the black-eyed peas and water into a large pot, then cook over medium heat for 25 minutes.
2. Add the carrot and beet to the pot and cook for 10 minutes more, adding more water as needed.
3. Add the turmeric, cayenne pepper, cumin, and parsley to the pot and cook for another 6 minutes, or until the vegetables are softened. Stir the mixture periodically. Season with salt, if desired.
4. Serve drizzled with the fresh lime juice.

PER SERVING

Calories: 89;Fat: 0.7g;Protein: 4.1g;Carbs: 16.6g.

Creamy Saffron Chicken with Ziti

Prep time: 5 minutes | Cook time: 35 minutes| Serves 4

- 3 tbsp butter
- 16 oz ziti
- 4 chicken breasts, cut into strips
- ½ tsp ground saffron threads
- 1 yellow onion, chopped
- 2 garlic cloves, minced
- 1 tbsp almond flour
- 1 pinch cardamom powder
- 1 pinch cinnamon powder
- 1 cup heavy cream
- 1 cup chicken stock
- ¼ cup chopped scallions
- 3 tbsp chopped parsley
- Salt and black pepper to taste

1. In a pot of boiling water, cook the ziti pasta for 8-10 minutes until al dente. Drain and set aside.
2. Melt the butter in a large skillet, season the chicken with salt, black pepper, and cook in the oil until golden brown on the outside, 5 minutes. Stir in the saffron, onion, garlic and cook until the onion softens and the garlic and saffron are fragrant, 3 minutes.
3. Stir in the almond flour, cardamom powder, and cinnamon powder, and cook for 1 minute to exude some fragrance. Add the heavy cream, chicken stock and cook for 2 to 3 minutes.
4. Adjust the taste with salt, pepper and mix in the ziti and scallions. Allow warming for 1-2 minutes and turn the heat off. Garnish with parsley.

PER SERVING

Calories: 775;Fat: 48g;Protein: 73g;Carbs: 3g.

Mustard Vegetable Millet

Prep time: 5 minutes | Cook time: 35 minutes| Serves 6

- 6 oz okra, cut into 1-inch lengths
- 3 tbsp olive oil
- 6 oz asparagus, chopped
- Salt and black pepper to taste
- 1 ½ cups whole millet
- 2 tbsp lemon juice
- 2 tbsp minced shallot
- 1 tsp Dijon mustard
- 6 oz cherry tomatoes, halved
- 3 tbsp chopped fresh dill
- 2 oz goat cheese, crumbled

1. In a large pot, bring 4 quarts of water to a boil. Add asparagus, snap peas, and salt and cook until crisp-tender, about 3 minutes.
2. Using a slotted spoon, transfer vegetables to a large plate and let cool completely, about 15 minutes. Add millet to water, return to a boil, and cook until grains are tender, 15-20 minutes.
3. Drain millet, spread in rimmed baking sheet, and let cool completely, 15 minutes. Whisk oil, lemon juice, shallot, mustard, salt, and pepper in a large bowl.
4. Add vegetables, millet, tomatoes, dill, and half of the goat cheese and toss gently to combine. Season with salt and pepper. Sprinkle with remaining goat cheese to serve.

PER SERVING

Calories: 315;Fat: 19g;Protein: 13g;Carbs: 35g.

Simple Green Rice

Prep time: 5 minutes | Cook time: 35 minutes| Serves 4

- 2 tbsp butter
- 4 spring onions, sliced
- 1 leek, sliced
- 1 medium zucchini, chopped
- 5 oz broccoli florets
- 2 oz curly kale
- ½ cup frozen green peas
- 2 cloves garlic, minced
- 1 thyme sprig, chopped
- 1 rosemary sprig, chopped
- 1 cup white rice
- 2 cups vegetable broth
- 1 large tomato, chopped
- 2 oz Kalamata olives, sliced

1. Melt the butter in a saucepan over medium heat. Cook the spring onions, leek, and zucchini for about 4-5 minutes or until tender.
2. Add in the garlic, thyme, and rosemary and continue to sauté for about 1 minute or until aromatic. Add in the rice, broth, and tomato. Bring to a boil, turn the heat to a gentle simmer, and cook for about 10-12 minutes.

3. Stir in broccoli, kale, and green peas, and continue cooking for 5 minutes. Fluff the rice with a fork and garnish with olives.

PER SERVING

Calories: 403;Fat: 11g;Protein: 9g;Carbs: 64g.

Milanese-style Risotto

Prep time: 5 minutes | Cook time: 15 minutes| Serves 4

- 2 tbsp olive oil
- 2 tbsp butter, softened
- 1 cup Arborio rice, cooked
- ½ cup white wine
- 1 onion, chopped
- Salt and black pepper to taste
- 2 cups hot chicken stock
- 1 pinch of saffron, soaked
- ½ cup Parmesan, grated

1. Warm the olive oil in a skillet over medium heat and sauté onion for 3 minutes. Stir in rice, salt, and pepper for 1 minute. Pour in white wine and saffron and stir to deglaze the bottom of the skillet.
2. Gradually add in the chicken stock while stirring; cook for 15-18 minutes. Turn off the heat and mix in butter and Parmesan cheese. Serve immediately.

PER SERVING

Calories: 250;Fat: 10g;Protein: 5g;Carbs: 18g.

Spicy Bean Rolls

Prep time: 5 minutes | Cook time: 25 minutes| Serves 4

1 tbsp olive oil
1 red onion, chopped
2 garlic cloves, minced
1 green bell pepper, sliced
2 cups canned cannellini beans
1 red chili pepper, chopped
1 tbsp cilantro, chopped
1 tsp cumin, ground
Salt and black pepper to taste
4 whole-wheat tortillas
1 cup mozzarella, shredded

1. Warm the olive oil in a skillet over medium heat and sauté onion for 3 minutes.
2. Stir in garlic, bell pepper, cannellini beans, red chili pepper, cilantro, cumin, salt, and pepper and cook for 15 minutes. Spoon bean mixture on each tortilla and top with cheese. Roll up and serve right away.

PER SERVING

Calories: 680;Fat: 15g;Protein: 38g;Carbs: 75g.

florentine Bean & Vegetable Gratin

Prep time: 5 minutes | Cook time: 55 minutes| Serves 4

- ½ cup Parmigiano Reggiano cheese, grated
- 4 pancetta slices
- 2 tbsp olive oil
- 4 garlic cloves, minced
- 1 onion, chopped
- ½ fennel bulb, chopped
- 1 tbsp brown rice flour
- 2 cans white beans
- 1 can tomatoes, diced
- 1 medium zucchini, chopped
- 1 tsp porcini powder
- 1 tbsp fresh basil, chopped
- ½ tsp dried oregano
- 1 tsp red pepper flakes
- Salt to taste
- 2 tbsp butter, cubed

1. Heat the olive in a skillet over medium heat. Fry the pancetta for 5 minutes until crispy. Drain on paper towels, chop, and reserve. Add garlic, onion, and fennel to the skillet and sauté for 5 minutes until softened. Stir in rice flour for 3 minutes.
2. Preheat oven to 350° F. Add the beans, tomatoes, and zucchini to a casserole dish and pour in the sautéed vegetable and chopped pancetta; mix well.
3. Sprinkle with porcini powder, oregano, red pepper flakes, and salt. Top with Parmigiano Reggiano cheese and butter and bake for 25 minutes or until the cheese is lightly browned. Garnish with basil and serve.

PER SERVING

Calories: 483;Fat: 28g;Protein: 19g;Carbs: 42g.

Pesto Fusilli with Broccoli

Prep time: 5 minutes | Cook time: 25 minutes| Serves 4

- ¼ cup olive oil
- 4 Roma tomatoes, diced
- 1 cup broccoli florets
- 1 lb fusilli
- 2 tsp tomato paste
- 2 garlic cloves, minced
- 1 tbsp chopped fresh oregano
- ½ tsp salt
- 1 cup vegetable broth
- 6 fresh basil leaves
- ¼ cup grated Parmesan cheese
- ¼ cup pine nuts

1. Place the pasta in a pot with salted boiling water and cook for 8-10 minutes until al dente. Drain and set aside. In a pan over medium heat, sauté tomato paste, tomatoes, broth, oregano, garlic, and salt for 10 minutes.

2. In a food processor, place basil, broccoli, Parmesan, olive oil, and pine nuts; pulse until smooth. Pour into the tomato mixture. Stir in pasta, cook until heated through and the pasta is well coated. Serve.

PER SERVING

Calories: 385;Fat: 22g;Protein: 12g;Carbs: 38g.

Israeli Style Eggplant and Chickpea Salad

Prep time: 5 minutes | Cook time: 25 minutes| Serves 6

- 2 tablespoons balsamic vinegar
- 2 tablespoons freshly squeezed lemon juice
- 1 teaspoon ground cumin
- ¼ teaspoon sea salt
- 2 tablespoons olive oil, divided
- 1 medium globe eggplant, stem removed, cut into flat cubes (about ½ inch thick)
- 1 can chickpeas, drained and rinsed
- ¼ cup chopped mint leaves
- 1 cup sliced sweet onion
- 1 garlic clove, finely minced
- 1 tablespoon sesame seeds, toasted

1. Preheat the oven to 550°F or the highest level of your oven or broiler. Grease a baking sheet with 1 tablespoon of olive oil.
2. Combine the balsamic vinegar, lemon juice, cumin, salt, and 1 tablespoon of olive oil in a small bowl. Stir to mix well.
3. Arrange the eggplant cubes on the baking sheet, then brush with 2 tablespoons of the balsamic vinegar mixture on both sides.
4. Broil in the preheated oven for 8 minutes or until lightly browned. Flip the cubes halfway through the cooking time.
5. Meanwhile, combine the chickpeas, mint, onion, garlic, and sesame seeds in a large serving bowl. Drizzle with remaining balsamic vinegar mixture. Stir to mix well.
6. Remove the eggplant from the oven. Allow to cool for 5 minutes, then slice them into ½-inch strips on a clean work surface.
7. Add the eggplant strips in the serving bowl, then toss to combine well before serving.

PER SERVING

Calories: 125;Fat: 2.9g;Protein: 5.2g;Carbs: 20.9g.

Rice with Dried Fruit

Prep Time: 15 minutes| Cook Time: 30 minutes| Serves 4

- 1½ C. white rice, rinsed and drained
- 3 tbsp. olive oil
- ½ C. yellow onions, finely chopped
- 2 garlic cloves, minced
- ½ tsp. ground turmeric
- ½ tsp. ground cumin
- ¼ tsp. ground cinnamon
- 2¼ C. water
- Salt and ground black pepper, as required
- 2 tbsp. dried currants
- 2 tbsp. dried raisins
- 2 tbsp. dried apricots, finely chopped
- ¼ C. almonds, toasted and sliced

1. In a saucepan, heat olive oil over medium-low heat and sauté the onion for about 4 minutes.
2. Add the garlic and spices and sauté for about 1 minute.
3. Stir in the rice and cook for about 3 minutes, stirring continuously.
4. Stir in the water, salt, and black pepper and cook until boiling.
5. Adjust the heat to low and simmer, covered for about 15-18 minutes or until all the liquid is absorbed.
6. Remove from heat and immediately sprinkle the top of rice with dried fruit.
7. Immediately cover the pan and set aside for about 10 minutes.
8. Uncover the pan and stir in the almonds.
9. Serve immediately.

PER SERVING

Calories: 392; Fat: 12.2g;Carbs: 63.6g;Fiber: 2.6g;Protein: 6.9g

Rice & Lentil Casserole

Prep Time: 15 minutes| Cook Time: 1 hr. 10 minutes| Serves 4

- 2 turkey bacon slices, finely chopped
- 2 tbsp. olive oil
- 3 leeks, halved, cleaned and chopped
- ½ C. dry white wine
- 1 C. chicken broth
- Salt and ground black pepper, as required
- ¼ C. heavy cream
- Olive oil cooking spray
- 1 C. canned green lentils, drained and rinsed
- ¾ C. cooked long-grain white rice, rinsed and drained
- ¼ C. panko bread crumbs
- ¼ C. Parmesan cheese, grated

1. Heat a non-stick wok over medium-high heat and cook the bacon for about 8-10 minutes or until crispy.
2. with a slotted spoon, transfer the bacon onto a paper towel-lined plate.
3. Drain the bacon fat from wok.
4. In the same wok, heat olive oil over medium heat and sauté the leeks for about 5-6 minutes.
5. Stir in the wine and cook for about 2-3 minutes.
6. Stir in the broth, salt and black pepper and immediately cover wok.
7. Simmer for about 25-30 minutes.
8. Preheat your oven to 400 °F.
9. Grease a casserole dish with cooking spray.
10. In the wok of leek mixture, stir in the cream and cook for about 3-5 minutes or until mixture becomes thick, stirring continuously.
11. Remove from heat and stir in the lentils and rice.
12. Place the mixture into the prepared casserole dish evenly and sprinkle with bread crumbs, followed by cheese.
13. Bake for approximately 15 minutes.
14. Remove from oven and sprinkle with cooked bacon.
15. Set aside for about 5 minutes before serving.

PER SERVING

Calories: 349; Fat: 4.1g;Carbs: 48.2g;Fiber: 16g;Protein: 20.4g

Rice with Pork

Prep Time: 15 minutes| Cook Time: 10 minutes| Serves 4

- ¼ C. sun-dried tomato & oregano dressing, divided
- 1 C. frozen cut green beans
- 10 oz. chicken broth
- 1½ C. uncooked instant rice
- 1 (1-lb.) pork tenderloin, cut into 8 slices crosswise and pounded into ½-inch thickness
- 1 tsp. dried rosemary leaves, crushed
- 1 C. tomatoes, chopped
- 2 tbsp. Parmesan cheese, grated

1. In a medium-sized pan, add 2 tbsp. of the dressing over medium heat and cook for about 1-2 minutes or until heated through.
2. Stir in the beans and cook for about 1 minute.
3. Stir in the broth and cook until boiling.
4. Now, adjust the heat to medium-low and simmer for about 2-3 minutes.
5. Stir in the rice and cook until boiling.
6. Cover the pan and remove from heat.
7. Set aside, covered for about 5 minutes or until liquid is absorbed.
8. Sprinkle the pork slices with rosemary.
9. In a large-sized non-stick wok, add the remaining dressing over medium heat and cook for about 1-2 minutes or until heated through.
10. Stir in the pork slices and cook for about 4-5 minutes per side.
11. Add the tomato and cheese in the pan of rice and stir to combine.
12. Serve the pork with rice mixture.

PER SERVING

Calories: 515; Fat: 10.6g;Carbs: 62.2g;Fiber: 2.5g;Protein: 39.3g

Rice with Beans & Tomatoes

Prep Time: 15 minutes| Cook Time: 15 minutes| Serves 4

- 2 (15-oz.) cans red kidney beans, rinsed and drained
- ¾ C. uncooked instant rice
- 1 (14½-oz.) can stewed tomatoes, undrained
- 1 C. vegetable broth
- 1 tsp. Italian seasoning
- ¼ tsp. red pepper flakes, crushed
- 1 C. marinara sauce
- ¼ C. Parmesan cheese, grated

1. In a large-sized wok, add all ingredients except for marinara and Parmesan and stir to combine.
2. Place the pan over medium-high heat and cook until boiling.
3. Now, adjust the heat to low and simmer, covered or about 7-9 minutes or until rice is tender.
4. Stir in the marinara sauce and cook for about 2-3 minutes or until heated through, stirring occasionally.
5. Top with cheese and serve.

PER SERVING

Calories: 447; Fat: 5.6g;Carbs: 81.3g;Fiber: 13.8g;Protein: 18.6g

Baked Ziti

Prep Time: 15 minutes| Cook Time: 1 hr. 5 minutes| Serves 6

- Olive oil cooking spray
- 3 C. uncooked ziti pasta
- 1¾ C. meatless spaghetti sauce, divided
- 1½ C. part-skim mozzarella cheese, shredded and divided
- 1 C. cottage cheese
- 1 large egg, lightly beaten
- 2 tsp. dried parsley flakes
- ½ tsp. dried oregano
- ¼ tsp. garlic powder
- Ground black pepper, as required

1. Preheat your oven to 375 °F. Grease an 8-inch square baking dish with cooking spray.
2. In a large-sized saucepan of salted boiling water, add the pasta and cook for about 8-10 minutes.
3. Meanwhile, in a large-sized bowl, add ¾ C. of spaghetti sauce, 1 C. of mozzarella cheese, cottage cheese, egg, dried herbs, garlic powder and black pepper and mix well.
4. Drain the pasta well and stir with the cheese mixture.
5. In the bottom of the prepared baking dish, spread ¼ C. of spaghetti sauce and top with the pasta mixture, followed by the remaining sauce and mozzarella cheese.
6. Cover the baking dish and bake for approximately 45 minutes.
7. Serve hot.

PER SERVING

Calories: 291; Fat: 4.1g;Carbs: 45.5g;Fiber: 1.1g;Protein: 15.6g

Chapter 9
Vegetable Mains and Meatless Recipes

Baked Honey Acorn Squash

Prep time: 5 minutes | Cook time: 35 minutes| Serves 4

- 1 acorn squash, cut into wedges
- 2 tbsp olive oil
- 2 tbsp honey
- 2 tbsp rosemary, chopped
- 2 tbsp walnuts, chopped

1. Preheat oven to 400°F. In a bowl, mix honey, rosemary, and olive oil. Lay the squash wedges on a baking sheet and drizzle with the honey mixture.
2. Bake for 30 minutes until squash is tender and slightly caramelized, turning each slice over halfway through. Serve cooled sprinkled with walnuts.

PER SERVING

Calories: 136;Fat: 6g;Protein: 0.9g;Carbs: 20g.

Baked Beet & Leek with Dilly Yogurt

Prep time: 5 minutes | Cook time: 45 minutes| Serves 4

- 5 tbsp olive oil
- ½ lb leeks, thickly sliced
- 1 lb red beets, sliced
- 1 cup yogurt
- 2 garlic cloves, finely minced
- ¼ tsp cumin, ground
- ¼ tsp dried parsley
- ¼ cup parsley, chopped
- 1 tsp dill
- Salt and black pepper to taste

1. Preheat the oven to 390°F. Arrange the beets and leeks on a greased roasting dish. Sprinkle with some olive oil, cumin, dried parsley, black pepper, and salt. Bake in the oven for 25-30 minutes.
2. Transfer to a serving platter. In a bowl, stir in yogurt, dill, garlic, and the remaining olive oil. Whisk to combine. Drizzle the veggies with the yogurt sauce and top with fresh parsley to serve.

PER SERVING

Calories: 281;Fat: 18.7g;Protein: 6g;Carbs: 24g.

Garlicky Zucchini Cubes with Mint

Prep time: 5 minutes | Cook time: 15 minutes| Serves 4

- 3 large green zucchinis, cut into ½-inch cubes
- 3 tablespoons extra-virgin olive oil
- 1 large onion, chopped
- 3 cloves garlic, minced
- 1 teaspoon salt
- 1 teaspoon dried mint

1. Heat the olive oil in a large skillet over medium heat.
2. Add the onion and garlic and sauté for 3 minutes, stirring constantly, or until softened.
3. Stir in the zucchini cubes and salt and cook for 5

minutes, or until the zucchini is browned and tender.
4. Add the mint to the skillet and toss to combine, then continue cooking for 2 minutes.
5. Serve warm.

PER SERVING

Calories: 146;Fat: 10.6g;Protein: 4.2g;Carbs: 11.8g.

Stir-fried Kale with Mushrooms

Prep time: 5 minutes | Cook time: 15 minutes| Serves 4

- 1 cup cremini mushrooms, sliced
- 4 tbsp olive oil
- 1 small red onion, chopped
- 2 cloves garlic, thinly sliced
- 1 ½ lb curly kale
- 2 tomatoes, chopped
- 1 tsp dried oregano
- 1 tsp dried basil
- ½ tsp dried rosemary
- ½ tsp dried thyme
- Salt and black pepper to taste

1. Warm the olive oil in a saucepan over medium heat. Sauté the onion and garlic for about 3 minutes or until they are softened.
2. Add in the mushrooms, kale, and tomatoes, stirring to promote even cooking. Turn the heat to a simmer, add in the spices and cook for 5-6 minutes until the kale wilt.

PER SERVING

Calories: 221;Fat: 16g;Protein: 9g;Carbs: 19g.

Wilted Dandelion Greens with Sweet Onion

Prep time: 5 minutes | Cook time: 15 minutes| Serves 4

- 1 tablespoon extra-virgin olive oil
- 2 garlic cloves, minced
- 1 Vidalia onion, thinly sliced
- ½ cup low-sodium vegetable broth
- 2 bunches dandelion greens, roughly chopped
- Freshly ground black pepper, to taste

1. Heat the olive oil in a large skillet over low heat.
2. Add the garlic and onion and cook for 2 to 3 minutes, stirring occasionally, or until the onion is translucent.
3. Fold in the vegetable broth and dandelion greens and cook for 5 to 7 minutes until wilted, stirring frequently.
4. Sprinkle with the black pepper and serve on a plate while warm.

PER SERVING

Calories: 81;Fat: 3.9g;Protein: 3.2g;Carbs: 10.8g.

Baby Kale and Cabbage Salad

Prep time: 5 minutes | Cook time: 5 minutes| Serves 6

- 2 bunches baby kale, thinly sliced
- ½ head green savoy cabbage, cored and thinly sliced
- 1 medium red bell pepper, thinly sliced
- 1 garlic clove, thinly sliced
- 1 cup toasted peanuts
- Dressing:
- Juice of 1 lemon
- ¼ cup apple cider vinegar
- 1 teaspoon ground cumin
- ¼ teaspoon smoked paprika

1. In a large mixing bowl, toss together the kale and cabbage.
2. Make the dressing: Whisk together the lemon juice, vinegar, cumin and paprika in a small bowl.
3. Pour the dressing over the greens and gently massage with your hands.
4. Add the pepper, garlic and peanuts to the mixing bowl. Toss to combine.
5. Serve immediately.

PER SERVING

Calories: 199;Fat: 12.0g;Protein: 10.0g;Carbs: 17.0g.

Roasted Asparagus with Hazelnuts

Prep time: 5 minutes | Cook time: 25 minutes| Serves 4

- 2 tbsp olive oil
- 1 lb asparagus, trimmed
- ¼ cup hazelnuts, chopped
- 1 lemon, juiced and zested
- Salt and black pepper to taste
- ½ tsp red pepper flakes

1. Preheat oven to 425°F. Arrange the asparagus on a baking sheet. Combine olive oil, lemon zest, lemon juice, salt, hazelnuts, and black pepper in a bowl and mix well. Pour the mixture over the asparagus. Place in the oven and roast for 15-20 minutes until tender and lightly charred. Serve topped with red pepper flakes.

PER SERVING

Calories: 112;Fat: 10g;Protein: 3.2g;Carbs: 5.2g.

Tomatoes Filled with Tabbouleh

Prep time: 5 minutes | Cook time: 25 minutes| Serves 4

- 3 tbsp olive oil, divided
- 8 medium tomatoes
- ½ cup water
- ½ cup bulgur wheat
- 1 ½ cups minced parsley
- ⅓ cup minced fresh mint
- 2 scallions, chopped
- 1 tsp sumac
- Salt and black pepper to taste
- 1 lemon, zested

1. Place the bulgur wheat and 2 cups of salted water in a pot and bring to a boil. Lower the heat and simmer for 10 minutes or until tender. Remove the pot from the heat and cover with a lid. Let it sit for 15 minutes.
2. Preheat the oven to 400°F. Slice off the top of each tomato and scoop out the pulp and seeds using a spoon into a sieve set over a bowl. Drain and discard any excess liquid; chop the remaining pulp and place it in a large mixing bowl. Add in parsley, mint, scallions, sumac, lemon zest, lemon juice, bulgur, pepper, and salt, and mix well.
3. Spoon the filling into the tomatoes and place the lids on top. Drizzle with olive oil and bake for 15-20 minutes until the tomatoes are tender. Serve and enjoy!

PER SERVING

Calories: 160;Fat: 7g;Protein: 5g;Carbs: 22g.

Baked Vegetable Stew

Prep time: 5 minutes | Cook time: 65 minutes| Serves 6

- 1 can diced tomatoes, drained with juice reserved
- 3 tbsp olive oil
- 1 onion, chopped
- 2 tbsp fresh oregano, minced
- 1 tsp paprika
- 4 garlic cloves, minced
- 1 ½ lb green beans, sliced
- 1 lb Yukon Gold potatoes, peeled and chopped
- 1 tbsp tomato paste
- Salt and black pepper to taste
- 3 tbsp fresh basil, chopped

1. Preheat oven to 360°F. Warm the olive oil in a skillet over medium heat. Sauté onion and garlic for 3 minutes until softened. Stir in oregano and paprika for 30 seconds.
2. Transfer to a baking dish and add in green beans, potatoes, tomatoes, tomato paste, salt, pepper, and 1 ½ cups of water; stir well. Bake for 40-50 minutes. Sprinkle with basil. Serve.

PER SERVING

Calories: 121;Fat: 0.8g;Protein: 4.2g;Carbs: 26g.

Spicy Potato Wedges

Prep time: 5 minutes | Cook time: 35 minutes | Serves 4

- 1 ½ lb potatoes, peeled and cut into wedges
- 3 tbsp olive oil
- 1 tbsp minced fresh rosemary
- 2 tsp chili powder
- 3 garlic cloves, minced
- Salt and black pepper to taste

1. Preheat the oven to 370°F. Toss the wedges with olive oil, garlic, salt, and pepper. Spread out in a roasting sheet. Roast for 15-20 minutes until browned and crisp at the edges. Remove and sprinkle with chili powder and rosemary.

PER SERVING

Calories: 152;Fat: 7g;Protein: 2.5g;Carbs: 21g

Rustic Vegetable and Brown Rice Bowl

Prep time: 15 minutes | Cook time: 30 minutes | Serves 4

- Nonstick cooking spray
- 2 cups broccoli florets
- 2 cups cauliflower florets
- 1 (15-ounce) can chickpeas, drained and rinsed
- 1 cup carrots sliced 1 inch thick
- 2 to 3 tablespoons extra-virgin olive oil, divided
- Salt
- Freshly ground black pepper
- 2 to 3 tablespoons sesame seeds, for garnish
- 2 cups cooked brown rice
- FOR THE DRESSING
- 3 to 4 tablespoons tahini
- 2 tablespoons honey
- 1 lemon, juiced
- 1 garlic clove, minced
- Salt
- Freshly ground black pepper

1. Preheat the oven to 400°F. Spray two baking sheets with cooking spray.
2. Cover the first baking sheet with the broccoli and cauliflower and the second with the chickpeas and carrots. Toss each sheet with half of the oil and season with salt and pepper before placing in the oven.
3. Cook the carrots and chickpeas for 10 minutes, leaving the carrots still just crisp, and the broccoli and cauliflower for 20 minutes, until tender. Stir each halfway through cooking.
4. To make the dressing, in a small bowl, mix the tahini, honey, lemon juice, and garlic. Season with salt and pepper and set aside.
5. Divide the rice into individual bowls, then layer with vegetables and drizzle dressing over the dish.

PER SERVING

Calories: 454; Protein: 12g; Total Carbohydrates: 62g; Sugars: 12g; Fiber: 11g; Total Fat: 18g; Saturated Fat: 3g; Cholesterol: 0mg; Sodium: 61mg

Quinoa with Almonds and Cranberries

Prep time: 15 minutes | Cook time: 10 minutes | Serves 4

- 2 cups cooked quinoa
- ⅓ teaspoon cranberries or currants
- ¼ cup sliced almonds
- 2 garlic cloves, minced
- 1¼ teaspoons salt
- ½ teaspoon ground cumin
- ½ teaspoon turmeric
- ¼ teaspoon ground cinnamon
- ¼ teaspoon freshly ground black pepper

1. In a large bowl, toss the quinoa, cranberries, almonds, garlic, salt, cumin, turmeric, cinnamon, and pepper and stir to combine. Enjoy alone or with roasted cauliflower.

PER SERVING

Calories: 194; Protein: 7g; Total Carbohydrates: 31g; Sugars: <1g; Fiber: 4g; Total Fat: 6g; Saturated Fat: <1g; Cholesterol: 0mg; Sodium: 727mg

Mediterranean Baked Chickpeas

Prep time: 15 minutes | Cook time: 20 minutes | Serves 4

- 1 tablespoon extra-virgin olive oil
- ½ medium onion, chopped
- 3 garlic cloves, chopped
- 2 teaspoons smoked paprika
- ¼ teaspoon ground cumin
- 4 cups halved cherry tomatoes
- 2 (15-ounce) cans chickpeas, drained and rinsed
- ½ cup plain, unsweetened, full-fat Greek yogurt, for serving
- 1 cup crumbled feta, for serving

1. Preheat the oven to 425°F.
2. In an oven-safe sauté pan or skillet, heat the oil over medium heat and sauté the onion and garlic. Cook for about 5 minutes, until softened and fragrant. Stir in the paprika and cumin and cook for 2 minutes. Stir in the tomatoes and chickpeas.
3. Bring to a simmer for 5 to 10 minutes before placing in the oven.
4. Roast in oven for 25 to 30 minutes, until bubbling and thickened. To serve, top with Greek yogurt and feta.

PER SERVING

Calories: 412; Protein: 20g; Total Carbohydrates: 51g; Sugars: 7g; Fiber: 13g; Total Fat: 15g; Saturated Fat: 7g; Cholesterol: 37mg; Sodium: 444mg

Falafel Bites

Prep time: 15 minutes | Cook time: 20 minutes| Serves 4

- 1⅔ cups falafel mix
- 1¼ cups water
- Extra-virgin olive oil spray
- 1 tablespoon pickled onions (optional)
- 1 tablespoon pickled turnips (optional)
- 2 tablespoons tzatziki sauce (optional)

1. In a large bowl, carefully stir the falafel mix into the water. Mix well. Let stand 15 minutes to absorb the water. Form mix into 1-inch balls and arrange on a baking sheet.
2. Preheat the broiler to high.
3. Take the balls and flatten slightly with your thumb (so they won't roll around on the baking sheet). Spray with olive oil, and then broil for 2 to 3 minutes on each side, until crispy and brown.
4. To fry the falafel, fill a pot with ½ inch of cooking oil and heat over medium-high heat to 375°F. Fry the balls for about 3 minutes, until brown and crisp. Drain on paper towels and serve with pickled onions, pickled turnips, and tzatziki sauce (if using).

PER SERVING

Calories: 166; Protein: 17g; Total Carbohydrates: 30g; Sugars: 5g; Fiber: 8g; Total Fat: 2g; Saturated Fat: 0g; Cholesterol: 0mg; Sodium: 930mg

Quick Vegetable Kebabs

Prep time: 15 minutes | Cook time: 20 minutes| Serves 4

- 4 medium red onions, peeled and sliced into 6 wedges
- 4 medium zucchini, cut into 1-inch-thick slices
- 4 bell peppers, cut into 2-inch squares
- 2 yellow bell peppers, cut into 2-inch squares
- 2 orange bell peppers, cut into 2-inch squares
- 2 beef steak tomatoes, cut into quarters
- 3 tablespoons herbed oil

1. Preheat the oven or grill to medium-high or 350°F.
2. Thread 1 piece red onion, zucchini, different colored bell peppers, and tomatoes onto a skewer. Repeat until the skewer is full of vegetables, up to 2 inches away from the skewer end, and continue until all skewers are complete.
3. Put the skewers on a baking sheet and cook in the oven for 10 minutes or grill for 5 minutes on each side. The vegetables will be done with they reach your desired crunch or softness.
4. Remove the skewers from heat and drizzle with herbed oil.

PER SERVING

Calories: 240; Protein: 6g; Total Carbohydrates: 34g; Sugars: 15g; Fiber: 9g; Total Fat: 12g; Saturated Fat: 2g; Cholesterol: 0mg; Sodium: 38mg

Tortellini in Red Pepper Sauce

Prep time: 15 minutes | Cook time: 10 minutes| Serves 4

- 1 (16-ounce) container fresh cheese tortellini (usually green and white pasta)
- 1 (16-ounce) jar roasted red peppers, drained
- 1 teaspoon garlic powder
- ¼ cup tahini
- 1 tablespoon red pepper oil (optional)

1. Bring a large pot of water to a boil and cook the tortellini according to package directions.
2. In a blender, combine the red peppers with the garlic powder and process until smooth. Once blended, add the tahini until the sauce is thickened. If the sauce gets too thick, add up to 1 tablespoon red pepper oil (if using).
3. Once tortellini are cooked, drain and leave pasta in colander. Add the sauce to the bottom of the empty pot and heat for 2 minutes. Then, add the tortellini back into the pot and cook for 2 more minutes. Serve and enjoy!

PER SERVING

Calories: 350; Protein: 12g; Total Carbohydrates: 46g; Sugars: 2g; Fiber: 4g; Total Fat: 11g; Saturated Fat: 2g; Cholesterol: 44mg; Sodium: 192mg

Freekeh, Chickpea, and Herb Salad

Prep time: 15 minutes | Cook time: 10 minutes| Serves 4

- 1 (15-ounce) can chickpeas, rinsed and drained
- 1 cup cooked freekeh
- 1 cup thinly sliced celery
- 1 bunch scallions, both white and green parts, finely chopped
- ½ cup chopped fresh flat-leaf parsley
- ¼ cup chopped fresh mint
- 3 tablespoons chopped celery leaves
- ½ teaspoon kosher salt
- ⅓ cup extra-virgin olive oil
- ¼ cup freshly squeezed lemon juice
- ¼ teaspoon cumin seeds
- 1 teaspoon garlic powder

1. In a large bowl, combine the chickpeas, freekeh, celery, scallions, parsley, mint, celery leaves, and salt and toss lightly.
2. In a small bowl, whisk together the olive oil, lemon juice, cumin seeds, and garlic powder. Once combined, add to freekeh salad.

PER SERVING

Calories: 350; Protein: 9g; Total Carbohydrates: 38g; Sugars: 1g; Fiber: 9g; Total Fat: 19g; Saturated Fat: 2g; Cholesterol: 0mg; Sodium: 329mg

Kate's Warm Mediterranean Farro Bowl

Prep time: 15 minutes | Cook time: 10 minutes| Serves 4

- ⅓ cup extra-virgin olive oil
- ½ cup chopped red bell pepper
- ⅓ cup chopped red onions
- 2 garlic cloves, minced
- 1 cup zucchini, cut in ½-inch slices
- ½ cup canned chickpeas, drained and rinsed
- ½ cup coarsely chopped artichokes
- 3 cups cooked farro
- Salt
- Freshly ground black pepper
- ¼ cup sliced olives, for serving (optional)
- ½ cup crumbled feta cheese, for serving (optional)
- 2 tablespoons fresh basil, chiffonade, for serving (optional)
- 3 tablespoons balsamic reduction, for serving (optional)

1. In a large sauté pan or skillet, heat the oil over medium heat and sauté the pepper, onions, and garlic for about 5 minutes, until tender.
2. Add the zucchini, chickpeas, and artichokes, then stir and continue to sauté vegetables, approximately 5 more minutes, until just soft.
3. Stir in the cooked farro, tossing to combine and cooking enough to heat through. Season with salt and pepper and remove from the heat.
4. Transfer the contents of the pan into the serving vessels or bowls.
5. Top with olives, feta, and basil (if using). Drizzle with balsamic reduction (if using) to finish.

PER SERVING

Calories: 367; Protein: 9g; Total Carbohydrates: 51g; Sugars: 2g; Fiber: 9g; Total Fat: 20g; Saturated Fat: 2g; Cholesterol: 0mg; Sodium: 87mg

Creamy Chickpea Sauce with Whole-Wheat Fusilli

Prep time: 15 minutes | Cook time: 20 minutes| Serves 4

- ¼ cup extra-virgin olive oil
- ½ large shallot, chopped
- 5 garlic cloves, thinly sliced
- 1 (15-ounce) can chickpeas, drained and rinsed, reserving ½ cup canning liquid
- Pinch red pepper flakes
- 1 cup whole-grain fusilli pasta
- ¼ teaspoon salt
- ⅛ teaspoon freshly ground black pepper
- ¼ cup shaved fresh Parmesan cheese
- ¼ cup chopped fresh basil
- 2 teaspoons dried parsley
- 1 teaspoon dried oregano
- Red pepper flakes

1. In a medium pan, heat the oil over medium heat, and sauté the shallot and garlic for 3 to 5 minutes, until the garlic is golden. Add ¾ of the chickpeas plus 2 tablespoons of liquid from the can, and bring to a simmer.
2. Remove from the heat, transfer into a standard blender, and blend until smooth. At this point, add the remaining chickpeas. Add more reserved chickpea liquid if it becomes thick.
3. Bring a large pot of salted water to a boil and cook pasta until al dente, about 8 minutes. Reserve ½ cup of the pasta water, drain the pasta, and return it to the pot.
4. Add the chickpea sauce to the hot pasta and add up to ¼ cup of the pasta water. You may need to add more pasta water to reach your desired consistency.
5. Place the pasta pot over medium heat and mix occasionally until the sauce thickens. Season with salt and pepper.
6. Serve, garnished with Parmesan, basil, parsley, oregano, and red pepper flakes.

PER SERVING (1 CUP PASTA)

Calories: 310; Protein: 10g; Total Carbohydrates: 33g; Sugars: 1g; Fiber: 7g; Total Fat: 17g; Saturated Fat: 3g; Cholesterol: 5mg; Sodium: 243mg

Linguine and Brussels Sprouts

Prep time: 15 minutes | Cook time: 30 minutes| Serves 4

- 8 ounces whole-wheat linguine
- ⅓ cup, plus 2 tablespoons extra-virgin olive oil, divided
- 1 medium sweet onion, diced
- 2 to 3 garlic cloves, smashed
- 8 ounces brussels sprouts, chopped
- ½ cup chicken stock, as needed
- ⅓ cup dry white wine
- ½ cup shredded Parmesan cheese
- 1 lemon, cut in quarters

1. Bring a large pot of water to a boil and cook the pasta according to package directions. Drain, reserving 1 cup of the pasta water. Mix the cooked pasta with 2 tablespoons of olive oil, then set aside.
2. In a large sauté pan or skillet, heat the remaining ⅓ cup of olive oil on medium heat. Add the onion to the pan and cook for about 5 minutes,
3. Add the Brussels sprouts and cook covered for 15 minutes. Add chicken stock as needed to prevent burning. Once Brussels sprouts have wilted and are fork-tender, add white wine and cook down for about 7 minutes, until reduced.
4. Add the pasta to the skillet and add the pasta water as needed.
5. Serve with the Parmesan cheese and lemon for squeezing over the dish right before eating.

PER SERVING

Calories: 502; Protein: 15g; Total Carbohydrates: 50g; Sugars: 3g; Fiber: 9g; Total Fat: 31g; Saturated Fat: 5g; Cholesterol: 10mg; Sodium: 246mg

Mozzarella and Sun-Dried Portobello Mushroom Pizza

Prep time: 15 minutes | Cook time: 10 minutes| Serves 4

- 4 large portobello mushroom caps
- 3 tablespoons extra-virgin olive oil
- Salt
- Freshly ground black pepper
- 4 sun-dried tomatoes
- 1 cup mozzarella cheese, divided
- ½ to ¾ cup low-sodium tomato sauce

1. Preheat the broiler on high.
2. On a baking sheet, drizzle the mushroom caps with the olive oil and season with salt and pepper. Broil the portobello mushrooms for 5 minutes on each side, flipping once, until tender.
3. Fill each mushroom cap with 1 sun-dried tomato, 2 tablespoons of cheese, and 2 to 3 tablespoons of sauce. Top each with 2 tablespoons of cheese. Place the caps back under the broiler for a final 2 to 3 minutes, then quarter the mushrooms and serve.

PER SERVING

Calories: 218; Protein: 11g; Total Carbohydrates: 12g; Sugars: 3g; Fiber: 2g; Total Fat: 16g; Saturated Fat: 5g; Cholesterol: 15mg; Sodium: 244mg

---

Pesto and Roasted Pepper Pizza

Prep time: 1 hour and 10 minutes (1 hour inactive)| Cook time: 20 minutes| Serves 4

- 1½ cups warm water
- 1 teaspoon active dry yeast
- ¼ cup extra-virgin olive oil
- 2 tablespoons sugar
- 2 teaspoons kosher salt
- 4 cups all-purpose flour
- 10 ounces fresh mozzarella, shredded
- ⅓ cup pesto
- ⅓ cup chopped roasted red peppers
- ⅓ cup crumbled feta

1. In a small bowl, microwave the water for about 15 seconds, just until it's warm. Sprinkle the yeast into the warm water and let it stand for 10 minutes, until the top layer is foamy.
2. In a large bowl, whisk together the oil, sugar, and salt. Stir this into the yeast mix, then pour it back into the large bowl and add the flour.
3. Gently combine the flour mixture with a whisk or wooden spoon. Mix in the bowl until almost all the flour is incorporated and a ball of dough is formed. Cover the bowl with a heavy kitchen towel and let stand for 1 hour at room temperature.
4. Once the hour has passed, preheat the oven to 400°F and put a baking sheet upside-down in the oven.
5. Next, flour an area of the kitchen counter well and cut the pizza dough in half, reserving half for another pizza. Gently roll out half of the dough into a circle about 1 inch thick. The second half of the pizza dough will last for about 6 months in the freezer or 2 to 3 days in the refrigerator.
6. Remove the pizza from the oven and add mozzarella cheese first. Put it back into the oven and cook for 7 to 10 minutes. This will help dry out the wet, fresh mozzarella.
7. After 7 to 10 minutes, remove the pizza and add the pesto followed by the peppers and put it back into the oven for an additional 10 minutes.
8. Remove the pizza and let it rest for 5 minutes; while it's cooling, add the crumbled feta.

PER SERVING

Calories: 705; Protein: 23g; Total Carbohydrates: 78g; Sugars: 6g; Fiber: 3g; Total Fat: 32g; Saturated Fat: 12g; Cholesterol: 49mg; Sodium: 1,401mg

---

Lentil Burgers

Prep time: 15 minutes | Cook time: 10 minutes| Serves 4

- 1 cup cooked green lentils, divided
- ½ cup plain, unsweetened, full-fat Greek yogurt
- ½ lemon, zested and juiced
- ½ teaspoon garlic powder, divided
- ⅛ teaspoon kosher salt, divided
- 6 ounces cremini mushrooms, finely chopped
- 3 tablespoons extra-virgin olive oil, divided
- ¼ teaspoon tablespoon white miso
- ¼ teaspoon smoked paprika
- ¼ cup gluten-free flour

1. In a blender, pour in ½ cup of lentils and partially puree until somewhat smooth, but with many whole lentils still remaining.
2. Meanwhile, in a small bowl, combine the yogurt, lemon zest and juice, ¼ teaspoon garlic powder, and half the salt. Season and set aside.
3. In a medium bowl, combine the mushrooms, 2 tablespoons of olive oil, miso, paprika, and the remaining ¼ teaspoon of garlic powder. Add all the lentils and stir. Vigorously stir in flour until the mixture holds together when squeezed; if it doesn't, continue to mash the lentils until it does and add 1 to 2 tablespoons flour if needed. Form into 6 patties about ¾ inch thick.
4. In a large nonstick sauté pan or skillet, working in batches, heat the remaining 1 tablespoon of olive oil over medium heat. Cook until the patties are deeply browned and very crisp on the bottom side, about 3 minutes. Carefully turn and repeat on second side, adding more oil as needed to maintain a light coating around patties in skillet. Repeat with remaining patties, adding more oil to the pan if needed.
5. Spread the reserved yogurt mixture into a pita. Top with patties and Pickled Onions.

PER SERVING

Calories: 216; Protein: 10g; Total Carbohydrates: 19g; Sugars: 3g; Fiber: 5g; Total Fat: 13g; Saturated Fat: 2g; Cholesterol: 4mg; Sodium: 69mg

Chapter 10
Pastas, Pizzas, and Breads

Herb-Topped Focaccia

Prep time: 2 hours | Cook time: 20 minutes | Serves 10

- 1 tablespoon dried rosemary or 3 tablespoons minced fresh rosemary
- 1 tablespoon dried thyme or 3 tablespoons minced fresh thyme leaves
- ½ cup extra-virgin olive oil
- 1 teaspoon sugar
- 1 cup warm water
- 1 (¼-ounce) packet active dry yeast
- 2½ cups flour, divided
- 1 teaspoon salt

1. In a small bowl, combine the rosemary and thyme with the olive oil.
2. In a large bowl, whisk together the sugar, water, and yeast. Let stand for 5 minutes.
3. Add 1 cup of flour, half of the olive oil mixture, and the salt to the mixture in the large bowl. Stir to combine.
4. Add the remaining 1½ cups flour to the large bowl. Using your hands, combine dough until it starts to pull away from the sides of the bowl.
5. Put the dough on a floured board or countertop and knead 10 to 12 times. Place the dough in a well-oiled bowl and cover with plastic wrap. Put it in a warm, dry space for 1 hour.
6. Oil a 9-by-13-inch baking pan. Turn the dough onto the baking pan, and using your hands gently push the dough out to fit the pan.
7. Using your fingers, make dimples into the dough. Evenly pour the remaining half of the olive oil mixture over the dough. Let the dough rise for another 30 minutes.
8. Preheat the oven to 450°F. Place the dough into the oven and let cook for 18 to 20 minutes, until you see it turn a golden brown.

PER SERVING

Calories: 199; Protein: 3g; Total Carbohydrates: 23g; Sugars: 0g; Fiber: 1g; Total Fat: 11g; Saturated Fat: 2g; Cholesterol: 0mg; Sodium: 233mg

Caramelized Onion Flatbread with Arugula

Prep time: 10 minutes | Cook time: 25 minutes | Serves 4

- 4 tablespoons extra-virgin olive oil, divided
- 2 large onions, sliced into ¼-inch-thick slices
- 1 teaspoon salt, divided
- 1 sheet puff pastry
- 1 (5-ounce) package goat cheese
- 8 ounces arugula
- ½ teaspoon freshly ground black pepper

1. Preheat the oven to 400°F.
2. In a large skillet over medium heat, cook 3 tablespoons olive oil, the onions, and ½ teaspoon of salt, stirring, for 10 to 12 minutes, until the onions are translucent and golden brown.
3. To assemble, line a baking sheet with parchment paper. Lay the puff pastry flat on the parchment paper. Prick the middle of the puff pastry all over with a fork, leaving a ½-inch border.
4. Evenly distribute the onions on the pastry, leaving the border.
5. Crumble the goat cheese over the onions. Put the pastry in the oven to bake for 10 to 12 minutes, or until you see the border become golden brown.
6. Remove the pastry from the oven, set aside. In a medium bowl, add the arugula, remaining 1 tablespoon of olive oil, remaining ½ teaspoon of salt, and ½ teaspoon black pepper; toss to evenly dress the arugula.
7. Cut the pastry into even squares. Top the pastry with dressed arugula and serve.

PER SERVING

Calories: 501; Protein: 12g; Total Carbohydrates: 29g; Sugars: 5g; Fiber: 4g; Total Fat: 40g; Saturated Fat: 10g; Cholesterol: 44mg; Sodium: 878mg

Quick Shrimp Fettuccine

Prep time: 10 minutes | Cook time: 10 minutes | Serves 4

- 8 ounces fettuccine pasta
- ¼ cup extra-virgin olive oil
- 3 tablespoons garlic, minced
- 1 pound large shrimp (21-25), peeled and deveined
- ⅓ cup lemon juice
- 1 tablespoon lemon zest
- ½ teaspoon salt
- ½ teaspoon freshly ground black pepper

1. Bring a large pot of salted water to a boil. Add the fettuccine and cook for 8 minutes.
2. In a large saucepan over medium heat, cook the olive oil and garlic for 1 minute.
3. Add the shrimp to the saucepan and cook for 3 minutes on each side. Remove the shrimp from the pan and set aside.
4. Add the lemon juice and lemon zest to the saucepan, along with the salt and pepper.
5. Reserve ½ cup of the pasta water and drain the pasta.
6. Add the pasta water to the saucepan with the lemon juice and zest and stir everything together. Add the pasta and toss together to evenly coat the pasta. Transfer the pasta to a serving dish and top with the cooked shrimp. Serve warm.

PER SERVING

Calories: 615; Protein: 33g; Total Carbohydrates: 89g; Sugars: 3g; Fiber: 4g; Total Fat: 17g; Saturated Fat: 2g; Cholesterol: 145mg; Sodium: 407mg

Roasted Ratatouille Pasta

Prep time: 5 minutes | Cook time: 35 minutes | Serves 2

- 1 small eggplant
- 1 small zucchini
- 1 portobello mushroom
- 1 Roma tomato, halved
- ½ medium sweet red pepper, seeded
- ½ teaspoon salt, plus additional for the pasta water
- 1 teaspoon Italian herb seasoning
- 1 tablespoon olive oil
- 2 cups farfalle pasta
- 2 tablespoons minced sun-dried tomatoes in olive oil with herbs
- 2 tablespoons prepared pesto

1. Slice the ends off the eggplant and zucchini. Cut them lengthwise into ½-inch slices.
2. Place the eggplant, zucchini, mushroom, tomato, and red pepper in a large bowl and sprinkle with ½ teaspoon of salt. Using your hands, toss the vegetables well so that they're covered evenly with the salt. Let them rest for about 10 minutes.
3. While the vegetables are resting, preheat the oven to 400°F. Line a baking sheet with parchment paper.
4. When the oven is hot, drain off any liquid from the vegetables and pat them dry with a paper towel. Add the Italian herb seasoning and olive oil to the vegetables and toss well to coat both sides.
5. Lay the vegetables out in a single layer on the baking sheet. Roast them for 15 to 20 minutes, flipping them over after about 10 minutes or once they start to brown on the underside. When the vegetables are charred in spots, remove them from the oven.
6. While the vegetables are roasting, fill a large saucepan with water. Add salt and cook the pasta until al dente, about 8 to 10 minutes. Drain the pasta, reserving ½ cup of the pasta water.
7. When cool enough to handle, cut the vegetables into large chunks and add them to the hot pasta.
8. Stir in the sun-dried tomatoes and pesto and toss everything well. Serve immediately.

PER SERVING

Calories: 613;Fat: 16.0g;Protein: 23.1g;Carbs: 108.5g.

Simple Pesto Pasta

Prep time: 10 minutes | Cook time: 10 minutes | Serves 4

- 1 pound spaghetti
- 4 cups fresh basil leaves, stems removed
- 3 cloves garlic
- 1 teaspoon salt
- ½ teaspoon freshly ground black pepper
- ¼ cup lemon juice
- ½ cup pine nuts, toasted
- ½ cup grated Parmesan cheese
- 1 cup extra-virgin olive oil

1. Bring a large pot of salted water to a boil. Add the spaghetti to the pot and cook for 8 minutes.
2. Put basil, garlic, salt, pepper, lemon juice, pine nuts, and Parmesan cheese in a food processor bowl with chopping blade and purée.
3. While the processor is running, slowly drizzle the olive oil through the top opening. Process until all the olive oil has been added.
4. Reserve ½ cup of the pasta water. Drain the pasta and put it into a bowl. Immediately add the pesto and pasta water to the pasta and toss everything together. Serve warm.

PER SERVING

Calories: 1,067; Protein: 23g; Total Carbohydrates: 91g; Sugars: 3g; Fiber: 6g; Total Fat: 72g; Saturated Fat: 11g; Cholesterol: 10mg; Sodium: 817mg

Za'atar Pizza

Prep time: 10 minutes | Cook time: 15 minutes | Serves 4

- 1 sheet puff pastry
- ¼ cup extra-virgin olive oil
- ⅓ cup za'atar seasoning

1. Preheat the oven to 350°F.
2. Put the puff pastry on a parchment-lined baking sheet. Cut the pastry into desired slices.
3. Brush the pastry with olive oil. Sprinkle with the za'atar.
4. Put the pastry in the oven and bake for 10 to 12 minutes or until edges are lightly browned and puffed up. Serve warm or at room temperature.

PER SERVING

Calories: 374; Protein: 3g; Total Carbohydrates: 20g; Sugars: 1g; Fiber: 1g; Total Fat: 30g; Saturated Fat: 6g; Cholesterol: 0mg; Sodium: 166mg

White Pizza with Prosciutto and Arugula

Prep time: 10 minutes | Cook time: 15 minutes | Serves 4

- 1 pound prepared pizza dough
- ½ cup ricotta cheese
- 1 tablespoon garlic, minced
- 1 cup grated mozzarella cheese
- 3 ounces prosciutto, thinly sliced
- ½ cup fresh arugula
- ½ teaspoon freshly ground black pepper

1. Preheat the oven to 450°F. Roll out the pizza dough on a floured surface.
2. Put the pizza dough on a parchment-lined baking sheet or pizza sheet. Put the dough in the oven and bake for 8 minutes.
3. In a small bowl, mix together the ricotta, garlic, and mozzarella.
4. Remove the pizza dough from the oven and spread the cheese mixture over the top. Bake for another 5 to 6 minutes.
5. Top the pizza with prosciutto, arugula, and pepper; serve warm.

PER SERVING

Calories: 435; Protein: 20g; Total Carbohydrates: 51g; Sugars: 0g; Fiber: 4g; Total Fat: 17g; Saturated Fat: 8g; Cholesterol: 53mg; Sodium: 1,630mg

Flat Meat Pies

Prep time: 20 minutes | Cook time: 15 minutes | Serves 4

- ½ pound ground beef
- 1 small onion, finely chopped
- 1 medium tomato, finely diced and strained
- ½ teaspoon salt
- ½ teaspoon freshly ground black pepper
- 2 sheets puff pastry

1. Preheat the oven to 400°F.
2. In a medium bowl, combine the beef, onion, tomato, salt, and pepper. Set aside.
3. Line 2 baking sheets with parchment paper. Cut the puff pastry dough into 4-inch squares and lay them flat on the baking sheets.
4. Scoop about 2 tablespoons of beef mixture onto each piece of dough. Spread the meat on the dough, leaving a ½-inch edge on each side.
5. Put the meat pies in the oven and bake for 12 to 15 minutes until edges are golden brown.

PER SERVING

Calories: 577; Protein: 18g; Total Carbohydrates: 41g; Sugars: 2g; Fiber: 2g; Total Fat: 38g; Saturated Fat: 10g; Cholesterol: 35mg; Sodium: 541mg

Meaty Baked Penne

Prep time: 10 minutes | Cook time: 40 minutes | Serves 8

- 1 pound penne pasta
- 1 pound ground beef
- 1 teaspoon salt
- 1 (25-ounce) jar marinara sauce
- 1 (1-pound) bag baby spinach, washed
- 3 cups shredded mozzarella cheese, divided

1. Bring a large pot of salted water to a boil, add the penne, and cook for 7 minutes. Reserve 2 cups of the pasta water and drain the pasta.
2. Preheat the oven to 350°F.
3. In a large saucepan over medium heat, cook the ground beef and salt. Brown the ground beef for about 5 minutes.
4. Stir in marinara sauce, and 2 cups of pasta water. Let simmer for 5 minutes.
5. Add a handful of spinach at a time into the sauce, and cook for another 3 minutes.
6. To assemble, in a 9-by-13-inch baking dish, add the pasta and pour the pasta sauce over it. Stir in 1½ cups of the mozzarella cheese. Cover the dish with foil and bake for 20 minutes.
7. After 20 minutes, remove the foil, top with the rest of the mozzarella, and bake for another 10 minutes. Serve warm.

PER SERVING

Calories: 497; Protein: 31g; Total Carbohydrates: 54g; Sugars: 7g; Fiber: 5g; Total Fat: 18g; Saturated Fat: 8g; Cholesterol: 68mg; Sodium: 1,083mg

Cheesy Spaghetti with Pine Nuts

Prep time: 10 minutes | Cook time: 10 minutes | Serves 4

- 8 ounces spaghetti
- 4 tablespoons (½ stick) unsalted butter
- 1 teaspoon freshly ground black pepper
- ½ cup pine nuts
- 1 cup fresh grated Parmesan cheese, divided

1. Bring a large pot of salted water to a boil. Add the pasta and cook for 8 minutes.
2. In a large saucepan over medium heat, combine the butter, black pepper, and pine nuts. Cook for 2 to 3 minutes or until the pine nuts are lightly toasted.
3. Reserve ½ cup of the pasta water. Drain the pasta and put it into the pan with the pine nuts.
4. Add ¾ cup of Parmesan cheese and the reserved pasta water to the pasta and toss everything together to evenly coat the pasta.
5. To serve, put the pasta in a serving dish and top with the remaining ¼ cup of Parmesan cheese.

PER SERVING

Calories: 542; Protein: 20g; Total Carbohydrates: 46g; Sugars: 2g; Fiber: 2g; Total Fat: 32g; Saturated Fat: 13g; Cholesterol: 51mg; Sodium: 552mg

Creamy Garlic-Parmesan Chicken Pasta

Prep time: 5 minutes | Cook time: 25 minutes | Serves 4

- 2 boneless, skinless chicken breasts
- 3 tablespoons extra-virgin olive oil
- 1½ teaspoons salt
- 1 large onion, thinly sliced
- 3 tablespoons garlic, minced
- 1 pound fettuccine pasta
- 1 cup heavy cream
- ¾ cup freshly grated Parmesan cheese, divided
- ½ teaspoon freshly ground black pepper

1. Bring a large pot of salted water to a simmer.
2. Cut the chicken into thin strips.
3. Next add the salt, onion, and garlic to the pan with the chicken. Cook for 7 minutes.
4. Bring the pot of salted water to a boil and add the pasta, then let it cook for 7 minutes.
5. While the pasta is cooking, add the cream, ½ cup of Parmesan cheese, and black pepper to the chicken; simmer for 3 minutes.
6. Reserve ½ cup of the pasta water. Drain the pasta and add it to the chicken cream sauce.
7. Add the reserved pasta water to the pasta and toss together. Let simmer for 2 minutes. Top with the remaining ¼ cup Parmesan cheese and serve warm.

PER SERVING

Calories: 879; Protein: 35g; Total Carbohydrates: 90g; Sugars: 7g; Fiber: 5g; Total Fat: 42g; Saturated Fat: 19g; Cholesterol: 129mg; Sodium: 1,336mg

Roasted Tomato Pita Pizzas

Prep time: 10 minutes |Cook time: 20 minutes| Serves 6

- 2 pints grape tomatoes (about 3 cups), halved
- 1 tablespoon extra-virgin olive oil
- 2 garlic cloves, minced (about 1 teaspoon)
- 1 teaspoon chopped fresh thyme leaves (from about 6 sprigs)
- ¼ teaspoon freshly ground black pepper
- ¼ teaspoon kosher or sea salt
- ¾ cup shredded Parmesan cheese (about 3 ounces)
- 6 whole-wheat pita breads

1. Preheat the oven to 425°F.
2. In a baking pan, mix together the tomatoes, oil, garlic, thyme, pepper, and salt. Roast for 10 minutes. Pull out the rack, stir the tomatoes with a spatula or wooden spoon while still in the oven, and mash down the softened tomatoes to release more of their liquid. Roast for an additional 10 minutes.
3. While the tomatoes are roasting, sprinkle 2 tablespoons of cheese over each pita bread. Place the pitas on a large, rimmed baking sheet and toast in the oven for the last 5 minutes of the tomato cooking time.
4. Remove the tomato sauce and pita bread from the oven. Stir the tomatoes, spoon about ⅓ cup of sauce over each pita bread, and serve.

PER SERVING

Calories:139g, Total Fat:5g, Saturated Fat: 2g,Total Carbs:17 g, Fiber:2g, Protein:6g, Sugar:1g, Sodium:467mg,Phosphorus: 131mg,Potassium: 79mg,Cholesterol: 12mg,

Green and White Pizza

Prep time: 10 minutes |Cook time: 20 minutes| Serves 4

- 1 pound refrigerated fresh pizza dough
- Nonstick cooking spray
- 2 tablespoons extra-virgin olive oil, divided
- ½ cup thinly sliced onion (about ¼ medium onion)
- 2 garlic cloves, minced (about 1 teaspoon)
- 3 cups baby spinach (about 3 ounces)
- 3 cups arugula (about 3 ounces)
- ¼ teaspoon freshly ground black pepper
- 1 tablespoon water
- 1 tablespoon freshly squeezed lemon juice (from ½ medium lemon)
- all-purpose flour, for dusting
- ½ cup crumbled goat cheese (about 2 ounces)
- ½ cup shredded Parmesan cheese (about 2 ounces)

1. Preheat the oven to 500°F. Take the pizza dough out of the refrigerator. Coat a large, rimmed baking sheet with nonstick cooking spray.
2. In a large skillet over medium heat, heat 1 tablespoon of oil. Add the onion and cook for 4 minutes, stirring often. Add the garlic and cook for 1 minute, stirring often. Add the spinach, arugula, pepper, and water. Cook for about 2 minutes, stirring often, especially at the beginning, until all the greens are coated with oil and they start to cook down (they will shrink considerably). Remove the pan from the heat and mix in the lemon juice.
3. On a lightly floured surface, form the pizza dough into a 12-inch circle or a 10-by-12-inch rectangle, using a rolling pin or by stretching with your hands. Place the dough on the prepared baking sheet. Brush the dough with the remaining tablespoon of oil. Spread the cooked greens on top of the dough to within ½ inch of the edge. Crumble the goat cheese on top, then sprinkle with the Parmesan cheese.
4. Bake for 10 to 12 minutes, or until the crust starts to brown around the edges. Remove from the oven, and slide the pizza onto a wooden cutting board. Cut into eight pieces with a pizza cutter or a sharp knife and serve.

PER SERVING

Calories:521g, Total Fat:31g, Saturated Fat: 12g,Total Carbs:38 g, Fiber:4g, Protein:23g, Sugar:6g, Sodium:1073mg,Phosphorus: 450mg,Potassium: 465mg,Cholesterol: 50mg,

White Clam Pizza Pie

Prep time: 10 minutes |Cook time: 20 minutes| Serves 4

- 1 pound refrigerated fresh pizza dough
- Nonstick cooking spray
- 2 tablespoons extra-virgin olive oil, divided
- 2 garlic cloves, minced (about 1 teaspoon)
- ½ teaspoon crushed red pepper
- 1 (10-ounce) can whole baby clams, drained, ⅓ cup of juice reserved
- ¼ cup dry white wine
- All-purpose flour, for dusting
- 1 cup diced fresh or shredded mozzarella cheese (about 4 ounces)
- 1 tablespoon grated Pecorino Romano or Parmesan cheese
- 1 tablespoon chopped fresh flat-leaf (Italian) parsley

1. Preheat the oven to 500°F. Take the pizza dough out of the refrigerator. Coat a large, rimmed baking sheet with nonstick cooking spray.
2. In a large skillet over medium heat, heat 1½ tablespoons of the oil. Add the garlic and crushed red pepper and cook for 1 minute, stirring frequently to prevent the garlic from burning. Add the reserved clam juice and wine. Bring to a boil over high heat. Reduce to medium heat so the sauce is just simmering and cook for 10 minutes, stirring occasionally. The sauce will cook down and thicken.
3. Stir in the clams and cook for 3 minutes, stirring occasionally.
4. While the sauce is cooking, on a lightly floured surface, form the pizza dough into a 12-inch circle or into a 10-by-12-inch rectangle with a rolling pin or by stretching with your hands. Place the dough on the prepared baking sheet. Brush the dough with the remaining ½ tablespoon of oil. Set aside until the clam sauce is ready.
5. Spread the clam sauce over the prepared dough within ½ inch of the edge. Top with the mozzarella cheese, then sprinkle with the Pecorino Romano.
6. Bake for 10 minutes, or until the crust starts to brown around the edges. Remove the pizza from the oven and slide onto a wooden cutting board. Top with the parsley, cut into eight pieces with a pizza cutter or a sharp knife, and serve.

PER SERVING

Calories:484g, Total Fat:22g, Saturated Fat: 7g,Total Carbs:46 g, Fiber:4g, Protein:26g, Sugar:5g, Sodium:1111mg,Phosphorus: 483mg,Potassium: 492mg,Cholesterol: 30mg,

Mediterranean Veggie Pizza with Pourable Thin Crust

Prep time: 15 minutes |Cook time: 15 minutes| Serves 4

- Nonstick cooking spray
- 3 tablespoons cornmeal
- 1 cup white whole-wheat flour or regular whole-wheat flour
- ½ cup all-purpose flour
- 1 tablespoon dried oregano, crushed between your fingers
- ¼ teaspoon kosher or sea salt
- 1 cup plus 2 tablespoons 2% milk
- 2 large eggs, beaten
- 1 large bell pepper, sliced into ⅛-inch-thick rounds
- 1 (2.25-ounce) can sliced olives, any type of green or black, drained (about ½ cup)
- 3 whole canned artichoke hearts, drained and quartered
- ⅓ cup thinly sliced red onion (about onion)
- ½ cup feta cheese (about 2 ounces), crumbled
- Extra-virgin olive oil, for topping (optional)

1. Place one oven rack about 4 inches below the broiler element. Preheat the oven to 400°F. Spray a large, rimmed baking sheet with nonstick cooking spray. Sprinkle it with the cornmeal and set aside.
2. In a large bowl, whisk together the flours, oregano, and salt. In a small bowl, whisk together the milk and eggs; mix into the flour mixture until well combined.
3. Pour the mixture onto the prepared baking sheet. Using a rubber scraper, carefully spread the batter evenly to the corners of the pan. Arrange the bell pepper slices evenly over the batter.
4. Bake on any oven rack for 10 to 12 minutes, or until the crust is dry on top. Remove the pizza crust from the oven.
5. Turn the oven broiler to high.
6. Top the pizza crust with the olives, artichoke hearts, and onion. Top with the feta cheese.
7. Place the pizza on the upper oven rack under the broiler. Broil until the cheese is melted and golden, rotating the pan halfway through and watching carefully to prevent burning. Top with a drizzle of olive oil.

PER SERVING

Calories:364g, Total Fat:17g, Saturated Fat: 7g,Total Carbs:33 g, Fiber:3g, Protein:20g, Sugar:5g, Sodium:1981mg,Phosphorus: 303mg,Potassium: 471mg,Cholesterol: 147mg,

Triple-Green Pasta

Prep time: 5 minutes |Cook time: 15 minutes| Serves 4

- 8 ounces uncooked penne
- 1 tablespoon extra-virgin olive oil
- 2 garlic cloves, minced (1 teaspoon)
- ¼ teaspoon crushed red pepper
- 2 cups chopped fresh flat-leaf (Italian) parsley, including stems
- 5 cups loosely packed baby spinach (about 5 ounces)
- ¼ teaspoon ground nutmeg
- ¼ teaspoon freshly ground black pepper
- ¼ teaspoon kosher or sea salt
- ⅓ cup Castelvetrano olives (or other green olives), pitted and sliced (about 12)
- ⅓ cup grated Pecorino Romano or Parmesan cheese (about 1 ounce)

1. In a large stockpot, cook the pasta according to the package directions, but boil 1 minute less than instructed. Drain the pasta, and save ¼ cup of the cooking water.
2. While the pasta is cooking, in a large skillet over medium heat, heat the oil. Add the garlic and crushed red pepper, and cook for 30 seconds, stirring constantly. Add the parsley and cook for 1 minute, stirring constantly. Add the spinach, nutmeg, pepper, and salt, and cook for 3 minutes, stirring occasionally, until the spinach is wilted.
3. Add the pasta and the reserved ¼ cup pasta water to the skillet. Stir in the olives, and cook for about 2 minutes, until most of the pasta water has been absorbed. Remove from the heat, stir in the cheese, and serve.

PER SERVING

Calories:262g, Total Fat:4g, Saturated Fat: 4g,Total Carbs:51 g, Fiber:13g, Protein:15g, Sugar:32g, Sodium:1180mg,Phosphorus: 246mg,Potassium:1902 mg,Cholesterol: 3mg,

No-Drain Pasta alla Norma

Prep time: 5 minutes | Cook time: 25 minutes | Serves 6

- 1 medium globe eggplant (about 1 pound), cut into ¾-inch cubes
- 1 tablespoon extra-virgin olive oil
- 1 cup chopped onion (about ½ medium onion)
- 8 ounces uncooked thin spaghetti
- 1 (15-ounce) container part-skim ricotta cheese
- 3 Roma tomatoes, chopped (about 2 cups)
- 2 garlic cloves, minced (about 1 teaspoon)
- ¼ teaspoon kosher or sea salt
- ½ cup loosely packed fresh basil leaves
- Grated Parmesan cheese, for serving (optional)

1. Lay three paper towels on a large plate, and pile the cubed eggplant on top. (Don't cover the eggplant.) Microwave the eggplant on high for 5 minutes to dry and partially cook it.
2. In a large stockpot over medium-high heat, heat the oil. Add the eggplant and the onion and cook for 5 minutes, stirring occasionally.
3. Add the spaghetti, ricotta, tomatoes, garlic, and salt. Cover with water by a ½ inch (about 4 cups of water). Cook uncovered for 12 to 15 minutes, or until the pasta is just al dente (tender with a bite), stirring occasionally to prevent the pasta from sticking together or sticking to the bottom of the pot.
4. Remove the pot from the heat and let the pasta stand for 3 more minutes to absorb more liquid while you tear the basil into pieces. Sprinkle the basil over the pasta and gently stir. Serve with Parmesan cheese, if desired.

PER SERVING

Calories:206g, Total Fat:8g, Saturated Fat: 4g,Total Carbs:23 g, Fiber:6g, Protein:13g, Sugar:6g, Sodium:201mg,Phosphorus: 220mg,Potassium: 501mg,Cholesterol: 25mg,

Zucchini with Bow Ties

Prep time: 5 minutes | Cook time: 25 minutes | Serves 4

- 3 tablespoons extra-virgin olive oil
- 2 garlic cloves, minced (about 1 teaspoon)
- 3 large or 4 medium zucchini, diced (about 4 cups)
- ½ teaspoon freshly ground black pepper
- ¼ teaspoon kosher or sea salt
- ½ cup 2% milk
- ¼ teaspoon ground nutmeg
- 8 ounces uncooked farfalle (bow ties) or other small pasta shape
- ½ cup grated Parmesan or Romano cheese (about 2 ounces)
- 1 tablespoon freshly squeezed lemon juice (from ½ medium lemon)

1. In a large skillet over medium heat, heat the oil. Add the garlic and cook for 1 minute, stirring frequently. Add the zucchini, pepper, and salt.

Stir well, cover, and cook for 15 minutes, stirring once or twice.
2. While the zucchini is cooking, in a large stockpot, cook the pasta according to the package directions.
3. Drain the pasta in a colander, saving about 2 tablespoons of pasta water. Add the pasta and pasta water to the skillet. Mix everything together and remove from the heat. Stir in the cheese and lemon juice and serve.

PER SERVING

Calories:190g, Total Fat:10g, Saturated Fat: 3g,Total Carbs:20 g, Fiber:3g, Protein:7g, Sugar:2g, Sodium:475mg,Phosphorus:163 mg,Potassium: 149mg,Cholesterol: 18mg,

Roasted Asparagus Caprese Pasta

Prep time: 10 minutes | Cook time: 15 minutes | Serves 6

- 8 ounces uncooked small pasta, like orecchiette (little ears) or farfalle (bow ties)
- 1½ pounds fresh asparagus, ends trimmed and stalks chopped into 1-inch pieces (about 3 cups)
- 1 pint grape tomatoes, halved (about 1½ cups)
- 2 tablespoons extra-virgin olive oil
- ¼ teaspoon freshly ground black pepper
- ¼ teaspoon kosher or sea salt
- 2 cups fresh mozzarella, drained and cut into bite-size pieces (about 8 ounces)
- ⅓ cup torn fresh basil leaves
- 2 tablespoons balsamic vinegar

1. Preheat the oven to 400°F.
2. In a large stockpot, cook the pasta according to the package directions. Drain, reserving about ¼ cup of the pasta water.
3. While the pasta is cooking, in a large bowl, toss the asparagus, tomatoes, oil, pepper, and salt together. Spread the mixture onto a large, rimmed baking sheet and bake for 15 minutes, stirring twice as it cooks.
4. Remove the vegetables from the oven, and add the cooked pasta to the baking sheet. Mix with a few tablespoons of pasta water to help the sauce become smoother and the saucy vegetables stick to the pasta.
5. Gently mix in the mozzarella and basil. Drizzle with the balsamic vinegar. Serve from the baking sheet or pour the pasta into a large bowl.
6. If you want to make this dish ahead of time or to serve it cold, follow the recipe up to step 4, then refrigerate the pasta and vegetables. When you are ready to serve, follow step 5 either with the cold pasta or with warm pasta that's been gently reheated in a pot on the stove.

PER SERVING

Calories:147g, Total Fat:3g, Saturated Fat:1 g,Total Carbs:17 g, Fiber:5g, Protein:16g, Sugar:4g, Sodium:420mg,Phosphorus: 337mg,Potassium: 290mg,Cholesterol: 8mg,

Pasta with Tomatoes

Prep Time: 15 minutes| Cook Time: 15 minutes| Serves 4

1 (8-oz.) package linguini pasta
2 tbsp. olive oil
1 tbsp. garlic, minced
1 tbsp. dried oregano, crushed
1 tbsp. dried basil, crushed
1 tsp. dried thyme, crushed
2 C. tomatoes, chopped

1. In a large-sized saucepan of lightly salted boiling water, add the pasta and cook for about 8-10 minutes or according to package's directions.
2. Drain the pasta well.
3. In a large-sized wok, heat oil over medium heat and sauté the garlic for about 1 minute.
4. Stir in herbs and sauté for about 1 minute more.
5. Add the pasta and cook for about 2-3 minutes or until heated completely.
6. Fold in tomatoes and remove from heat.
7. Serve hot.

PER SERVING

Calories: 301; Fat: 8.9g;Carbs: 47.7g;Fiber: 6.7g;Protein: 8.5g

Spicy Pork and Zucchini Pasta

Prep time: 10 minutes | Cook time: 20 minutes | Serves 6

- 1 pound whole wheat rotini
- 1 tablespoon extra-virgin olive oil
- 1 yellow onion, chopped
- 2 garlic cloves, minced
- 1 pound lean ground pork
- 2 medium zucchini, sliced
- 1 teaspoon salt
- 1 teaspoon dried oregano
- ½ or ⅓ teaspoon red pepper flakes
- ¼ teaspoon cayenne pepper
- 1 (15-ounce) can stewed tomatoes
- 1 (15-ounce) fire-roasted tomatoes

1. Cook the pasta according to the package instructions. Drain the noodles, return them to the pot, and set them aside.
2. While the pasta is cooking, in a large sauté pan, heat the oil over medium-high heat. Add the onion and garlic and cook for 3 to 4 minutes, or until the onion has softened.
3. Add the ground pork to the pan and continue cooking until the pork is browned and cooked through.
4. Stir in the zucchini, salt, oregano, red pepper flakes, and cayenne pepper, and continue cooking for 5 minutes, or until the zucchini has softened.
5. Add the stewed tomatoes and fire-roasted tomatoes. Reduce the heat to medium-low and simmer the sauce for 5 minutes.
6. Pour the sauce over the cooked pasta. Stir to coat the noodles in the sauce and serve.

PER SERVING

Calories: 428; Fat: 7g; Protein: 30g; Carbohydrates: 168g; Fiber: 11g; Sugar: 8g; Sodium: 478mg

Mini Cucumber & Cream Cheese Sandwiches

Prep time: 5 minutes | Cook time: 5 minutes| Serves 4

- 4 bread slices
- 1 cucumber, sliced
- 2 tbsp cream cheese, soft
- 1 tbsp chives, chopped
- ¼ cup hummus
- Salt and black pepper to taste

1. In a bowl, mix hummus, cream cheese, chives, salt, and pepper until well combined. Spread the mixture onto bread slices.
2. Top with cucumber and cut each sandwich into three pieces. Serve immediately.

PER SERVING

Calories: 190;Fat: 13g;Protein: 9g;Carbs: 5g

Pecan & Raspberry & Frozen Yogurt Cups

Prep time: 5 minutes | Cook time: 15 minutes| Serves 4

- 2 cups fresh raspberries
- 4 cups vanilla frozen yogurt
- 1 lime, zested
- ¼ cup chopped praline pecans

1. Divide the frozen yogurt into 4 dessert glasses.
2. Top with raspberries, lime zest, and pecans. Serve immediately.

PER SERVING

Calories: 142;Fat: 3.4g;Protein: 3.7g;Carbs: 26g

Chocolate and Avocado Mousse

Prep time: 5 minutes | Cook time: 5 minutes| Serves 4

- 8 ounces dark chocolate, chopped
- ¼ cup unsweetened coconut milk
- 2 tablespoons coconut oil
- 2 ripe avocados, deseeded
- ¼ cup raw honey
- Sea salt, to taste

1. Put the chocolate in a saucepan. Pour in the coconut milk and add the coconut oil.
2. Cook for 3 minutes or until the chocolate and coconut oil melt. Stir constantly.
3. Put the avocado in a food processor, then drizzle with honey and melted chocolate. Pulse to combine until smooth.
4. Pour the mixture in a serving bowl, then sprinkle with salt. Refrigerate to chill for 30 minutes and serve.

PER SERVING

Calories: 654;Fat: 46.8g;Protein: 7.2g;Carbs: 55.9g

Berry Sorbet

Prep time: 5 minutes | Cook time: 15 minutes| Serves 4

- 1 tsp lemon juice
- ¼ cup honey
- 1 cup fresh strawberries
- 1 cup fresh raspberries
- 1 cup fresh blueberries

1. Bring 1 cup of water to a boil in a pot over high heat. Stir in honey until dissolved. Remove from the heat and mix in berries and lemon juice; let cool.
2. Once cooled, add the mixture to a food processor and pulse until smooth. Transfer to a shallow glass and freeze for 1 hour. Stir with a fork and freeze for 30 more minutes. Repeat a couple of times. Serve in dessert dishes.

PER SERVING

Calories: 115;Fat: 1g;Protein: 1g;Carbs: 29g

Lovely Coconut-covered Strawberries

Prep time: 5 minutes | Cook time: 15 minutes| Serves 4

- 1 cup chocolate chips
- ¼ cup coconut flakes
- 1 lb strawberries
- ½ tsp vanilla extract
- ½ tsp ground nutmeg
- ¼ tsp salt

1. Melt chocolate chips for 30 seconds. Remove and stir in vanilla, nutmeg, and salt. Let cool for 2-3 minutes.
2. Dip strawberries into the chocolate and then into the coconut flakes. Place on a wax paper-lined cookie sheet and let sit for 30 minutes until the chocolate dries. Serve.

PER SERVING

Calories: 275;Fat: 20g;Protein: 6g;Carbs: 21g

Honey & Spice Roasted Almonds

Prep time: 5 minutes | Cook time: 15 minutes| Serves 4

- 2 tbsp olive oil
- 3 cups almonds
- 1 tbsp curry powder
- ¼ cup honey
- 1 tsp salt

1. Preheat oven to 260 °F. Coat almonds with olive oil, curry powder, and salt in a bowl; mix well. Arrange on a lined with aluminum foil sheet and bake for 15 minutes.
2. Remove from the oven and let cool for 10 minutes. Drizzle with honey and let cool at room temperature. Enjoy!

PER SERVING

Calories: 134;Fat: 8g;Protein: 1g;Carbs: 18g

Mint Raspberries Panna Cotta

Prep time: 5 minutes | Cook time: 15 minutes| Serves 4

- 2 tbsp warm water
- 2 tsp gelatin powder
- 2 cups heavy cream
- 1 cup raspberries
- 2 tbsp sugar
- 1 tsp vanilla extract
- 4 fresh mint leaves

1. Pour 2 tbsp of warm water into a small bowl. Stir in the gelatin to dissolve. Allow the mixture to sit for 10 minutes. In a large bowl, combine the heavy cream, raspberries, sugar, and vanilla.
2. Blend with an immersion blender until the mixture is smooth and the raspberries are well puréed. Transfer the mixture to a saucepan and heat over medium heat until just below a simmer.
3. Remove from the heat and let cool for 5 minutes. Add in the gelatin mixture, whisking constantly until smooth. Divide the custard between ramekins and refrigerate until set, 4-6 hours. Serve chilled garnished with mint leaves.

PER SERVING

Calories: 431;Fat: 44g;Protein: 4g;Carbs: 7g

Salty Spicy Popcorn

Prep time: 5 minutes | Cook time: 15 minutes| Serves 6

- 3 tbsp olive oil
- ¼ tsp garlic powder
- Salt and black pepper to taste
- ½ tsp dried thyme
- ½ tsp chili powder
- ½ tsp dried oregano
- 12 cups plain popped popcorn

1. Warm the olive oil in a large pan over medium heat. Add the garlic powder, black pepper, salt, chili powder, thyme, and stir oregano until fragrant, 1 minute.
2. Place the popcorn in a large bowl and drizzle with the infused oil over. Toss to coat.

PER SERVING

Calories: 183;Fat: 12g;Protein: 3g;Carbs: 19g

Orange Mug Cakes

Prep time: 5 minutes | Cook time: 5 minutes| Serves 2

- 6 tablespoons flour
- 2 tablespoons sugar
- 1 teaspoon orange zest
- ½ teaspoon baking powder
- Pinch salt
- 1 egg
- 2 tablespoons olive oil
- 2 tablespoons unsweetened almond milk
- 2 tablespoons freshly squeezed orange juice
- ½ teaspoon orange extract
- ½ teaspoon vanilla extract

1. Combine the flour, sugar, orange zest, baking powder, and salt in a small bowl.
2. In another bowl, whisk together the egg, olive oil, milk, orange juice, orange extract, and vanilla extract.
3. Add the dry ingredients to the wet ingredients and stir to incorporate. The batter will be thick.
4. Divide the mixture into two small mugs. Microwave each mug separately. The small ones should take about 60 seconds, and one large mug should take about 90 seconds, but microwaves can vary.
5. Cool for 5 minutes before serving.

PER SERVING

Calories: 303;Fat: 16.9g;Protein: 6.0g;Carbs: 32.5g

Mascarpone Baked Pears

Prep time: 5 minutes | Cook time: 20 minutes| Serves 2

- 2 ripe pears, peeled
- 1 tablespoon plus 2 teaspoons honey, divided
- 1 teaspoon vanilla, divided
- ¼ teaspoon ground coriander
- ¼ cup minced walnuts
- ¼ cup mascarpone cheese
- Pinch salt
- Cooking spray

1. Preheat the oven to 350°F. Spray a small baking dish with cooking spray.
2. Whisk together 1 tablespoon of honey, ½ teaspoon of vanilla, ginger, and coriander in a small bowl. Pour this mixture evenly over the pear halves.
3. Scatter the walnuts over the pear halves.
4. Bake in the preheated oven for 20 minutes, or until the pears are golden and you're able to pierce them easily with a knife.
5. Meanwhile, combine the mascarpone cheese with the remaining 2 teaspoons of honey, ½ teaspoon of vanilla, and a pinch of salt. Stir to combine well.
6. Divide the mascarpone among the warm pear halves and serve.

PER SERVING

Calories: 308;Fat: 16.0g;Protein: 4.1g;Carbs: 42.7g

Flourless Chocolate Brownies with Raspberry Balsamic Sauce

Prep Time: 10 minutes, plus 5 minutes to cool | **Cook Time:** 20 minutes | **Serves 2**

FOR THE RASPBERRY SAUCE

- ¼ cup good-quality balsamic vinegar
- 1 cup frozen raspberries
- For the brownie
- ½ cup black beans with no added salt, rinsed
- 1 large egg
- 1 tablespoon olive oil
- ½ teaspoon vanilla extract
- 4 tablespoons unsweetened cocoa powder
- ¼ cup sugar
- ¼ teaspoon baking powder
- Pinch salt
- ¼ cup dark chocolate chips

TO MAKE THE RASPBERRY SAUCE

- Combine the balsamic vinegar and raspberries in a saucepan and bring the mixture to a boil. Reduce the heat to medium and let the sauce simmer for 15 minutes, or until reduced to ½ cup. If desired, strain the seeds and set the sauce aside until the brownie is ready.

TO MAKE THE BROWNIE

1. Preheat the oven to 350°F and set the rack to the middle position. Grease two 8-ounce ramekins and place them on a baking sheet.
2. In a food processor, combine the black beans, egg, olive oil, and vanilla. Purée the mixture for 1 to 2 minutes, or until it's smooth and the beans are completely broken down. Scrape down the sides of the bowl a few times to make sure everything is well-incorporated.
3. Add the cocoa powder, sugar, baking powder, and salt and purée again to combine the dry ingredients, scraping down the sides of the bowl as needed.
4. Stir the chocolate chips into the batter by hand. Reserve a few if you like, to sprinkle over the top of the brownies when they come out of the oven.
5. Pour the brownies into the prepared ramekins and bake for 15 minutes, or until firm. The center will look slightly undercooked. If you prefer a firmer brownie, leave it in the oven for another 5 minutes, or until a toothpick inserted in the middle comes out clean.
6. Remove the brownies from the oven. If desired, sprinkle any remaining chocolate chips over the top and let them melt into the warm brownies.
7. Let the brownies cool for a few minutes and top with warm raspberry sauce to serve.

PER SERVING

Calories: 510; Total fat: 16g; Total carbs: 88g; Fiber: 14g; Sugar: 64g; Protein: 10g; Sodium: 124mg; Cholesterol: 94mg

Spiced Baked Pears with Mascarpone

Prep Time: 10 minutes | **Cook Time:** 20 minutes | **Serves 2**

- 2 ripe pears, peeled
- 1 tablespoon plus 2 teaspoons honey, divided
- 1 teaspoon vanilla, divided
- ¼ teaspoon ginger
- ¼ teaspoon ground coriander
- ¼ cup minced walnuts
- ¼ cup mascarpone cheese
- Pinch salt

1. Preheat the oven to 350°F and set the rack to the middle position. Grease a small baking dish.
2. Cut the pears in half lengthwise. Using a spoon, scoop out the core from each piece. Place the pears with the cut side up in the baking dish.
3. Combine 1 tablespoon of honey, ½ teaspoon of vanilla, ginger, and coriander in a small bowl. Pour this mixture evenly over the pear halves.
4. Sprinkle walnuts over the pear halves.
5. Bake for 20 minutes, or until the pears are golden and you're able to pierce them easily with a knife.
6. While the pears are baking, mix the mascarpone cheese with the remaining 2 teaspoons honey, ½ teaspoon of vanilla, and a pinch of salt. Stir well to combine.
7. Divide the mascarpone among the warm pear halves and serve.

PER SERVING

Calories: 307; Total fat: 16g; Total carbs: 43g; Fiber: 6g; Sugar: 31g; Protein: 4g; Sodium: 89mg; Cholesterol: 18mg

Orange Olive Oil Mug Cakes

Prep Time: 10 minutes | **Cook Time:** 2 minutes | **Serves 2**

- 6 tablespoons flour
- 2 tablespoons sugar
- ½ teaspoon baking powder
- Pinch salt
- 1 teaspoon orange zest
- 1 egg
- 2 tablespoons olive oil
- 2 tablespoons freshly squeezed orange juice
- 2 tablespoons milk
- ½ teaspoon orange extract
- ½ teaspoon vanilla extract

1. In a small bowl, combine the flour, sugar, baking powder, salt, and orange zest.
2. In a separate bowl, whisk together the egg, olive oil, orange juice, milk, orange extract, and vanilla extract.
3. Divide the mixture into two small mugs that hold at least 6 ounces each, or one 12-ounce mug.
4. Microwave each mug separately. The small ones should take about 60 seconds, and one large mug should take about 90 seconds, but microwaves can vary. The cake will be done when it pulls away from the sides of the mug.

PER SERVING

Calories: 302; Total fat: 17g; Total carbs: 33g; Fiber: 1g; Sugar: 14g; Protein: 6g; Sodium: 117mg; Cholesterol: 83mg

Dark Chocolate Bark with Fruit and Nuts

Prep Time: 15 minutes, plus 1 hour to cool | **Serves 2**

- 2 tablespoons chopped nuts (almonds, pecans, walnuts, hazelnuts, pistachios, or any combination of those)
- 3 ounces good-quality dark chocolate chips (about ⅔ cup)
- ¼ cup chopped dried fruit (apricots, blueberries, figs, prunes, or any combination of those)

1. Line a sheet pan with parchment paper.
2. Place the nuts in a skillet over medium-high heat and toast them for 60 seconds, or just until they're fragrant.
3. Place the chocolate in a microwave-safe glass bowl or measuring cup and microwave on high for 1 minute. Stir the chocolate and allow any unmelted chips to warm and melt. If necessary, heat for another 20 to 30 seconds, but keep a close eye on it to make sure it doesn't burn.
4. Pour the chocolate onto the sheet pan. Sprinkle the dried fruit and nuts over the chocolate evenly and gently pat in so they stick.
5. Transfer the sheet pan to the refrigerator for at least 1 hour to let the chocolate harden.
6. When solid, break into pieces. Store any leftover chocolate in the refrigerator or freezer.

PER SERVING

Calories: 284; Total fat: 16g; Total carbs: 39g; Fiber: 2g; Sugar: 31g; Protein: 4g; Sodium: 2mg; Cholesterol: 0mg

Grilled Fruit Kebabs with Honey Labneh

Prep Time: 15 minutes, plus overnight if making the labneh | **Cook Time:** 10 minutes | **Serves 2**

- ⅔ cup prepared labneh, or, if making your own, ⅔ cup full-fat plain Greek yogurt
- 2 tablespoons honey
- 1 teaspoon vanilla extract
- Pinch salt
- 3 cups fresh fruit cut into 2-inch chunks (pineapple, cantaloupe, nectarines, strawberries, plums, or mango)

1. If making your own labneh, place a colander over a bowl and line it with cheesecloth. Place the Greek yogurt in the cheesecloth and wrap it up. Put the bowl in the refrigerator and let sit for at least 12 to 24 hours, until it's thick like soft cheese.
2. Mix honey, vanilla, and salt into labneh. Stir well to combine and set it aside.
3. Thread the fruit onto skewers and grill for 4 minutes on each side, or until fruit is softened and has grill marks on each side.
4. Serve the fruit with labneh to dip.

PER SERVING

Calories: 292; Total fat: 6g; Total carbs: 60g; Fiber: 4g; Sugar: 56g; Protein: 5g; Sodium: 131mg; Cholesterol: 17mg

Blueberry Pomegranate Granita

Prep Time: 5 minutes | **Cook Time:** 10 minutes, plus 30 minutes to cool and 2 hours to freeze | **Serves 2**

- 1 cup frozen wild blueberries
- 1 cup pomegranate or pomegranate blueberry juice
- ¼ cup sugar
- ¼ cup water

1. Combine the frozen blueberries and pomegranate juice in a saucepan and bring to a boil. Reduce the heat and simmer for 5 minutes, or until the blueberries start to break down.
2. While the juice and berries are cooking, combine the sugar and water in a small microwave-safe bowl. Microwave for 60 seconds, or until it comes to a rolling boil. Stir to make sure all of the sugar is dissolved and set the syrup aside.
3. Pour the mixture into an 8-by-8-inch baking pan or a similar-sized bowl. The liquid should come about ½ inch up the sides. Let the mixture cool for 30 minutes, and then put it into the freezer.
4. Every 30 minutes for the next 2 hours, scrape the granita with a fork to keep it from freezing solid.
5. Serve it after 2 hours, or store it in a covered container in the freezer.

PER SERVING

Calories: 214; Total fat: 0g; Total carbs: 54g; Fiber: 2g; Sugar: 48g; Protein: 1g; Sodium: 15mg; Cholesterol: 0mg

Mini Mixed Berry Crumbles

Prep Time: 15 minutes | Cook Time: 30 minutes | Serves 2

- 1½ cups frozen mixed berries, thawed
- 1 tablespoon butter, softened
- 1 tablespoon brown sugar
- ¼ cup pecans
- ¼ cup oats

1. Preheat the oven to 350°F and set the rack to the middle position.
2. Divide the berries between 2 (8-ounce) ramekins
3. In a food processor, combine the butter, brown sugar, pecans, and oats, and pulse a few times, until the mixture resembles damp sand.
4. Divide the crumble topping over the berries.
5. Place the ramekins on a sheet pan and bake for 30 minutes, or until the top is golden and the berries are bubbling.

PER SERVING

Calories: 267; Total fat: 17g; Total carbs: 27g; Fiber: 6g; Sugar: 13g; Protein: 4g; Sodium: 43mg; Cholesterol: 15mg

Chocolate Turtle Hummus

Prep Time: 15 minutes | Serves 2

FOR THE CARAMEL
- 2 tablespoons coconut oil
- 1 tablespoon maple syrup
- 1 tablespoon almond butter
- Pinch salt
- For the hummus
- ½ cup chickpeas, drained and rinsed
- 2 tablespoons unsweetened cocoa powder
- 1 tablespoon maple syrup, plus more to taste
- 2 tablespoons almond milk, or more as needed, to thin
- Pinch salt
- 2 tablespoons pecans

TO MAKE THE CARAMEL

1. To make the caramel, put the coconut oil in a small microwave-safe bowl. If it's solid, microwave it for about 15 seconds to melt it.
2. Stir in the maple syrup, almond butter, and salt.
3. Place the caramel in the refrigerator for 5 to 10 minutes to thicken.

TO MAKE THE HUMMUS

1. In a food processor, combine the chickpeas, cocoa powder, maple syrup, almond milk, and pinch of salt, and process until smooth. Scrape down the sides to make sure everything is incorporated.
2. If the hummus seems too thick, add another tablespoon of almond milk.
3. Add the pecans and pulse 6 times to roughly chop them.
4. Transfer the hummus to a serving bowl and when the caramel is thickened, swirl it into the hummus. Gently fold it in, but don't mix it in completely.
5. Serve with fresh fruit or pretzels.

PER SERVING

Calories: 321; Total fat: 22g; Total carbs: 30g; Fiber: 6g; Sugar: 15g; Protein: 7g; Sodium: 100mg; Cholesterol: 0mg

Lemon Panna Cotta with Blackberries

Prep Time: 20 minutes | Cook Time: 10 minutes, plus 6 hours to set | Serves 2

- ¾ cup half-and-half, divided
- 1 teaspoon unflavored powdered gelatin
- ½ cup heavy cream
- 3 tablespoons sugar
- 1 teaspoon lemon zest
- 1 tablespoon freshly squeezed lemon juice
- 1 teaspoon lemon extract
- ½ cup fresh blackberries
- Lemon peels to garnish (optional)

1. Place ¼ cup of half-and-half in a small bowl.
2. Sprinkle the gelatin powder evenly over the half-and-half and set it aside for 10 minutes to hydrate.
3. In a saucepan, combine the remaining ½ cup of half-and-half, the heavy cream, sugar, lemon zest, lemon juice, and lemon extract. Heat the mixture over medium heat for 4 minutes, or until it's barely simmering—don't let it come to a full boil. Remove from the heat.
4. When the gelatin is hydrated (it will look like applesauce), add it into the warm cream mixture, whisking as the gelatin melts.
5. If there are any remaining clumps of gelatin, strain the liquid or remove the lumps with a spoon.
6. Pour the mixture into 2 dessert glasses or stemless wineglasses and refrigerate for at least 6 hours, or up to overnight.
7. Serve with the fresh berries and garnish with some strips of fresh lemon peel, if desired.

PER SERVING

Calories: 422; Total fat: 33g; Total carbs: 28g; Fiber: 2g; Sugar: 21g; Protein: 6g; Sodium: 64mg; Cholesterol: 115mg

Goat Cheese Stuffed Pears with Hazelnuts

Prep time: 5 minutes | Cook time: 20 minutes | Serves 4

- 1 tablespoon extra-virgin olive oil
- 2 ripe medium pears, halved lengthwise, cored and hollowed out with a spoon
- ½ cup water
- 4 tablespoons goat cheese
- 2 ounces firm tofu
- 2 tablespoons honey
- ¼ cup roughly chopped hazelnuts

1. Preheat the oven to 350°F.
2. In a medium skillet, heat the olive oil over medium heat.
3. Place the pears in the skillet, skin-side up, and lightly brown them, about 2 minutes.
4. Place the pears in an 8 x 8-inch square baking dish, hollow-side up, and pour the water into the baking dish, taking care not to get any in the hollow part of the pears.
5. Roast the pears until softened, about 10 minutes. Remove the pears from the oven.
6. Mash together the goat cheese and tofu until well combined. Then stir in the honey and hazelnuts.
7. Evenly divide the goat cheese mixture among the four pear halves and put them back in the oven for 5 minutes.
8. Serve warm. Refrigerate the leftovers in an airtight container for 3 to 4 days.

PER SERVING

Calories: 197; Total Fat: 11g; Saturated Fat: 2g; Cholesterol: 3mg; Sodium: 36mg; Potassium: 193mg; Magnesium: 28mg; Carbohydrates: 24g; Sugars: 9g; Fiber: 4g; Protein: 5g; Added Sugars: 9g; Vitamin K: 7mcg

Spiced Oranges with Dates

Prep time: 15 minutes | Serves 4

- 4 large oranges
- 2 large blood oranges or cara cara oranges
- ¼ cup coarsely chopped Medjool dates
- ⅛ teaspoon ground cloves
- 2 tablespoons chopped hazelnuts

1. Use a sharp paring knife to cut the skin and pith off the oranges so you have just the flesh. Follow the membranes to cut out the sections of the oranges, and place them in a medium bowl. Squeeze any remaining juice from the membranes into the bowl with the fruit.
2. Add the dates, cloves, and hazelnuts to the bowl and toss to combine.
3. Serve spooned into individual bowls.
4. Prep in advance or store leftovers by refrigerating in an airtight container for 3 to 5 days.

PER SERVING

Calories: 178; Total Fat: 3g; Saturated Fat: 0g;

Cholesterol: 0mg; Sodium: 0mg; Potassium: 584mg; Magnesium: 37mg; Carbohydrates: 40g; Sugars: 32g; Fiber: 8g; Protein: 3g; Added Sugars: 0g; Vitamin K: 1mcg

Protein-Packed Chocolate Mousse

Prep time: 10 minutes, plus 30 minutes to chill | Serves 4

- ¼ cup semisweet chocolate chips
- ⅔ cup unsweetened soy milk
- ½ (16-ounce) package silken tofu
- ½ cup cocoa powder
- 2 teaspoons honey
- 2 teaspoons vanilla extract
- Berries of your choice, for garnish (optional)
- Fresh mint, for garnish (optional)
- Shaved chocolate, for garnish (optional)

1. Melt the chocolate chips on the stove using a double boiler or in the microwave in a microwave-safe bowl.
2. In a food processor or blender, combine the soy milk, tofu, cocoa powder, honey, and vanilla. Transfer the melted chocolate to the food processor and blend until smooth.
3. Scoop the mixture into four dishes. Refrigerate for 30 minutes. To serve, garnish with berries (if using), mint (if using), and shaved chocolate (if using).
4. Prep in advance or store leftovers by refrigerating them in an airtight container for up to 4 days.

PER SERVING

Calories: 136; Total Fat: 7g; Saturated Fat: 3g; Cholesterol: 1mg; Sodium: 23mg; Potassium: 442mg; Magnesium: 86mg; Carbohydrates: 16g; Sugars: 5g; Fiber: 4g; Protein: 7g; Added Sugars: 3g; Vitamin K: 2mcg

Oatmeal Dark Chocolate Chip Peanut Butter Cookies

Prep time: 15 minutes | Cook time: 10 minutes| Makes 24

- 1½ cups natural creamy peanut butter
- ½ cup dark brown sugar
- 2 large eggs
- 1 cup old-fashioned rolled oats
- 1 teaspoon baking soda
- ½ teaspoon salt
- ½ cup dark chocolate chips

1. Preheat the oven to 350°F. Line a baking sheet with parchment paper.
2. In the bowl of a stand mixer fitted with the paddle attachment, whip the peanut butter until very smooth. Continue beating and add the brown sugar and then one egg at a time, until fluffy. Beat in the oats, baking soda, and salt until combined. Fold in the dark chocolate chips.
3. Use a small cookie scoop or teaspoon to place spoonfuls of the cookie dough on the baking sheet, about 2 inches apart. Bake for 8 to 10 minutes depending on your preferred level of doneness.
4. Store at room temperature in an airtight container for up to 7 days.

PER SERVING (1 COOKIE)

Calories: 156; Total Fat: 11g; Saturated Fat: 2g; Cholesterol: 16mg; Sodium: 110mg; Potassium: 171mg; Magnesium: 59mg; Carbohydrates: 12g; Sugars: 1g; Fiber: 2g; Protein: 5g; Added Sugars: 5g; Vitamin K: 0mcg

Coconut Date Energy Bites

Prep time: 10 minutes | Makes 15

- 12 pitted Medjool dates
- ½ cup unsweetened shredded coconut
- ½ cup chopped walnuts or almonds
- 1½ tablespoons melted coconut oil

1. Place the dates, coconut, walnuts, and coconut oil in a food processor and pulse until the mixture becomes a paste. Form 2-inch bites, place in an airtight container, and store in the refrigerator for up to 2 weeks.

PER SERVING (1 BALL)

Total Calories: 110; Total Fat: 6g; Saturated Fat: 3g; Cholesterol: 0mg; Sodium: 1mg; Potassium: 151mg; Total Carbohydrate: 16g; Fiber: 2g; Sugars: 13g; Protein: 1g

Melon-Lime Sorbet

Prep time: 15 minutes, plus 4 to 6 hours to freeze and 30 minutes to set| Serves 8

- 1 small honeydew melon, peeled, seeded, and cut into 1-inch chunks
- 1 small cantaloupe, peeled, seeded, and cut into 1-inch chunks
- 2 tablespoons honey
- 2 tablespoons freshly squeezed lime juice
- Pinch cinnamon
- Water as needed

1. Spread the honeydew and cantaloupe out on a baking sheet lined with parchment paper. Place the baking sheet in the freezer for 4 to 6 hours until the fruit is frozen.
2. In a food processor, combine the frozen melon chunks, honey, lime juice, and cinnamon.
3. Pulse until smooth, adding water (a tablespoon at a time) if needed to puree the melon.
4. Transfer the mixture to a resealable container and place it in the freezer until set, about 30 minutes.
5. Freeze in an airtight "freezer" container for up to 1 month.

PER SERVING

Calories: 81; Total Fat: 0g; Saturated Fat: 0g; Cholesterol: 0mg; Sodium: 32mg; Potassium: 439mg; Magnesium: 20mg; Carbohydrates: 21g; Sugars: 15g; Fiber: 2g; Protein: 1g; Added Sugars: 4g; Vitamin K: 5mcg

Fruit-Topped Meringues

Prep time: 15 minutes, plus 1 hour cooling time | Cook time: 50 minutes| Makes 24 cookies

- 4 large egg whites, at room temperature
- ¼ teaspoon cream of tartar
- Pinch salt
- ½ cup honey
- 1 cup raspberries

1. Preheat the oven to 200°F. Line two baking sheets with parchment paper and set aside.
2. In a large stainless steel bowl, beat the egg whites until they are frothy.
3. Beat in the cream of tartar and salt until soft peaks form, 4 to 5 minutes.
4. Beat in the honey, 1 tablespoon at a time, until stiff glossy peaks form.
5. Spoon the meringue batter onto the baking sheets using a tablespoon and create a small well in the center of each with the back of a spoon.
6. Bake until firm, 45 to 50 minutes. Turn off the heat in the oven and prop the door open to cool the meringues in the oven for at least 1 hour.
7. Refrigerate in an airtight container for up to 1 week and serve with a raspberry in the center of each meringue.

PER SERVING (2 MERINGUES)

Calories: 54; Total Fat: 0g; Saturated Fat: 0g; Cholesterol: 0mg; Sodium: 32mg; Potassium: 52mg; Magnesium: 4mg; Carbohydrates: 13g; Sugars: 0g; Fiber: 1g; Protein: 1g; Added Sugars: 12g; Vitamin K: 1mcg

Individual Apple Pockets

Prep time: 5 minutes | Cook time: 15 minutes| Serves 6

- 1 organic puff pastry, rolled out, at room temperature
- 1 Gala apple, peeled and sliced
- ¼ cup brown sugar
- ⅛ teaspoon ground cinnamon
- ⅛ teaspoon ground cardamom
- Nonstick cooking spray
- honey, for topping

1. Preheat the oven to 350°F.
2. Cut the pastry dough into four even discs.
3. In a small bowl, toss the apple slices with brown sugar, cinnamon, and cardamom.
4. Spray a muffin tin very well with cooking spray. Be sure to spray only the muffin holders you plan to use.
5. Once sprayed, line the bottom of the muffin tin with the dough and place 1 or 2 broken apple slices on top. Fold the remaining dough over the apple and drizzle with honey.
6. Bake for 15 minutes or until brown and bubbly.
7. Store at room temperature in an airtight container for up to 2 days.

PER SERVING

Calories: 276; Total Fat: 16g; Saturated Fat: 4g; Cholesterol: 0mg; Sodium: 105mg; Potassium: 70mg; Magnesium: 9mg; Carbohydrates: 32g; Sugars: 3g; Fiber: 1g; Protein: 3g; Added Sugars: 9g; Vitamin K: 7mcg

Key Lime Cherry "Nice" Cream

Prep time: 10 minutes | Serves 4

- 4 frozen bananas, peeled
- 1 cup frozen dark sweet cherries
- Grated zest and juice of 1 lime, divided
- ½ teaspoon vanilla extract
- ¼ teaspoon salt

1. Place the bananas, cherries, lime juice, vanilla, and salt in a food processor and puree until smooth, scraping the sides as needed.
2. Transfer the nice cream to bowls and top with the lime zest.
3. For leftovers, place the nice cream in airtight containers and store in the freezer for up to 1 month. Let it thaw for 30 minutes, until it reaches a soft-serve ice cream texture, before serving.

PER SERVING

Calories: 134; Total Fat: 0g; Saturated Fat: 0g; Cholesterol: 0mg; Sodium: 147mg; Potassium: 522mg; Magnesium: 37mg; Carbohydrates: 34g; Sugars: 20g; Fiber: 4g; Protein: 2g; Added Sugars: 0g; Vitamin K: 2mcg

Chapter 12
Staples

Walnut Basil Pesto

Makes 1 cup | Prep time: 15 minutes | Makes 1 cup

- 2 cups packed chopped fresh basil
- 3 garlic cloves, peeled
- ¼ cup chopped walnuts
- ½ cup extra-virgin olive oil
- ½ teaspoon salt
- ⅓ cup grated Parmesan cheese

1. In a food processor or high-powered blender, combine the basil, garlic, and walnuts. Pulse until the mixture is coarsely chopped.
2. Add the oil, salt, and Parmesan cheese. Process on high for 5 minutes, or until mixture is well mixed and smooth.
3. Refrigerate in a covered container for up to 3 weeks, or store in the freezer for up to 1 month.

PER SERVING (1 TABLESPOON)

Calories: 82; Fat: 9g; Protein: 1g; Carbohydrates: 1g; Fiber: 0g; Sugar: 0g; Sodium: 98mg

Quick Garlic Hummus

Makes 3 cups | Prep time: 10 minutes | Makes 3 cups

- 1 (28-ounce) can low-sodium chickpeas, drained and rinsed
- 3 garlic cloves, peeled
- ⅓ cup extra-virgin olive oil
- 2 tablespoons freshly squeezed lemon juice
- 2 tablespoons water
- ¼ teaspoon salt
- ¼ teaspoon ground cumin

1. In a food processor, combine the chickpeas, garlic, oil, lemon juice, water, salt, and cumin. Puree on high until the mixture is smooth, scraping down the sides as needed.
2. Refrigerate for up to 1 week in a covered container.

PER SERVING (¼ CUP HUMMUS)

Calories: 107; Fat: 7g; Protein: 3g; Carbohydrates: 9g; Fiber: 2g; Sugar: 2g; Sodium: 129mg

Roasted Garlic

Makes 1 bulb | Prep time: 5 minutes | Cook time: 40 minutes | Makes 1 bulb

- 1 head garlic
- 1 teaspoon extra-virgin olive oil
- Salt

1. Preheat the oven to 400°F. Place a rack in the middle of the oven.
2. Slice off the top quarter of the head of garlic and discard. Wrap the remaining head of garlic in aluminum foil, leaving the top open, and place it in a small, oven-safe ramekin.
3. Drizzle the oil over the top of the garlic and sprinkle it with salt. Wrap the garlic completely with foil.
4. Place the ramekin containing the garlic on the middle rack of the preheated oven. Bake for 40 minutes, or until the garlic cloves are golden and softened.

PER SERVING

Calories: 93; Fat: 5g; Protein: 2g; Carbohydrates: 12g; Fiber: 1g; Sugar: 0g; Sodium: 161mg

Lemony Greek Dressing

Makes ½ cup | Prep time: 5 minutes | Makes 1 cup

- ¼ cup extra-virgin olive oil
- ¼ cup freshly squeezed lemon juice
- 2 garlic cloves, minced
- 1 teaspoon dried oregano
- 1 teaspoon Dijon mustard
- ½ teaspoon salt
- ¼ teaspoon freshly ground pepper

1. In a liquid measuring cup, whisk together the oil, lemon juice, garlic, oregano, mustard, salt, and pepper.
2. Refrigerate in an airtight container for up to 1 week. Let sit at room temperature for 3 minutes, then shake well before using.

PER SERVING (2 TABLESPOONS)

Calories: 126; Fat: 14g; Protein: 0g; Carbohydrates: 2g; Fiber: 0g; Sugar: 0g; Sodium: 305mg

Simple French Vinaigrette

Makes ½ cup | Prep time: 5 minutes | Makes 1 cup

¼ cup extra-virgin olive oil
¼ cup white vinegar
2 garlic cloves, minced
½ teaspoon salt
1 teaspoon Dijon mustard
1 teaspoon honey

1. In a liquid measuring cup, whisk the oil, vinegar, garlic, salt, mustard, and honey.
2. Refrigerate in an airtight container for up to 1 week.

PER SERVING (2 TABLESPOONS)

Calories: 130; Fat: 14g; Protein: 0g; Carbohydrates: 2g; Fiber: 0g; Sugar: 1g; Sodium: 305mg

Balsamic Glaze

Makes ½ cup | Cook time: 20 minutes| Makes 1 cup

- 2 cups balsamic vinegar

1. Pour the vinegar into a large saucepan and bring it to a boil over medium heat.
2. Reduce the heat to medium-low and continue simmering, stirring occasionally, for 20 minutes, or until the vinegar is reduced by about half and thickened.
3. Let the glaze cool completely, then refrigerate it in an airtight container for up to 1 week.

PER SERVING (1 TABLESPOON)

Calories: 56; Fat: 0g; Protein: 0g; Carbohydrates: 11g; Fiber: 0g; Sugar: 10g; Sodium: 15mg

Balsamic Caramelized Onions

Makes 3 cups | Prep time: 5 minutes | Cook time: 15 minutes| Makes 3 cups

- 1 tablespoon extra-virgin olive oil
- 2 large red onions, thinly sliced
- Water
- ¼ teaspoon salt
- 2 tablespoons balsamic vinegar

1. In a large skillet, heat the oil over medium-high heat. Add the onions and stir to coat them with oil.
2. Cook, stirring often, for 10 to 12 minutes, or until the onions are soft and translucent. Add a tablespoon of water at a time if the onions start to stick.
3. Add the salt and vinegar. Cook for another 1 to 2 minutes, or until the vinegar has
4. evaporated.

PER SERVING (¼ CUP)

Calories: 22; Fat: 1g; Protein: 0g; Carbohydrates: 3g; Fiber: 0g; Sugar: 1g; Sodium: 50mg

Easy Tzatziki

Makes 1 cup | Prep time: 10 minutes| Makes 1 cup

½ English cucumber
1 cup low-fat plain Greek yogurt
2 garlic cloves, minced
2 tablespoons chopped fresh dill
1½ tablespoons freshly squeezed lemon juice
1 tablespoon extra-virgin olive oil
½ teaspoon salt

1. Using a box grater, grate the cucumber and squeeze out the excess water. Place the cucumber in a large bowl.
2. Add the yogurt, garlic, dill, lemon juice, oil, and salt, and mix well.
3. Cover and refrigerate until ready to serve, or up to 3 days.

PER SERVING (2 TABLESPOONS)

Calories: 39; Fat: 2g; Protein: 2g; Carbohydrates: 3g; Fiber: 0g; Sugar: 3g; Sodium: 167mg

Super-Fluffy Quinoa

Makes 3 cups | Prep time: 5 minutes | Cook time: 25 minutes| Makes 2 cups

- 1 cup quinoa, rinsed
- 2 cups water
- Salt

1. In a large stockpot, combine the rinsed quinoa and water and bring to a boil over medium-high heat.
2. Reduce the heat to medium-low and simmer for 20 minutes, or until all the liquid has been absorbed.
3. Remove the pan from the heat, and cover for 5 minutes. Fluff with a fork and season with salt before serving.

PER SERVING (1 CUP COOKED)

Calories: 208; Fat: 3g; Protein: 8g; Carbohydrates: 36g; Fiber: 4g; Sugar: 0g; Sodium: 55mg

Appendix 1 Measurement Conversion Chart

Volume Equivalents (Dry)	
US STANDARD	METRIC (APPROXIMATE)
1/8 teaspoon	0.5 mL
1/4 teaspoon	1 mL
1/2 teaspoon	2 mL
3/4 teaspoon	4 mL
1 teaspoon	5 mL
1 tablespoon	15 mL
1/4 cup	59 mL
1/2 cup	118 mL
3/4 cup	177 mL
1 cup	235 mL
2 cups	475 mL
3 cups	700 mL
4 cups	1 L

Volume Equivalents (Liquid)		
US STANDARD	US STANDARD (OUNCES)	METRIC (APPROXIMATE)
2 tablespoons	1 fl.oz.	30 mL
1/4 cup	2 fl.oz.	60 mL
1/2 cup	4 fl.oz.	120 mL
1 cup	8 fl.oz.	240 mL
1 1/2 cup	12 fl.oz.	355 mL
2 cups or 1 pint	16 fl.oz.	475 mL
4 cups or 1 quart	32 fl.oz.	1 L
1 gallon	128 fl.oz.	4 L

Temperatures Equivalents	
FAHRENHEIT(F)	CELSIUS(C) APPROXIMATE)
225 °F	107 °C
250 °F	120 ° °C
275 °F	135 °C
300 °F	150 °C
325 °F	160 °C
350 °F	180 °C
375 °F	190 °C
400 °F	205 °C
425 °F	220 °C
450 °F	235 °C
475 °F	245 °C
500 °F	260 °C

Weight Equivalents	
US STANDARD	METRIC (APPROXIMATE)
1 ounce	28 g
2 ounces	57 g
5 ounces	142 g
10 ounces	284 g
15 ounces	425 g
16 ounces (1 pound)	455 g
1.5 pounds	680 g
2 pounds	907 g

Appendix 2 The Dirty Dozen and Clean Fifteen

The Environmental Working Group (EWG) is a nonprofit, nonpartisan organization dedicated to protecting human health and the environment Its mission is to empower people to live healthier lives in a healthier environment. This organization publishes an annual list of the twelve kinds of produce, in sequence, that have the highest amount of pesticide residue-the Dirty Dozen-as well as a list of the fifteen kinds ofproduce that have the least amount of pesticide residue-the Clean Fifteen.

THE DIRTY DOZEN	
The 2016 Dirty Dozen includes the following produce. These are considered among the year's most important produce to buy organic:	
Strawberries	Spinach
Apples	Tomatoes
Nectarines	Bell peppers
Peaches	Cherry tomatoes
Celery	Cucumbers
Grapes	Kale/collard greens
Cherries	Hot peppers
The Dirty Dozen list contains two additional itemskale/collard greens and hot peppers-because they tend to contain trace levels of highly hazardous pesticides.	

THE CLEAN FIFTEEN	
The least critical to buy organically are the Clean Fifteen list. The following are on the 2016 list:	
Avocados	Papayas
Corn	Kiw
Pineapples	Eggplant
Cabbage	Honeydew
Sweet peas	Grapefruit
Onions	Cantaloupe
Asparagus	Cauliflower
Mangos	
Some of the sweet corn sold in the United States are made from genetically engineered (GE) seedstock. Buy organic varieties of these crops to avoid GE produce.	

Appendix 3 Index

Printed in Great Britain
by Amazon

14606850R00079